Auntie Jean's Jug

by

PATRICIA ECKER

P R E Books Limited

Published by
P R E Books Limited CV22 7NP

Illustrations: Patricia Ecker
Copyright © R. Ecker 1995
ISBN 0 9525169 0 X

British Library Cataloguing in Publication Data
A Catalogue record for this book is available from
The British Library

Typeset and Printed
by
Cramphorn Colour Printers Limited, 15C Paynes Lane, Rugby CV21 2UH

Auntie Jean's Jug was a cherished ornament throughout my childhood and is standing before me as I write now. Its quaint Victorian shape and raised pattern of birds and blossoming branches are among my earliest memories. We used to drop into its capacious belly all sorts of little things we found lying about, and every so often, someone would empty it out. There among the rusty pins and twists of string we would find old treasures we had forgotten, a charm from a cracker, a bent brooch, beads from a broken necklace, or a tiny pencil on a silk tasselled cord, from a dance programme.

My memory is like Auntie Jean's Jug. I dip into it for something I know is there and bring up a dozen other things I had forgotten. Old friends come crowding back out of the dark, until a whole decade of my life revives, events, sensation and emotion. These pages tell part of what I have re-discovered.

AUNTIE JEAN'S JUG

CONTENTS

1. EARLY MORNING

he world began in the middle of a sunny Saturday morning when I was one and a half. It was summer, and Mother was pushing me in the pram across the back yard, to go shopping. I was sitting up, with my legs dangling - but only just - into the central well of the pram where the leather cushion had been lifted out. Above my head a sash window was thrust up and my brother, who was nearly eight, leaned out. "Mummy", he wheedled, "bring us back some stodge from Town".

My sensations, and the words Gerald spoke, are among my active, first-level memories, the sort you can actually re-experience by closing your eyes and drifting backwards. I think this must be about the earliest memory I have because the blue pram in which I sat was sold when I was eighteen months old and replaced by a brown American-cloth push chair that was low and rattled, and had a vicious folding wooden foot-board that trapped my ankles.

Gerald was not at school so it must have been Saturday. He was trying out the latest schoolboy slang. "Stodge", I understood without being told, meant sweets, or sticky buns, or a "Nelson", that was a very filling and cheap cake made by a local baker. It was stale fruit-cake re-cycled and cooked in a thick wodge between two layers of sugary pastry - very good value for a penny.

I understood Gerald's words; after all, I must have heard him hinting for

7

sweets from Town before. But I did not speak myself. I could follow quite a lot of talk before I actually tried to communicate much in return, just as we can often follow a conversation in a foreign language even when we can only speak half a dozen words of it ourselves. So I can remember being a small silent person, but knowing precisely what Gerald meant by "stodge" and having my attention caught by the word, so far unknown.

There is no before or after to this memory. As I sit in the pram which is beginning to move across the dark blue bricks of the yard, I can see the opening of the side passage but I do not remember being wheeled down it. It is later memories (we lived in that house until I was four) that tell me about the laurel bush in the next garden, the dark grating under the front window, the low wall and its cast iron railings, and the step down to the footpath.

We lived in three houses in my childhood; '16' where I was born, '62' where we moved when I was four, and '106' which Father built when I was nine. Gerald had been born in the village where I now live, but the long bicycle ride in to School, on an elderly boneshaker over unmade roads, had been too tiring for Father, and they moved in to town, just across the road from the Grammar School, where he taught Classics and Modern Languages.

I can only remember isolated features of '16', the earliest house- the painted panel on the wardrobe, scorched by the gas jet, the red and blue glass in the landing window, the rusty pump in the yard, and the turn of the stairs where I saw a fairy man dancing- but these few are all clear and brilliant as dewdrops.

There is a low cubby-hole in the wall by the range. It is only about as high as me. It smells strongly of wax and turpentine and the sweet sourness of leather, for it is here we keep our shoes for cleaning and the box of shoe polish and brushes. I have a little pair of real shoes, not soft pram bootees. They are almost square, like little boxes, and are made of glossy black patent leather. They have each flat mother-of-pearl buttons ornamenting the toe and one of these has a vein of deep red fire in it. It burns dark and wonderful when you tilt it, and suffuses the rest of the button with a pink glow. I hold my hands out for the shoes, to study and brood over my little jewel of fire. "Pretty", I croon. "Yes. Pretty shoes", says Mother. "Be careful of them".

I am aware that she and I are not on the same wavelength. She thinks I love the shoes, as she does, as pretty articles of dress. But all I care about really is that flake of dark fire in the mother-of-pearl. I would like to get it off but it resists my tugging. That is why she says "Be careful". But it does not seem worth the trouble of explaining. What she thinks I think does not matter, but I am quite clear inside my head that Mother and I are thinking quite different things about those shoes.

"Ride a cock horse
To Banbury Cross
To see a fine lady on a white horse.
With rings on her fingers and bells on her toes,
She shall have music wherever she goes".

I sat astride Mother's ankle and she bounced me up and down. I must still have been very small; Mother was no Goliath. The tune was less compelling than the words. I could understand "Rings on her fingers". Mother wore a wedding ring and sometimes a half-hoop of tiny diamonds called "a gagementing". But I had never seen anyone with bells on their toes. I had silvery bobbles of sleighbells on my reins when I walked, but if you hung them on your toes you would not be able to put your shoes on. It was odd, but no odder than most things, and in the meantime, it was very pleasant to jiggle about on Mother's foot as she crossed her legs at the knee and tossed me gently up and down. I would giggle, then begin to shriek with delight, and when she stopped, would demand "More, more".

"No more. Not now. I've got a bone in my leg".

That sounded sinister and always silenced me. A bone, like the chalk-white hollow bone in the Sunday joint. I would look at her leg in its cotton stocking, wrinkled where I had sat on it, and wonder if the harsh bone was about to burst out hideously from the smooth line of her skin.

I remember my drop-side iron cot too, but I slept in it until I was four. It was painted white with chips, and when a determined toddler stood up in it and, taking a firm hold on the sides, shook and rocked it, it made a noise not unlike a train thundering through a tunnel. The walls of '16' were thin, and the rumble and clank of me taking bed-time exercise was too much for our neighbours. When I was bursting with energy, especially on long light summer evenings, Mr Smythe, the Monumental Mason who lived next door, would reach the end of his endurance and Mrs Smythe would come, embarrassed, to our door to say, "Please, could you get Pat to keep quiet. The noise is making our heads ache!"

The thinness of the party-wall was a trial to Mother, especially on the days when she had to wash my hair. As an infant I had tight curly 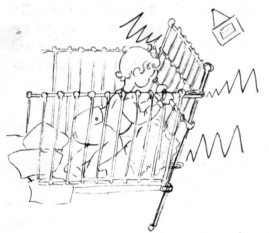 hair that tangled very easily. I loathed hair-washing. The soap got in my eyes and stung and it was even worse when Mother tried to wipe it out. Her knuckles and her wedding ring pummelled my skull, and when she began to rinse, I was sure it meant more soap. I screamed steadily all through. She would dry me with a thick scratchy towel like a door-mat, and then began the torture of brushing and combing my tangles. She went at it fairly roughly because, as I screamed hysterically whatever she did, there was some virtue in getting it over as fast as possible. It was pandemonium, and Mother herself would be almost in tears from exasperation and frustration by the time I was knot-free and tidy. The noise was so bad that after one shame-making evening when Mrs Smythe had come to the door anxiously to ask if Pat had had an accident and could they help in any way, Mother used to send the maid round to warn them that she was only washing my hair, not beating me to a jelly with the poker. (She must have been sorely tempted once or twice!)

The problem of getting me to settle down and go to sleep once I was in my cot was solved in the end by Mother reading to me. As I grew larger and stronger and my cot-shakings threatened to tumble both '16' and '18' to their flimsy foundations, I had somehow to be kept quiet until sleep overtook me. Mother must have grudged the time for she had plenty other things to do, but anything was better than being on bad terms with the neighbours. She read me story books but they were not much of a success. I could not really concentrate at that age for long enough to be able to follow a story. The problem was solved in a most unlikely way.

Someone gave Mother a cookery book like no other I have seen. I have a tattered copy myself now and still find it fascinating. It is full of entertaining recipes, household hints and a delightful section called "Wrinkles for the Cook". Mother must have explained to me the two meanings of 'wrinkles' and taught me to find it funny and crow with delight when she read it out. I kept her busy reading my favourite bits.

There was "Bible Cake" which began:

Take ½lb Judges V, verse 25
½lb Jeremiah VI, v 20
1 tablespoonful I Samuel XIV, v 25
and so on.

There were Medical Hints:

"Excessive smoking is often the cause of blindness and nervous breakdown"

"Cure for Anaemia

1 pint stout
1 gill portwine
1 gill black beer
½ noggin brandy.
Take half a wineglassful twice a day".

(At least you would enjoy being anaemic)

At the foot of every page was a proverb or saying:

"The best physicians are Dr Diet, Dr Quiet and Dr Merryman".
"A bad workman quarrels with his tools".

(Unexpected ideas cropped up)

"Sleep to induce

Potassium bromide, 1 drachm
Chloralmide, 1 drachm
Tincture of orange, 3 drachms
Chloroform water, enough to make 4 ozs".

(Chloroform! That's what Mother needed for me!)

"To Catch Wasps.

He hath found an old bottle, I cannot say where,
And tied it with skill to the back of a chair,
Full of mild ale so balmy and sugar so brown,
And he'll trap them by dozens, I'll bet you a crown.
(N.B. 1 inch of beer will suffice)".

In the middle of a page of soup recipes you would suddenly find a story. "Two sailors went into a restaurant. The waiter put down two plates of unappetizing, watery stuff before them. One tasted it. 'What's this?' he asked. 'Soup, sir', said the waiter. 'Fancy that, Bill', he said to his companion 'All our lives we've been sailing on soup and we never knew it'."

Fancy that, indeed!

These snippets were just long enough to hold my attention and make me ask for more. I think the truth is that Mother was so amused herself that I laughed by infection. Whatever the reason, the book was a riotous success, and when Mother judged I had had enough, she would say, "Now, what shall we have for the last, the very last?"

My reply was always the same. "Toad-in-the-Hole". The name of this dish struck me at three as the ultimate in humour, and in order to

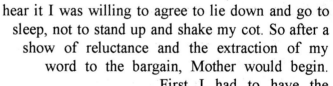

hear it I was willing to agree to lie down and go to sleep, not to stand up and shake my cot. So after a show of reluctance and the extraction of my word to the bargain, Mother would begin. First I had to have the proverb from the foot of the page:-
"I oft have heard defended, little said, soonest mended." Then I would lie down, be covered up and wait.

"Toad-in-the-Hole (Savoury)

7 slices of cold mutton
2 or 3 sheep's kidneys
Few mushrooms, if liked
1 teaspoonful ketchup or sauce
6 ozs. flour
1 pint of milk
2 eggs
Little pepper, pinch of salt.

Stew kidneys until tender in a little gravy or water. Put meat and kidneys into a buttered pie dish. Make a batter of the flour, milk and eggs. Pour over the meat. Bake 1½ hours. Serve in the dish".

And if Mother had gone reasonably slowly, I would be sound asleep before the meat was in the buttered pie-dish.

2. LITTLE MONSTER

was not a very nice child. That may be a left-handed way of patting myself on the back and saying "I am nice now". Well - reasonably nice. Experience, and imagination, do make us feel more for others. But small children are not normally sympathetic. Wordsworth, I'm afraid, was just plain wrong when he said of the infant Babe:-

> "already shades
> Of pity cast from inward tenderness
> Do fall around him upon aught that bears
> Unsightly marks of violence or harm."

Small children shun the malformed and the injured, and judging from myself, have no real care for the well-being of others except as it will affect themselves. When I threw the stool at the policeman, it was to protect myself against my father being taken away. When I hung from a train screaming because he had disappeared to buy papers, it was because the train might go off without him and then what would happen to ME?

As the baby I knew myself to be indulged, and quite early on I realised that if something went wrong when we were together, ten year old Gerald would be blamed, not angelic-looking little Pat with her golden curls. Gerald was a singularly good-natured boy and rarely took it out on me, unfair though it all was, especially as I can remember clearly plotting with conscious malice to get him into trouble when he had dented my self-importance.

One day when we still lived at '16', Gerald and his friend Geoffrey wanted to go out together one morning and little sister grizzled and whined to go with the big boys. Of course they did not want a brat tagging along while they boasted and laughed insanely and shoved each other about, but Mother said "Take her with you - don't be selfish". And take me they had to.

We went up a nearby side-street where the houses faced straight on to the footpath without even a slip of a garden. The front doors were set back in arched porches. I was annoyed with Gerald for not wanting to take me along. I ran on ahead of him and Geoffrey and nicely calculating when I was too far away to be stopped, I slipped into a house doorway and rang the bell. By the time the housewife had come to the door and opened it, two small boys were outside - clearly they were the offenders! She turned on them, accusing them of rudeness, of wasting her time when she was busy, of being little nuisances, ringing decent people's bells and then running away.

Gerald opened and shut his mouth like a fish as he realised what

I had done and at last spluttered, "But it wasn't us - truly - it was my little sister". And he pointed accusingly at me as I stood shyly hanging my head. I waited confidently for the expected reaction and it came, just as I had known it would. The housewife looked at me. "Rubbish", she said. "Don't you try to get out of it like that! As if that little innocent would do such a thing! Be off with you both or I'll come and find your mother and complain. I know where you live - just round the corner".

That was enough. Gerald and Geoffrey were not going to push their luck any further. Gerald grabbed my hand and whisked me off on a slant up the street and out of sight. Once well away, those two boys gave me such a wigging about the sin of ringing strangers' doorbells that they did effectively scare me off it for the rest of my life, and whoever else played 'knock-down-Ginger' it wasn't me!

Perhaps with Jenny it was more forgiveable. I meant to get Jenny into trouble but she had frightened me and I knew that she knew that she had done wrong. We were still at '16' so I was three. She was our current daily maid - the one before Elsie. At fifteen it can't have been much fun in our little flagged kitchen all day, with only the delivery boys coming to the back door for company, so she was glad enough to be sent out to do a few errands and take me for an afternoon airing in the push-chair. It must have been winter; it was dusk before we left the park, and the gaslight was on over the tea-table when my father called Jenny to account after he got home.

Caldecott Park was at the other end of town. It had a big grove of trees in the middle, surrounding a large pond. A tarmac path ran through the trees all round, and once you got away from the main drive, you were out of sight - almost lost in a wood - until you came round to the bandstand at the far end. Jenny had pushed me a few yards up this path, while the thin winter sunlight filtered through the bare branches and glittered on the pond. I was well wrapped up with leggings and fur mittens and a waterproof cover buttoned down over my legs. Jenny was lingering - glancing back. We were joined by a tall figure in the clumsy khaki of a private's uniform. We moved on slowly to the furthest point beyond the pond. The talk and scuffling behind my head did not interest me - there were ducks on the water. The push chair stopped. In a few moments Jenny said, "Now you wait here and be a good girl. I won't be long". And she and the soldier pushed through the screening evergreens and vanished.

A little time passed. No one came. Not even any footsteps on the distant drive. The glitter disappeared off the water. The brightness left the sky. A greyness filled the air and on the chill breeze wafts of bonfire smoke were carried. I called quaveringly, "Jenny?". No reply. I sat waiting, then again, more urgently I tried. "Jenny, Jenny". Still no one came. I was strapped in my push chair and did not know how to get out, and I was abandoned in a lonely place. I wanted to go home. Somebody <u>must</u> come! I began to scream her name hysterically, and it seemed to me the sky grew darker every moment.

At last the silly girl must have heard me and given over kissing and cuddling with her soldier. Or maybe the two of them had

17

wandered out of earshot. Anyway, footsteps pounded, branches crackled and Jenny came flying red-faced down the path. I was too glad to see her to do anything but cry, and she pushed me along, scolding and embarrassed, up the North Street Hill and past the parish Church. By the time we got near father's school, it was deep dusk, and I had stopped making a fuss. Instead I was brooding quietly on revenge. I deliberately held my fire and when we turned in at '16' I had my coat and leggings removed, and sat on the fender to turn the butter in the dish to soften without a word of complaint against Jenny. I would wait until Daddy was there to hear my tale.

The gas was lighted with a little 'plop'. Father came home rubbing his hands for warmth. The steaming tea pot was extinguished under its big padded cosy, scorched where it had been stood on the range to 'draw'. Boiled egg, bread and butter soldiers and 'milk with a little tea in it'. Then I dropped my bomb, now when Daddy was here. I could be sure he would take more notice than Mummy. "Jenny left me in the Park. Ever so long. She went with a soldier".

Questions. Growing indignation. Smugly I piled on the guilt for Jenny. "I was frightened. It was dark. I cried".

"They were very late back. I was worried", said Mother.

"Jenny!" My father's voice was the authoritative bellow I had heard him use on Sports Day at school, but not at home.

Jenny appeared, scrunching her apron in damp hands. In the inquisition that followed, I kept my eyes down and messed my egg about, as Jenny alternated between remorse and cheeky defiance. The latter predominated as she realised she was going to lose her place anyway.

I felt justified. She was supposed to look after me. She shouldn't have left me.

Jenny departed the next day, and shortly afterwards it transpired that several pairs of my mother's silk stockings and some of her choicer lingerie had departed with her.

She was succeeded by Elsie - the first of the aptly named

Darlings, who came to us one after another for almost twelve years. Elsie was a rock, a reassurance, and she was also the eldest of a long family, and knew a good deal more about spoiled children than I knew myself. The calculating little beast who exploited her baby looks and golden curls was about to get her come-uppance.

We had moved to '62' - a much bigger house, but with the same basic design. The dining room at the back was flanked by a windowless flagged passage that led to the kitchen. I was getting older and my bossiness was no longer amusing. It was a bore. Father had a theory that it was bad for digestion to drink with your meals, so we did not have water on the table. If we were really thirsty, we had to fetch a glass of water ourselves. We had

Jacobean pattern tumblers in the sideboard, and I had an identical glass but in the 'whisky tot' size. This miniature of the grown-ups' tumblers gave me immense joy. I loved almost passionately those few things which were child-size, like my little wooden rolling-pin and mixing bowl that had been a Christmas present. I wanted a drink of water at dinner one day - or more likely I wanted the pleasure of handling my little tumbler. Elsie had just passed the vegetables through the hatch and taken her own plate of dinner back to the kitchen.

"I want a drink of water".

"Well, get your little glass out of the cupboard and go and ask Elsie to fill it for you".

I slipped down off the shiny dark red seat of the dining chair, turned the little key in the sideboard doors, and carefully took out my cherished glass. I went down the dark passage to the quarry tiled kitchen where Elsie was eating her dinner, while it was hot. I demanded water imperiously.

"Say 'please' ", replied Elsie.

I asked again, a little more politely, but Elsie felt I was getting too overbearing. She told me to wait while she finished her plateful. I saw no reason whatsoever why Elsie, who was the maid, should enjoy her dinner in peace, while I had to wait around for a glass of water which I didn't really want. I eyed her angrily.

"Elsie", I said, in a threatening tone, "if you don't give me my water now, I'll break my tumbler on the floor".

That would move her! My tumbler was special, - precious, one of the most treasured items in the household. She would never dare to let it get broken. I held it menacingly above the flags.

Elsie looked at me calmly and went on chewing. "Go ahead and break it then", she said. "It won't bother me".

Enraged I hurled it. It shattered on the red tiles. My heart nearly stopped beating. I gazed at what I had done - my treasure - ruined - by me! And I suddenly saw that it was my own fault. I did not have the power to order other people about and I had destroyed my little tumbler all for nothing. I wept.

Mother came to enquire. "Did she drop it?"

"No", said Elsie calmly. "She threw it on the floor in a temper because I wouldn't get up at once and get her the water."

And there my babyhood ended. I was not consoled, I was scolded. Elsie was not to be ordered about by me. I was not important. And if I had smashed my little tumbler, I would just have

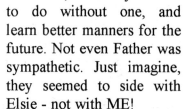

to do without one, and learn better manners for the future. Not even Father was sympathetic. Just imagine, they seemed to side with Elsie - not with ME!

'Sin' was hard to define in my early years. I could really only judge the wickedness of my actions by the scale of the row when I was found out, and that could be misleading. When

I helped myself to three half-pence from Mother's purse, left unattended on the kitchen table, and Mother immediately noticed, (that gives an idea of the value of money in those days) there was trouble, prolonged and bitter. I certainly learned not to steal. But the upset and scoldings were just as bad when I innocently told Sally's mother that we didn't have tea-towels with a nice coloured stripe down the middle and the word 'Glass' woven in; ours were made of old bedsheets that had been sides-to-middled and wouldn't mend any more. My sin here had apparently been showing the family up in public by talking about our private economies. In some strange way it was shameful to make economies, although I was always being told at home that we must never be wasteful, and many things I craved were dismissed as "too expensive. We can't afford things like that". There was a splendid row about the tea-towels but every bit as bad was the row over Pussy and the Ovaltine.

I had had whooping-cough, and it left me racked by fits of dry coughing that kept me awake night after night until I began to have plum-coloured bags under my eyes. Mother decided to give me a bedtime drink of Ovaltine in the hopes that the hot milk would make me drowsy, and cheat the coughing. Surprisingly, it worked, and a cup of Ovaltine last thing became a routine for me. Mother would bring it to the dining-room just before my bed-time, and I would disappear with it to my private refuge, under the table, hidden by the long crimson cloth. It was here that I had been discovered at the age of three, happily stuffing myself with half-a-pound of best Maypole butter that had unaccountably vanished from the fireside, where it had been put down on a plate to soften. I like butter!

So I, and my cup and saucer crept into the pleasant gloom under the table, and very soon, Pussy would sidle in purring. Pussy liked sweet Ovaltine as well. I poured her a saucerful and put it down for her to drink while I sipped and nursed my cup. Pussy, of course, was just like myself; we shared everything. Well, I can't say I ate her mice, or the six raw herrings she stole off the kitchen table one day, but cake, or bread-and-butter, or pudding we shared bite and bite about, and if she did not want all the Ovaltine, I would pour the remainder back into my cup and finish it quite happily. I suppose

I ought to have been warned by the day when Mother steadfastly refused to let me put a dinner-plate straight back on the dresser with the others, even when I pointed out that Pussy had licked it so clean it shone just as much as the ones Margery had washed up.

The day came when Mother, laying the table for supper, saw me tilting Pussy's dregs back into my cup. The storm burst. What a disgusting thing to do! Surely I knew perfectly well that animals were dirty! I could catch dreadful diseases doing that. I must never do it again! Did I hear? NEVER. I must not eat off a plate an animal had used, or touch any food it had left.

My chief feeling, after bewilderment, was resentment. How could she call Pussy dirty? Pussy's sparkling shirt front and smart white socks were spotless, and she washed her face and hands after every meal far more conscientiously than I ever did. But I was scolded off to bed, and told that I must not share my Ovaltine with her any more. Judging by the storm, I would have classed my action as a sin.

Sins had an uncomfortable way of being found out. 'Making a long nose' or 'pulling snooks' was a gesture we picked up from children in the side-streeets, who despised us as soppy, when my friends Carl and Ursula and I went carefully, hand in hand across the road, to spend a penny on sweets at the shop where they sold Sharp's Eton Toffee. It was RUDE, and we were NEVER to do it. So of course, we longed to, and one day, when he had gone over the railway and along our road where it petered out into a country walk, with big trees and shallow dry ditches each side, we wriggled down out of sight in the ditch, and popped up, three shameless urchins in a row, to thumb our noses enthusiastically at the few passing cars. A stately limousine came down the road, chauffeur-driven and with two ladies in high feather chatting in the back. Carl nudged us. "Now", he said, and up we jumped, derisively, six thumbs and twenty-four fingers waggling as we danced and pulled faces as rudely as we knew how. Well satisfied with our afternoon's sport, we returned home about an hour later. I knew as soon as I shut the door that there was trouble; Mother's face was dark with doom. The afternoon's sins were repeated to me. I was shown up - shamed, scolded, disgraced. But how had Mother found out? We had been a mile and a half from home and she was safely here and couldn't see us.

Carl and Ursula had come in for identical trouble when they got in, too, but they at least could solve the mystery. That last limousine had been a hired car, containing Giulia's mother who was entertaining a visiting Italian Princess, and had been shocked and humiliated before her when three rude children had sprung out of the ditch making a vulgar gesture, but when she had recognised the children as school friends of her daughter, she had swooped down on our mothers to complain, the very instant she had returned the Princess safely to her hotel. And so the avenging angel had already served us up on toast, before we even opened the doors of our homes.

We learned. We learned to be more canny, more secretive, and to take care, when we were planning something the grown-ups would class as wicked, to do it somewhere safer from prying eyes. When the small boys who lived along the Lane organised a match to see who could pee the furthest, we girls were interested spectators, but we made sure that the competition took place behind the garages, where we were out of sight, and we posted a sentry at both ends. Carl won.

Sin was not actually confined to children, I realised in time. Grown-ups committed sins as well, but there was a difference. They did not get into rows if they were found out. My own parents sinned, and they talked about it openly. It was in my first summer in Guernsey, and the sin was smuggling.

As the time neared for us to go home from the Cottage, Father and our friends talked about ways they might manage to get more than the allowance of duty free tobacco back to England. Father was a heavy smoker. Perfume and spirits did not interest either of my parents. The bottle of 4711 Cologne which Mother could take home quite legally was ample to see her through the modest demands of a whole year. For her and the other ladies, the temptation was silk. Fine tussore and shantung came to the island by way of France, and were untaxed. Pure silk at five shillings a yard, a third or quarter of what it would cost in England, was rousing a lust in Mother, but cut lengths of silk would never get past the Customs. Then Auntie Elsie made a brilliant suggestion. They should buy dress lengths, cut them in half and seam them roughly up into tubes. Then, with a couple of judiciously placed darts, two ribbon shoulder-straps and a trimming of cheap machine lace round the hem, they could become petticoats or nightdresses for the benefit of the Customs, and be unpicked for the dressmaker in England. Father considered it. It might work, he conceded, but she had better wash the petticoats, and iron them a bit roughly, so that they would look as though they had been worn. Satisfied, Mother went off to St Peter Port to buy ravishing lengths of pale rose and soft cream tussore. I enquired of Gerald, "What is smuggling?"

I was stunned to hear from him that it was wrong - it was against the law, and yet he and my highly moral parents were not only going to do it, they were enjoying it!

For the last week of the holiday, the ladies sat in the sun on the beach, stitching up cobbled run-and-fell seams and whipping lace edging round the hems of the tubes of silk. Actually, they were perfectly wearable as petticoats in those days, when dresses were little-more than tubes either. The plan worked very well and Mother was able to have the indulgence of pure silk summer dresses and blouses she could never have afforded on her ten shillings a week allowance if they had been bought in England. In later years she and Wyn collaborated in crime, splitting lengths between them, to throw the Customs men off the scent, and returning the halves to each other after we all got home. Some of these tubular garments were still folded in a drawer, waiting to be used, when I grew up, and I had one crisp shantung blouse when I was married, that had never paid its just dues to the Customs and Excise.

I grew used to hearing this petty smuggling spoken of as a kind of sport, and offered a few ideas of my own for concealing tobacco and cigarettes. It was Sin, and yet it was not Sin, because the grown-ups did it. It was later, though, not at this time, that Father told me his best smuggling story.

He was in Germany on a language course, in the summer of 1912.

25

One of his fellow students was a young English curate called Jim. They had digs together and Jim was very good company, though a bit wild. He had three sisters, two youngish aunts and his mother at home, and he had promised them that he would bring back to every one of them a really big bottle of perfume. Two or three days before they were due to come home, he went out and spent nearly all his remaining cash on these presents and ranged the bottles - nearly half a pint each, on the mantlepiece when he returned. Father looked at them doubtfully. "You'll have to pay a fortune in Duty on those, Jim".

"Shan't pay a penny", said Jim cheerfully. "Smuggle them in".

"You'll never do it. They're much too big!"

"You wait, my boy. Jim'll manage".

Father and Jim were going to travel together, and Father, who was by now a responsible young schoolmaster with a reputation to lose, did not relish the idea of being embroiled in Jim's shady affairs when he was detected at the Customs, with three clanking pints of perfume in his suitcase. "Well, anyway," he said rather sourly, "I hope you won't wear your dog-collar to travel. I don't think your Vicar would like it!"

"Black suit, dog-collar, shovel hat. The lot", returned Jim.

And so it proved. As they travelled across Germany, Jim was the very picture of pious good principles. They had a roughish sea-crossing and reached England in the early morning weary and a bit dishevelled. They heaved their suitcases on to the Customs bench, and Father opened his up - "Anything to declare?", enquired the officers running a practised hand through the layers of Father's belongings. Father displayed the cigars he had brought and the bottle of brandy. They were within the allowance. Apart from his ticket, Father had on this occasion precisely six-pence halfpenny left, and had known he could not afford to run any risks over having to pay for excess goods. His case was closed, scrawled in blue chalk and he was free to move on.

Meanwhile, Jim had been standing bemused beside his strapped and locked suitcase, fingering his little pocket diary, which somehow or other had the air of being a book of prayer. He had made no move to unlock his case, but seemed abstracted. "Anything to declare, sir?", the officer asked.

"No - oh, no", Jim replied.

The Customs man drummed his fingers on the locked case and eyed Jim. "Are you sure there's nothing, sir?"

"No", said Jim; then he caught the man's eye on him and looked embarrassed. "Oh, dear", he said. "How dreadful of me! What am I saying? I suppose I ought ... Well, actually, yes. I have six bottles of perfume for my sisters, and my mother, you know".

"Can I see them, please", said the Customs man wearily, exchanging a resigned glance with his colleague. Father was both relieved that Jim had decided to be honest, and alarmed that the duty involved might be more than the two of them could muster. Sixpence half-penny would not go far.

Jim went into a routine of not being able to find his keys, while the queue behind him built up and grew impatient. When he did finally get the case unlocked and unstrapped, he was desperately helpful and rummaged all through his underwear, insisting that he knew just where he had packed them. By this time the counter was littered with an embarrassing display of Jim's vests and long woolly pants and the Customs man was nearing ignition point. At last, with a cry of triumph, Jim drew out of his case a small flat cardboard box with a pretty picture on the lid. "There we are", he said, flipping it open for inspection. "Six bottles of perfume".

Inside were six tiny sample-sized phials, each of a different scent, and the whole quantity not adding up to more than a wine glass full. The crowd shuffled impatiently and the lady next to Jim pointedly averted her eyes from Jim's underwear. The Customs man shrugged and chalked on the open lid. Father began stuffing Jim's belongings back into the case, while Jim beamed happily.

"It's all right, is it?" he asked. "No duty to pay? Really that is so very..... Thank you so much. My Mother, you know, and three sisters, and two aunts. All dear girls, but it does come a little expensive. So kind, Oh, thank you, Tom - that's everything, I think. Now I'll just do up the straps. Lock it? Yes. I'm sure.... Oh, no! How fortunate you noticed ... "

At last, Father, fuming, was able to get him safely away, still smiling and thanking the Customs man profusely. As they ran for the Boat Train, Jim prodded Father in the side.

"Told you I would, didn't I, boy?"

"You DEVIL", said Father.

3. SEA, AND SUN, AND SAND

t was all grey - the clear cold grey of half-melted ice- on a sunless day in August. The featureless northern sea stretched like a low wall widely on either hand. The shore sand was greyish and chill. Slung between Mummy and Auntie Charlotte, I was shivering with cold and aversion. I might have come to terms with the water except that it wouldn't stay still. It kept surging up towards me, rearing and showing its grey teeth. With every surge, the rug of brown seaweed, clothing the boulders, would heave and lurch, reaching out a myriad snakey fingers for my legs. I would pull back and Mummy would tug me forward. Fine cold spray, whipped along the surface by the bustling wind, covered me with a clammy chill. Blown sand stung my face. I was naked, attacked and it was cold, cold, COLD. My whimpers grew. A scream began to form. It took hold of me and possessed me. It was not something I controlled - it was extra, invading my body, swelling and pushing me out. I was trapped - held by the grownups outwardly, and crowded out inwardly by the huge gasping screams that pulsed and grew, bursting over me like great waves.

They gave up. I was whisked up the beach to the dry sand of the dunes, where the wind was stifled, and a towel wrapped me safely from the unfriendly world. In some obscure way I was held to have disgraced myself. Daddy would be disappointed. "Pat wouldn't paddle. Other children love paddling, but she stood on the edge and screamed!"

And there it must have rested. My first encounter with the ocean had been with the chilly water of the Irish Sea, in pebble-strewn sand, on a grey and breezy day. I was three, and very near to ground level.

29

To me, the sea seemed a low vertical wall, granite coloured, but a wall that moved about, and went for me if I got too near. The whole episode is certainly exaggerated in my mind. My mother would never have tried to coax a toddler into the sea on a really rough day. She wasn't all that partial to waves herself. The breakers that ground their teeth at me may have been all of six inches high. But it was a new, unstable, unreliable world, frightening to the tender bones and shrinking skin of the child first meeting that grey northern sea.

They must have accepted that "Pat was afraid of the water", for the next summer, in a warm and peaceful Devon cove, I was let alone with my bucket and spade while the rest of the party bathed. Fat,contented and spreading like a pancake, I sat on a sandcastle with our friends' baby and watched the blue-green sea stretch like a cat with the rising tide, and the dark woods on either side of Coombe Martin cove, eye themselves in the still water. The sea was not a wall here but a cosy, almost enclosed silk mat.

There was an abandoned wooden fishing boat, tarred and mastless, rising and falling a little in the bay, and my general mistrust of the water was not lessened when, one hot afternoon, a slender boy dived from the abandoned hulk and did not surface again. I hardly noticed the stir of concern, and was only mildly interested when the few men bathing all struck out frantically for the vessel. After many dives, three of them gasped to the surface, bringing up the white body of the boy, boneless and bowed back like boiled macaroni. He had stunned himself, hitting the sandy bottom in shallow water. Was he dead? I never knew. I remember artificial respiration on the beach, then I was hurried away. But if it was a corpse they manhandled out of the shallows on to the warm sand, his was the first, and only, dead body I ever saw. I think he may well have been drowned, as there was a marked reticence about his fate that cast a shadow over the holiday.

You could keep the sea - I didn't want it, but I knew the joys of sand and my horizons were widening. One day we went - by train - to Woolacombe. The name remained in my mind for years as pure magic. As far as I could see stretched golden, flat, perfect sands. No rocks, no shingle, no seaweed. A child let loose in a sweet-shop, or a gold miner who has struck a rich lode - they alone might feel as I felt when I saw that limitless paradise. I can see it now as I saw it then; flat, pale gold and filling my eye. On the right, at the edge of my vision, is a thread of blue, the dreaded sea - but I scarcely notice. When you are so near the ground anyway, the sea is only a low brush line of colour.

One year more and all is changed. Guernsey.

A granite cottage with a thatched roof. It sits on a tiny headland between two bays. It is owned by a friend of an old colleague of Father's. I have been in the island before, but I was only six months old, and the rich Guernsey milk made me ill. Now I am five and open to all the new experiences and blisses the island pours out for me and Gerald and our Guernsey friend, Henry.

The biggest change is the sea.

Vazon Bay was like Woolacombe - not so big perhaps, but hotter, emptier, and lapped by a calm sea as obedient as a slave. The blazing sun baked the sands. The slow tide crept up and the shallow sea was warmed. The ripples at the edge were only little frills of froth. Seaweed had all been washed up, dried and deposited above the tide line. The rocks were half a mile away. You could run into the warm silky water and be breast deep without a single pebble or crab or strand of sea-lettuce impeding you. Then there was the TYRE. Daddy had begged an old lorry inner-tube from a garage-owning friend, and we leaped on it, lay on it, floated on it, swam in it, dived through it and paddled about in it through long, blissful mornings and afternoons. The pale green water shimmering over the sandy bottom, the nets of light and shade it cast, became my second world. The sea was my joy, my friend, my playground. I had no fear. I dog-paddled by instinct. I could hardly be dragged out of the water when at five o'clock it was judged best we should pack up and climb the thirty foot rise to the cottage for supper, oil-lamps and sleep.

The cottage, "La Giffardière", was our home only for a few weeks of our year, but for three or four years of my childhood it was so important that it elbowed out all the rest of my life. School, home, Christmas, Brownies, Sally - all were interesting but nothing came near to the solid reality, the primary importance, of life at "The Cottage". It fulfilled something in all of us, I believe. My father's growing awareness of the colourful beauty of the world around him and his power to pin it down in paintings, was sparked off by the fantastic colours of the Guernsey coast. My mother's quite natural desire to live for a little according to the Cottage simplicity of her Irish home, and not the middle-class pretentiousness she married into, found satisfaction in La Giffardière. For me the place was simply Paradise.

Here, in the easy conditions of those days, we lived and picnicked and made-shift. When the great thunder-storms swept over from France, and the rainwater poured in a river down the little front path from the road, under the front door, down the central passage where my bed was, and out to the back garden, we just opened the doors and let it wash through over the big grey stone flags that floored the dwelling. The roof was another matter. We did have to rush round putting buckets and basins under drips from the thatch, but over the

few summers that we rented the cottage, we grew quite smart at catching the dribbles before they soaked our beds or spoiled the polish on the wardrobes.

Guernsey, so near the French coast, had been fortified during the Napoleonic wars, and the bays were punctuated by Martello towers. The low headland on which the cottage stood had a granite platform at the end, like a nail on a fingertip; it had been a gun-battery, and a sauntering track led to it just across the road. You pushed your way between encroaching furze and tamarisk, feet confined to the threadlike sandy path, and after passing the enclosure where half a dozen contented geese grazed, you stepped on to the sun-baked granite slabs. Once there must have been a protective wall, but the shaped blocks had been carted away over the years for barns or byres, leaving only a foot-high, broad border, comfortable for sitting, springy with seathrift and short pink heather. The ground dropped beyond a slope of slippery grass that was a challenge to slide down, to the jumble of rocks below. A tiny bay curved in at one side and Vazon stretched peacefully on the other. It was dangerous coast, with reefs peering from the water at low tide, and the islet of L'Erée with its lighthouse on the far point. Here we would stroll down at eight or nine in the evening, to sit on the low granite blocks, still blood-warm from the day's scorching sun, and gaze out westwards to watch the spectacular sunsets. Some time about then there had been a great volcanic eruption and "they said" that the dust circling the earth for seasons afterwards caused these wonderful sunsets. I have never seen anything like them since. The breeze would drop and the utter calm that so often ends a summer day would smooth the sea to glass. It grew paler even than the sky, with a pearly sheen. Rocky outcrops, black against the west, were mirrored almost intact in the polished water. The sky would fade to faint green; then shell pink and rose would flush it over. Dusty gold would line the horizon, and any shreds of cloud would be mauve and lilac, mealy like the bloom on a grape. Moment by moment the colours would shift and blend, growing richer and deeper, until gradually the vibrant violet of dusk hooded us overhead and closed down on the west. Then we sighed and felt our way back to the cottage, looking into the eastern sky where the soft honey-yellow stars of heatwave blurred and blinked over the low trees and the glass-houses, and the daisy-wheels of the many windmills began to creak and turn idly as the night breeze awoke.

These sunsets were so glorious that Father, drunk with colour, determined somehow to capture them. There was no colour photography then, so he prepared papers, drawing in the outlines of the shadowy coast. and rock strewn sea and blocking in simply the features that would not change. Then, as sundown approached, he would take his board and paintbox and be ready on the battery wall as the sun dipped. The paper was soaked over with clear water and as the sunset grew into its rose and gold-tissued splendour, all he had to do was wash in each evening's panorama; lilac, turquoise and flame; silver gilt, rose and crimson; apricot and amethyst. A few of these sunsets still remain in our house, foxed with the damp of half a life-time in the loft, but breathing something of the miracle and wonder of those halcyon summer evenings.

Not all the evenings were still with a lambent sea. Storms came over from France, thunderstorms brawling over the Brittany coast, far enough away not to be frightening, but near enough to be a fireworks display like none other I had seen. The thunder muttered under its breath, but the lightning, in blue white zig-zags and lilac sheets, leaped like tigers from the pitchy black. The sea would suddenly stand out a milky plate while the electric bolts jerked their crazy legs in a frantic dance. Soon, the noise would grow louder and a new chill would envelop us. "Rain's coming!" and we would turn and race up the little hill to the cottage, and draw the orange linen curtains to shut out the flashes when they were right overhead. That might well be a night when we had to watch the rain sweep shallow over the flags from front door to back and when you had to remember to put your sandshoes on the chair, and stuff newspapers under the doors of the other rooms to keep the wet on its relatively harmless course into the back garden.

Spring tide and a high wind brought another sort of sea-drama for us to watch. Vazon Bay was shallow and above the high-tide mark, a band of boulders had been rolled by the winter seas, but not enough to protect the road and the grazing-land beyond. A sea wall of granite went all round the bay, and behind its shelter lay the road. In a storm the road was impassable. Great breakers as high as a house crowded into the bay and exploded on the sea wall. Tons of water smashed down on the road, to drain out slowly through the gullies. On nights of storm, we would wrap ourselves in waterproofs and, clinging to the tamarisks, edge our way to the top of the bluff to watch the show from above. The spray burst right up to our level, and the driving wind slapped it horizontally half the width of the bay, to soak us where we stood. When a great wave as big as a railway train rolled in and crashed on the sea-wall, the ground lurched and rang beneath our feet and the shockwaves jolted through my bones. Hour after hour the pounding and the riot went on, a primeval chaos, boiling with power and howling like a million demons.

If the gale blew itself out in the night, the shore the next morning would be a strange, forbidding place. The dry silvery sand that held its sunbaked warmth over each night would be hard, grey and chilly. Piles of sodden sea-weed would be flung like dirty clothes right up to the wall; bladder-wrack, hopping with a cloud of sand flies; broad, frilly-edged ribbon wrack with its tough rats'-tail anchor wrenched bodily from-the sea-bed; tattered and sordid rags of pale green sea-lettuce, crab shells and claws, driftwood and cuttlefish bone, all stinking of iodine. Distastefully we would haul them all into piles and clear a patch for our daily camp, where the sun could get at the sand and dry it out again, and warm the cold wall to comfort our backs. But several days would pass before we could again burrow our fists deep into the loose sand and find it still warm, then let it run between our fingers in a flashing salty shower, powder-dry and sweet smelling.

After a storm too, the edge of the sea was thick with a sludge of rubbish and weed hurled in by the waves, and taking days to be left high and dry or to be washed out to deep water again. Instead of clear pure ripples, where we could stand and laugh at our own feet looking bloated and white in the water, we had to prance through ten yards of swirling weed that clung horribly round the toes and ankles, and hid lurking nameless terrors. Your foot plunged through the murk and with a scurry and sickening wriggle, something would thrust itself away beneath your toes. You could advance cautiously, testing the sand as you went and giving fair warning to scuttling crab or lug-worm, but then the thin rags of sea-lettuce caught loathsomely in your toes, like wet lavatory-paper. Better to lift your feet high and bounce as fast as possible through the messy shallows to the clean, clear water beyond, where the sun rippled a net on the sandy bottom and you could see that there were no lurking pebbles to stab your tender instep.

I was two years older than the baby who had screamed at the edge of the grey Irish Sea, and this sea was warm - the shallows ran a long way out. There were no hidden dangers. Even before I could swim properly, I could boast to the other children when I went back to school that I was allowed to go in right up to my chin. Dog-paddle and duck-dive came naturally, well before the meticulous breast-stroke learned at the Public Baths, and anyway, my brother would never be far away. 'The Tyre' held us in a fascinated group, and was big and buoyant enough to be a sort of life raft as well as a toy and a gymnasium, for three or four of us. Here the water was warm silk, and its colours pale aquamarine, jade and purple. The red granite rocks and pale gold sand of the island turned the sea Mediterranean shades. Its hyacinth and turquoise and ultramarine were the colours of the sea in my lovely book of Greek myths. All winter long, I would pore over its pictures, seeing in the waves washing round poor Andromache, or floating Danae in her tub, the glass green of Vazon, or the royal blue of the deep water below the cliffs at Forêt

There were other bays in easy reach besides Vazon. If we felt like half-a-mile, instead of a hundred yards, there was Cobo. A mile would take us to Grandes Rocques, where our island friends had an old Army Hut as a summer dwelling. A jolting ride in the charabanc, with brass lamps, a canvas roof that pulled forwards in bad weather, and a door to every seat, would take us through the narrow sunken lanes and past the acres of glass houses, to St Peter Port, a steep little town tumbling on its nose into the sea. There we could pick up Auntie Elsie and Henry, and go on to the cliff side of the island, where shady water lanes curled down slowly to sea-level, funnels cut by the little streams through three hundred feet of cliff, and emerging, with their fresh water rills fanning across the crescents of sand. These coves faced due south and the sun burned into them all day until a curtain of shade from the western cliff angled across the sand and signalled time for home. Pack the baskets, roll up the wet bathing costumes in sausages of towel, and climb again slowly up the gullies, where meadowsweet still bloomed beside the stream-bed, along the open track of polished pebbles where the sun still shone, and into the arch of wind-knotted trees, stunted ilex and hazel, dark and cool, until at the top we came to the calm-faced old granite dwellings, cushioned all round with huge luxurious hydrangea bushes. Their flowers were as big as cauliflowers, and pale blue, pink and mauve bloomed side by side, all on the one bush. They had no scent, but their clear sugar-almond colours still seem to me the very essence of Guernsey.

In some of the bays, and Vazon was one, the chains and ribs of rock beyond the sand broke some of the force of the waves as they thundered up from Ushant to explode on the island's flank. Where the coast was lower and only sand dunes lay beyond the high-tide mark, groynes of heavy timber, tarred and buried deep in the sands, made a comb of black teeth, twenty feet apart, all along the vulnerable shore. These made charming little family camping grounds when we arrived to spend a day on the beach. We would take possession of our favourite groynes, and have a little low-walled room between them, with privacy for dressing and undressing, something to lean your back on, a place to hang bathing costumes to dry, and a gymnasium for the children to balance walk and vault over. They kept the wind off and we might boil a kettle for tea on the Primus, if our party was large enough to make it worth while. There are snapshots of us all on those blissful afternoons. Auntie Elsie was hooking a rug in orange and brown squares, and it was spread out on her knees amid the dry, crackly sea-weed and the salt sand. Mother was always content to savour the enchantment of having nothing to do - no darning, no silver

to polish - and would let the sand trickle endlessly through her fingers, burnishing her wedding ring to a white glitter, as the gentle chat and laughter passed between her and Elsie. Gerald and Henry and I would be lolling on towels, or hammocked in the red rubber tyre that we took into the sea. Father's panama, Mother's squashy straw beach hat that you could sit on and it would spring up again unharmed, my water wings, Auntie's woven rush market bag of tomatoes, cups and milk and bananas, Father's painting satchel, bathing caps, a paper-parasol and Mother's shabbiest handbag littered the sand around us, while the shapeless cotton sacks we called bathing costumes dried over the groyne behind us. It all looked as cosy and sordid as a wayside gypsy camp, especially if the Primus was going and the battered tin kettle spitting steam at the brown tea-pot waiting in the hot sand beside it.

Wool jersey bathing costumes were coming in during my childhood. They replaced the cotton suits which had no stretch and had to button on the shoulder, and hung loosely on the figure when dry. But once they were wet, they wrinkled like a prune and clung closer than skin, moulding themselves disgracefully to the body in all those areas where it would have been preferable for them not to cling. Looking at some of the family snapshots of us all bathing at Vazon or Petit Port, I feel that Regency courtesans who wore nothing but a gauze shift damped to follow their curves, were no more immodest than we!

Mother first, then Father, ventured into wool. He had a black Jantzen with yellow stripes round the waist. It was known as The Wasp and he wore it for forty years, and after he died, Mother took it over because it was easy to get in and out of on the beach. When

I first remember her bathing, she wore a tangerine cotton dress with its little frilly half-skirt embroidered in white. Gerald wore a nondescript black cotton bag, and I had a bright yellow one with black borders that was so big it took me three years to grow out of it and graduate to a neat red woollen Jantzen.

Honesty forces me to say, however, that I owe that dreadful yellow cotton some gratitude, although it embarrassed me so much when we went to the Baths from school, and everyone else had woollen suits. In Handwork at that time we were being taught to knit, and in the Spring we had all made square kettle-holders, except me. Mine was a wavy-edged rhomboid. We had been given thick wooden needles with twenty stitches cast on and told to knit a square. I took mine home and brought it back the next week, mysteriously expanded to fifty-three stitches. So when the other little girls, having mastered the art like a lot of old grannies, were promised that they could knit themselves bathing costumes for the summer, I was taken aside and told that they did not think I was quite ready to attempt that yet and I had better make a coat-hanger cover. I did not really mind. I found knitting dull anyway.

Three-ply wool was bought in the school green, and the cute little swim-suits begun. While I laboured at my two inch wide strip of royal blue, lurching from row to holey row, Sally and Betty and Jean clicked needles professionally and the Mickey Mouse costumes grew, with a bib in front and crossover braces at the back. When they were tried on they looked very jaunty and up to date and I thought privately about my ghastly yellow cotton clinging like the skin of a hippo, and how silly I was going to look among all the other little girls, darting and splashing in their smart cross-straps.

We had our first day at the Baths. I crept from my cubicle and withdrew half-way up the pool side, where I sat and dangled my toes in the pale green water, trying to look as though I did not belong to the green Mickey Mice at all. One by one they emerged, all alike and all smart. They gathered at the shallow end where steps led down into the water. Cautiously they descended and stood hugging themselves with preliminary shivers. The swimming instructress called them to order and obediently they all ducked and plunged forward to hold the rail at the side. I watched them and my mouth fell open in astonishment. Those swimming costumes, knitted in loose garter stitch and three-ply wool, grew sodden with water and enormously heavy. The weight and drag were too much, far too much, for the flimsy cross straps to support. They sagged and stretched and slithered off their wearer's shoulders as she swam, A dozen dark green bundles sank to the white tiles at the bottom, while a dozen shrieking and scarlet peeled shrimps floundered about in the glass-clear water, and I sat on the edge in my yellow horror and laughed and laughed and laughed.

Holiday food was one of the great attractions about Guernsey. The cottage had a small oil stove - the Hut only Primus stoves. Cooking was minimal and simple. All the things I disliked at home vanished for a few weeks. Brown stews with lumps of beef and carrot, the even worse grey stews with mutton and nasty sharp bones of scrag end, soggy greens, stewed prunes and custard, fried herrings - we could not have cooked them even if Mother had wanted to spend sunny hours coaxing an oil cooker when she could have been basking on the sand or 'swimming' with one leg on the bottom. Soon after breakfast, she would fill one of the wooden tomato baskets that were almost the island's symbol with thick crusty sandwiches, hunks of bread and farm butter, slapped together over corned beef or pink ham, with draggle-tailed petticoats of fat trailing out over the crust. She would pile in tomatoes, jolly and shining by the pound, whole lettuces, so clean from the ground that they only needed chopping in quarters to be munched, bananas, Jersey wonders, or, best of all to me, Lyons Cup Cakes (chocolate were the nicest). There was a special ritual for eating these delicious substitutes for pudding. They were baked in crinkly paper cases, and then icing was poured on so that they were table-flat on top. The icing was thick in the middle but luxurious round the edges. First you eased off the paper cup, carefully, but no matter how careful you were, some crumbs of icing would cling in the flutings, so you nibbled round and round the paper rim scraping the icing off with your front teeth. Next you turned the cake upside down and ate it upwards towards the cap of icing. A judiciously exploring tongue would lick out the final traces of cake and leave you with a delicious disc of fudgy icing, smooth and shiny on top and a good half-inch thick round the edges. This could be enjoyed just as slowly and stickily as a bar of chocolate and was an exotic and sensuous finish to a perfect meal, while the tide crawled lazily up the hot sand. Half an hour flat on your back, easing a full stomach into digestion, the sun beating down on closed eyelids, and we were ready to wriggle into our still damp cotton bathing suits for the long wallow and splash, paddle and duck, and dip and gasp and float of the afternoon in the sea. The water, warmed by the scorched sand was tepid, and very clear.

Little wavelets creamed over our insteps and tickled as we made our way in. Our feet looked white with huge bulbous toes; our shins seemed to bend half-way down and nets and loops of light shimmied  on the sandy bottom. Then with a scream and a flurry of splash Henry would go tearing past, showering me with spray, and dragging the coveted tyre behind him. I would launch myself after him, my water-wings pulling up under my armpits, and neck deep in the pale green water we would tumble and float for the long hot afternoon. No limit was put on the time we spent in the sea. Only tea-time and time to dress to go home put a stop to our play.

Not all our holidays were as paradisal as the Guernsey ones. I am lucky that in this span of eight years I am recalling, we had four Island summers. But there were others. When I was eight we went to Seascale, on the Lake District coast. Here we rented a dark little house in Railway Terrace. A footpath, but no road, ran along the front of the houses - then beyond a line of tall, spiked iron railings the embankment soared up at once. The trains ran along at roof level and we seemed to be living at the bottom of a well. It was a depressing house, smelling of lino and cabbages, and hardly ever glimpsing the sun.

The attraction of Seascale for Father was the scenery of the Lakes, and the nearness of the railway. At that time you could buy weekly 'Runabout' tickets which allowed you to go pretty well anywhere you liked by rail, provided you came back to your starting point the same day. There may also have been a limit on how far you travelled in the week - I do not remember - but the week's ticket cost 10/- and was very good value. With one of these tickets, Father could put his bicycle in the Guard's Van, go to some station like Keswick, and then have rides through the fells and time to have a few hours sketching. Sometimes he had to go back for a second day to finish the picture. Sometimes Gerald went too, and one week, we all had tickets and visited Friars Crag, Windermere and Wastwater (which overawed me with the desolation of grey barren screes and the black lake below).

We went to Coniston and climbed Old Man; this effectively put me off mountaineering for life. I was too young to care about scenery. The day was hot and we toiled and sweated up the slippery grass. Time and again I was heartened by seeing the last slope cut out against the sky, only to find on cresting it, that yet another tier of the hill lay beyond. I grew cross and tired and the whole expedition seemed pointless.

In our railway journeyings, we had passed Barrow-in-Furness, and seen Puffing Billy in his glass case on the platform, and had run along the coast behind Grange-over-Sands. As I was dragged unwillingly to one beauty spot after another, I kept in mind the enticing sweep of pale parchment beach that marked this resort, and begged, as each expedition was discussed, that we could go to Grange. After the Coniston day, Father must have felt I deserved a little indulgence and to Grange we went.

It should have been called Grange-over-Mud. Perhaps we were unlucky in our choice, but the part of the beach where we settled for an hour or two's castle building and swimming turned out to be grey slime and quicksands. As you slopped through the mud, strange transparent jellied atomies squirmed and leaped around you, slimy things that crawled with legs, or sprang against you with every sucking step. You dug your spade into what looked like clean damp sand, and produced a hole that filled at once with water. You ventured a few paces from the rocks where the family sat and the ground began to whirl and sink away beneath you and you were buried to your knees before Father could haul you out. It was disappointing and frightening, and I also felt guilty because it was my urgent begging that had brought us all here for a wasted day. We would have been better off staying at Seascale.

The Seascale beach was straight and narrow, stretching northwards towards St Bees' Head, backed by a thin line of dunes, and tormented all that August by a restless chill wind that brought grey rollers in growling off the Irish Sea. It was a stormy season and I felt the let down after the heat-waves of two successive summers in Guernsey. It was too cold to swim, though I was prepared to paddle if I could find a clean place to do so. I wore a thick vest and jersey and still the wind fingered through and nipped me with chill. The dunes were low and narrow. They did not offer the sheltered nooks we could find at Grandes Roques where the wind would be cut off and the sun have a chance. We sat on mackintoshes and huddled towels round our shoulders and over our legs, between forays down to the tide line to hunt shells, or to the end of the wooden jetty to dangle our toes shudderingly in the icy water. The sea-edge was unappetizing, thick with tangled and torn seaweed and scuttling small sea-creatures that scurried invisibly over your toes. The rough westerlies swept all the rubbish in on the tides and it washed in and out with the breaking waves but rarely cleared away. A couple of nights of storm filled the bay with jelly fish. In the morning the sands were strewn with thousands of rainbow blobs of jelly, helplessly stranded. They lay there like soap-bubbles, iridescent and delicately fringed, littering the sand, loathsome to tread on, and still drifting in millions in the water so that even paddling was too horrifying to attempt. Among them were a few of the plate-sized brown ones, segmented like an orange. These were the stinging jelly-fish, not really dangerous, but capable of raising a very nasty rash.

As the tide dropped, the ones left on the shore dehydrated in the wind. Their water drained away, their mesh of cell walls collapsed, and by mid-day all trace of them had gone except for circles cut in the sand as if with a pastry cutter, where their fringed edges had been the last to collapse and melt away into air, into thin air.

At Vazon we had picnicked on the beach, though the cottage was only a few hundred yards away. At Seascale, we were glad enough to go back to Railway Terrace for lunch; dark though the house was it offered at least shelter from the wind, and a hot meal. We ate as simply as we could, to give Mother a little rest from full scale housekeeping. Lunch would be corned beef and bread, with a huge boiling of sliced kidney beans, which Mother adored, well plastered with butter; or we had tomatoes, fruit and shop cake. After lunch as often as not, Mother would 'have a rest' and I would either read or mooch off by myself to glue my nose to small shop windows, or sit among the dunes gossiping with Jane and Lucy, two girls there with their widowed mother.

There was a newsagents at the end of Railway Terrace, and here Father bought me cheap shilling editions of novels to pass the time - H.G.Wells' "The Lady from the Sea", "The First Men on the Moon" and Jules Verne's "20,000 Leagues under the Sea" beguiled long chilly afternoons at Seascale, so it was not all loss.

The shore was safe and I had no desire to swim anyway, on those cold days when Mother preferred a quiet house with the eiderdown and a hotwater bottle to sitting chatting to Jane's and Lucy's mother amid the blown sand and the marram grass. So I could go to the beach unquestioned. But I preferred to roam the few streets and flatten my nose against plate glass windows. One tiny chemist's shop just around the corner by the sea drew me back day after day. Radox Bath Salts were specially recommended for soaking tired feet (a fairly common complaint in the Lake District in those days when 'hiking' was the newest popular craze). To encourage sales, they were giving away necklaces as free gifts and the window was decked with Radox boxes and strings of multi-coloured beads of many shapes so that each necklace looked like a swag of assorted sweets square, oval, lozenge, disc and ball, in puce, emerald, sky blue and the shattering shiny pink that pill boxes used to be covered in. I coveted them. I hung about for hours, breathing on the panes and trying to decide which tawdry string of glassy Liquorice Allsorts I would choose if only I had the money to buy a box of Radox to soak my corns! I tried to interest Mother. She had corns, but she was not smitten by the beauty of the beads as I was, so I had no luck. All the same, they drew me back, day after day, and

flash through my memory as the one streak of colour in an otherwise grey and melancholy summer.

Father's enormous square hands looked clumsy, but he could do the most delicate work in almost Chinese detail. He could make anything out of wood or silver but more and more he found pleasure in water-colours. It was the colours of the Guernsey coast that had started him off, when I was less than a year old, and by the time of the Seascale holiday eight years later, his pleasure lay in getting away from the rest of us and having long silent days of quiet independence, pinning down on tinted David Cox paper the blues and greys and myriad greens of the fells, and the shifting rainbows of mist and light that veiled receding mountains. It was a good summer for him, whatever it was for us, and anyway the next year we were back in Guernsey again, in a flat in the steep French streets of St Peter Port, and the whole island open to us as I grew taller and able to walk happily three or four miles to the unfrequented coves among the cliffs of the sunny south coast.

That third summer in Guernsey was a sociable time, when the Scout Troop from Father's school was there in camp, in charge of two masters, their wives and families, Clare and Wyn and their son who was Gerald's age, and small Léonie's parents. Léonie was the baby whose mother had inspired me, at the age of three, to take off my coat elegantly, with a cup of tea balanced on my lap, and Léonie by now was seven and as lively as a grasshopper. The family groups coalesced, along with our Guernsey friends who seemed to fit in as though they had always known everyone. There were always plenty of young folk to play with. This was the summer when Henry and I wandered off inland one day and found a delectable rocky place, with little cliffs broken into rough staircases, just right for climbing. We slithered in among them from the bracken and gorse bushes, finding every minute new crags to scale and new chimney routes to the top. I had recently been taken with the school, to see a film about Mallory and Irving climbing Everest, and was deeply impressed by it, because it had a sort of personal contact; 'Beaky', our teacher, had been at University with one of the two - I forget which - but secretly it had impressed me no end to find that one of my despised teachers knew

46

someone famous, although dead. Henry and I played Everest among the rocks happily until we became aware of someone shouting. Dazed and silly, we gazed about. A man in braces and shirt-sleeves was silhouetted against the sky on the far side of the rocky hollow. He was flailing his arms and dancing like a madman. "Run, you silly little buggers. Run", he kept shouting. I was always afraid of trespassing and being caught, so I prepared to scramble down the rocks and worm my way back to the beach unseen through the gorse. But Henry, who had a cooler head than mine, suddenly grabbed my arm and pulled me furiously the other way, up the last steps of rock, and over the lip. "Lie down", he shouted at me, throwing himself flat on the ground. I copied, bewildered, and the earth lurched and rang, as an explosion heaved the rock face below us. It was not just where we had been, but not so far away. In the silence after it, while my ears were still singing in my head, the slither and grate of falling shale whispered on the warm afternoon air. Henry lay still, his face greenish and shiny with sweat. He said nothing.

"What was it?", I asked at last.

"It's a quarry. They were blasting. We should have noticed the red flag". He nodded towards the bluff of rocks that nosed up out of the short turf on the other side. A flag pole, stayed with guy-ropes, flew a red square that hung limply in the heat. It meant nothing to me, and Henry had not known there was a working quarry on that coast - but he knew about red warning flags, because they were flown on the shooting butts at Grandes Rocques when the garrison was having target practice.

It was time we left. Two subdued and very thankful brats wriggled their way swiftly under bracken and crept unseen to the shore. "When we get back, put your jersey on", said Henry.

"Why? "

"So that man can't recognise your yellow blouse if he comes looking for us. We won't half get into trouble if he does!"

Maybe he did. I do not know. But we stayed close to the family party for the rest of the day, decorously clad in dark jerseys, sitting between the Mothers, who never suspected how nearly we had qualified as filling for Shepherd's Pie!

I brushed with death twice that summer.

Another camp on the island, not far from our Scouts, was a group of boys from a great orphanage. They were short of suitable clothes for an island camping holiday and someone, somewhere, had got hold of some lengths of furnishing cretonne, printed with chintzy designs of flowers, fruits and parrots. These had been made into shorts for the boys so that their good grey flannels should not be worn out. Nowadays, no one would turn for a second look at forty boys in cretonne shorts, unless out of envy, but then, the poor lads must have suffered torments of embarrassment and shame. Wherever they went on the island, a gasp greeted their arrival; the grownups quickly recovered their countenance, but the children had neither understanding nor pity. Jeers and catcalls followed them everywhere. Even if we, and the Scouts, had got used to them after a week, there were always new arrivals to look in astonishment or burst into rude laughter, and boys, both visitors and island boys, would follow the group's heels, shouting "Who stole the sofa cushions?" and "Got 'is mother's knickers on!". The two men who were in charge of the party must have had both sympathy and guts, for they nobly clad themselves in dark blue and tomato flowery knicks as well. As for the boys, they stuck together, and on the quiet and just round the corner out of sight, I reckon a few Island noses got bloodied and a few Island eyes bunged up.

One long hot day at Petit Port, our Scouts and the Flowery Boys had all been there, and the whole Staff group from school had gone over. Some of Henry's friends had joined us, and at the end of the day, when we had to go back up the three hundred and something steps to the top of the cliff, we young ones turned it into a race. The steps were shallow, sandy and irregular, edged with timber and twisting in dog-legged flights, with resting stages in between. As I was the youngest of the racing group, and a determined show-off, I was naturally intent on winning. The older ones, Gerald and Alec and Duncan, were not racing seriously; they had more sense, so I fairly easily overtook them and pelted on up the cliff, neck and neck with Henry, and passing batches of the Flowery Boys, toiling upward in the dusty sunshine that still struck dazzling on the upper face. Almost at the top, and very blown, I reached a landing and caught at the flimsy wooden rail that protected it from the steep drop that fell nearly sheer with rocky outcrops, and bracken to the boulders below.

Strange things began to happen. The horizon swung up and down,

the landscape seemed to close in from the sides, and then the day began to grow dim. I was observing the spinning scene with curiosity and saying aloud in an interested way, "How funny! Everything's going dark" when with a lurch I was yanked backwards.

Some minutes later I opened my eyes to find myself lying flat on the stony landing, with a group of Flowery Boys fanning me with towels. Father's head appeared above the steps and I was made to stay lying down while it was explained that the boys had arrived up the steps to hear me saying "Everything's going dark", and see me tilt and slump over the hand-rail, about to roll into the gulf below. They grabbed me and dragged me back, and almost certainly saved my life. Bless their little cotton shorts!

I felt perfectly well in a few minutes, but I was treated like fragile china, which I found embarrassing, and had to be examined by

a doctor friend also on holiday. He pronounced, on no grounds at all, that I was slightly anaemic, and for three years afterwards I was kept on a regime of iron pills, which were no trouble, and halibut liver oil which WAS. Five drops of the nauseating stuff every day. They used to put it on a piece of orange so I could get it down, but the taste remained, stomach turning and powerful, for six or seven hours. It was more than I could endure and I resorted to guile. As soon as lunch was over, I quickly learned to jump up, saying "I'll just take my halibut liver oil", and go to the kitchen where I would deftly put my five unspeakable drops straight down the sink.

4. HOUSES AND HOMES

have in front of me a picture in pastels (done by Father in 1931) of the living room of The Cottage - 'La Giffardière' where we spent long Guernsey holidays. It was everybody's dream cottage, granite built, thatched, with Dorothy Perkins roses crowding round the back door, and Gloire de Dijon round the front. A wicket gate up at road level led to a short stone path. You came in the green front door and the same wide grey flags floored the large passage straight through and out into the sunshine at the back. The second part of the passage could be cut off by a curtain and behind it there was just room for a crosslegged camp bed and a bare twelve inches to sidle past to the door. Here I slept. The big double bed in the only bedroom was for the parents, and you had to go through their bedroom to get to the lean-to kitchen beyond with an oil stove and a Primus for cooking. On the other side of the passage lay this lovely sitting room, the depth of the cottage, with windows deep set in the foot thick granite walls front and back. The fireplace was open nearly to the black beamed ceiling. We needed no fires in summer and it was set about with great brass and copper pans, and the shelf above it, frilled with orange linen, had willow-pattern plates and jugs. Blue and white china, old and faded, polished copper and brass, rush matting on the floor, gleaming dark oak table and ladderback chairs - all the picture postcard stuff, but real, genuine, plain, solid, and above all, loved. It was stepping back fifty years in time even in those days, and Father has it all pinned down on paper, the soft orange curtains, echoed by the great shallow bowl of marigolds and nasturtiums he had set on the round table, the straw coloured matting, the faded blue and white of the wing-chair. There was a fragrance and a peace about the place that I am glad to

have known. It was such a dwelling as Flora Thompson describes as being superseded by newer and shoddier ways even in her childhood in "Lark Rise". There was little in 'La Giffardière' that would have been out of the reach of a family who had lived in it and passed down their belongings over the generations. More dishes for ornament certainly, but little else. There were oil-lamps, that smoked and smelled if you were sluttish in your care of them, and we had to go to bed by candle-light. Sparrows got in the thatch, and water trickled through it in thunderstorms. The 'plumbing' was a bucket closet outside, that had to be emptied in a pit at the far end of the garden. In winter, driftwood burned in the basket grate of the hearth and no doubt the stone floors whistled with draughts. But there was a four-square sturdiness, a pride, independence and self-sufficiency about the place. We did not feel like summer visitors there. We felt we had slipped back into a place where we belonged not by right of inheritance, but because we too were only a generation removed from the tough life of these fishermen-farmers, and we had no sense of hardship in living this way. It was more a matter of wonder to us to be able to turn a switch and get electric light than to undress and go to bed in the dark because your candle had blown out.

The Islanders who built the cottage would have housed a whole family in those two rooms, but we spread a little further. I slept in the passage and Gerald had a bed in a wooden summer-house in the garden. Lucky Gerald. Sleeping in odd places was something I enjoyed. I remember being furious for a whole day when we had unexpected visitors to be put up overnight, and I had it worked out that if they had to have my room - which they did - I would sleep on the sitting-room sofa. But Authority had arranged it otherwise and decreed, most unreasonably, that fifteen year old Gerald should fold himself up on to the two-seater sofa while I had his bed. It was not just disappointing, it was so silly. I was much shorter and it would have been a positive pleasure to me. It was only a pain in the neck for him.

The rather surprising thing about fleas is that we were not tormented by them. A thatched roof, semi-wild garden, and plenty of livestock nearby ought to have meant at least something of a battle against them, but only once did we suffer. One flea, just one, got into the double bed. It was a feather bed, and that could make a flea a safe stronghold from which it could scarcely be dislodged. Mother's Olio Cookery Book said on the subject:-

"Fleas in a Bed (to Catch)

Remove the bedclothes gently. Take a piece of damp soap and dab onto the flea. This prevents it escaping".

Father followed the instructions to the letter. I can see him now removing the bedclothes gently. The trouble was, the flea had not read

the same book and played by different rules. It did not wait to be dabbed!

Anybody can pick up a flea living in the country, but Mother's childhood had been perilously poised just above the slope that led down to poverty and social degradation, and she was sensitive on such matters. We were earnestly enjoined never to mention that flea-especially not to anyone at home. Auntie Elsie, over from St Peter Port, could and did laugh uproariously at the picture of Father, gimlet-eyed and grasping his soap, pouncing fruitlessly on the nimble brown atomy on the bottom sheet, and Mother joined in the laughter - but the thought of Sally's mother knowing that we had a flea in the bed was too awful to be contemplated. For years I thought that fleas were unmentionable in polite society. I was so protected from this seamy side of life that I had never even heard of nits, and when a few years later, on holiday in Ireland, I was found to be absolutely crawling with them, I was astonished. I just thought sand in my hair was making my scalp itch. I did not know you could have lice.

My bed in the cottage was a canvas stretcher on two X shaped trestles and needed only to be unfolded to block the passage at night. When it rained very heavily, the other ceilings leaked from the thatch and the night was musical with the droppings of water into tin basins and galvanised buckets. Only when it was really torrential was I disturbed. Then the rain poured down the short path from the road, came under the front door, swept over the stone flags below my bed, and out again at the back. As long as your shoes or book or vest and knickers were not on the floor at the time it happened, it was quite fun to prop yourself on one elbow and enjoy the drama of going to bed in the middle of a river. Gerald in the woodshed had a tame time by comparison.

Gerald slept outside but we did most of our living out there as well. Only if it was too damp or windy would we eat at the round polished table in the pretty sitting room. Otherwise we had meals on a ricketty rustic table in the garden, just outside the kitchen door. The greater part of most days, anyway, was spent at one or other of the bays - usually our own Vazon, a mere two hundred yards away - and we took a picnic lunch.

The garden was divided into three little square plots of dried up lawn, with Dorothy Perkins roses in crude pink nodding pom-poms dividing them. Marigolds flopped untidily in the narrow borders, tamarisk bushes feathered the blue sky but gave no shade, and a pile of stones that might once have been a rockery was covered with a

54

juicy strident mass of nasturtiums. These delighted me. They were fiddly to pick and Mother did not want to be bothered, but I could pick as many as I liked - it only made them bloom more lavishly. If I ran in with both hands bulging with a top-heavy bunch of orange and yellow and cream, she would cram their stalks jam-packed into a willow-pattern jug, and we would place it in the sitting room - on the hearthstone to glow against the soot-blackened chimney back - on the wide deep window sill, or looking admiringly down at itself in the polish of the round oak table. Then we would sigh with pleasure, Mother at the picture of the 'perfect cottage' and wish she could live there for ever; I at the vivid colours, and the satisfaction of being able to pick flowers to my heart's content. Marigolds were nice, too, with their round flat seedheads, like crinkly buttons - but nasturtium seeds were best - little lobed green brains on juicy stalks that twisted round in a fascinating spiral when the flower faded.

No other holiday home we ever had came up to the Cottage. I think of it even now (I expect some millionaire owns it) as "home", not as a place we stayed in. I remember very well the agony of the last evening we were there when I was seven. The knowledge hung on me like an actual weight that tomorrow we would have to dress in our town clothes and the laced-up leather shoes that I had never put on since the outward journey, and locking the Cottage door behind us, start the long way back, deeper and deeper into gloom. Of course, much of the trouble was that I had sold my soul to the tabby cat and her three kittens, and my yearning to take them all back to England with us had been denied. "Don't worry - they are going to good homes." Dear little cats. How I long still to believe it was true.

There were the geese as well, who lived in a wired off enclosure down by the battery. I took my grief across the road and down the

55

little path to their run. They came cackling to the wire expecting the usual crusts, but we had emptied the breadcrock except for what was needed for breakfast, and I had only tufts of dry grass to give them. I can feel the mesh on my fingers, and the setting sun on my neck, as I stand too desperate even to cry, and knowing consciously for the first time the dead weight of the inescapable - this is the end.

We lived in another 'house' in Guernsey later. We called it "The Hut". It was left over from the Great War - circular, corrugated iron, with a shallow conical roof. The peak of this roof was an open hole, sheltered above by a little hat of tin. Directly underneath was the table and one day a mouse fell through the hole and plummetted neatly into a quart of milk providentially sitting in a jug below. Two pints of sweet milk we had to empty onto the grass, and the astonished little mouse must have been very well fed by the time it had groomed itself dry!

The Hut belonged to our friends in St Peter Port and they used it at weekends. Grandes Roques was not a village, just a handful of fisher cottages at one angle of the island and a big hotel in pepperpot Scottish Baronial style, on the headland beyond. It was two bays up from Vazon, a sandy cove, but the rocks were spectacular. There was a thin line of dune, then the 'coast road' - a single ribbon of sandy tarmac, then a shallow ditch, a low stone wall, and our field. The soil was pure sand, like the dunes and the grass thin and harsh, too sparse for cattle but I do seem to remember a few tethered goats from time to time.

Auntie Elsie, who came from Yorkshire, loved colour uninhibitedly as I did, and though the Hut was furnished only with the roughest furniture, camp-beds, sale room table and chairs, she had livened it all up with crazy patchwork. On the Yorkshire market stalls she could buy bundles of off-cuts of printed cottons, and these cut into rectangles and cobbled lightheartedly together on the sewing-machine, made cheap and cheerful curtains and bedspreads, so the effect was as welcoming as her own exuberant personality. The mouse in the milk was generously thrown in for good measure.

The Hut, of course, was nothing like the Cottage for beauty and charm, but it was one step up-market in having a chemical closet in a sentry-box against the outer wall. It smelled rawly of Jeyes Fluid, but was made bearable by the tantalising snippets of news on the squares of newspaper stacked beside it. Another, rather larger sentry box further round housed the kitchen and a compartment with two camp beds. These had curtained openings into the living space of the Hut. Washing was sketchy and largely superfluous since we all spent a great part of the day in the sea, but what we did was done at a battered table covered with American cloth, with an enamel bowl and mugs for teeth. The china was a glorious hotch-potch. You might get a thick white plate with S.S. Sarnia printed on its rim for your meat, a flat bottomed baby's bowl with "This Little Piggy went to Market" for your pudding, and drink your tea out of a Woolworths cup with a gold clover leaf, on a jazzy orange saucer. We had 'floating' spoons from Woolworths, aluminium and so light you almost had to tie them down. There was a honey pot like a straw bee-hive with a bee as large as a laying hen on the apex, by way of a knob. The tea-pot was a leery-looking tin one with a dent like a wink on one bow, and the mouse's milk jug came from a line of pub crockery, and had two Aberdeen terriers and "Black and White Whisky" printed on it.

This all encouraged a glorious gipsy life, like camping, but without the drawbacks. A colleague of Father's used to take the school Scouts camping on the island in summer, and one keen couple would often stay on after the boys had gone home. They brought their two ridge tents and put them up near our field, and I would go across in the early morning and find them tidying camp for the day. This meant bringing out the groundsheets and removing the slugs that had crawled under seeking damp in the night. Some were grey and some were cream-coloured but all were thick and as long as a jumbo sausage or a chocolate éclair, wrinkled and patterned all down their backs. The K's seemed quite unperturbed at sharing their tent with such humble folk but speaking for myself, I have taken care never to sleep in a tent on a groundsheet!

The year after The Hut we rented a flat in St Peter Port. Our part of the town is built on a hill - you could almost call it a cliff - and the only streets and roads there are have to run sideways, so you zigzag gradually down towards the harbour. But all over the older and steeper parts, flights of steps launch themselves down to the blue water, slotting between houses and the pink and grey granite walls of odd shaped back gardens. Looking down from Auntie Elsie's home, you stood dizzily above a landslide of pantiled roofs, rosy, terracotta and Indian red. Patches of cabbage, marigolds, and sweet peas smiled up at you, and ancient fig trees sprawled against the south walls of the houses. Diminishing and dog-legged steps beckoned you downwards and at the bottom, toy boats napped beside the harbour wall, idling in the sun.

Houses on the uphill side of the street, in this part of the town, had to have their ground floor dug into the hillside, and it was not until you got to the bedroom floor that you could have any windows at the back. It was here that we rented the flat. We had nothing to do with the ground floor, except to use the front door, but at the top of the steep brown lino-covered stairs, we had a sitting room looking over the street, with glimpses, between the houses opposite, of a sheet of grey satin sea hanging from a high pale horizon. From a door at the end of the bedroom corridor you stepped out onto a pierced iron work bridge that ran across the backs of several houses - and had a few steps at each end, leading down to the lowest terrace of the back gardens. The garden rose in steep jumps, and the houses in the next street up had their feet above our heads. It was a delightful confusion - like living in the reflections in a pool of water - you went up to get down.

Living here, Father was able to indulge himself in one of the little luxuries that were only rarely possible at home - breakfast with really fresh coffee. Further down the street, where the shops began, was an old fashioned grocers, where they roasted and ground their own coffee and after the fashion of the island which was more French than English, would have it ready in time for breakfast. Between us and the grocers, there was also a tiny bakery - they made Jersey Wonders - a delectable kind of super doughnut, oblong, sugary and turned inside out on itself - ambrosia! But they also baked their own small crusty rolls and these early in the morning came hot from the ovens. Father made an arrangement with their little delivery boy that each morning he should collect from the grocers a quarter of a pound of freshly roasted and ground coffee, and bring it along with our hot rolls, crackling sweetly as the crust cooled inside the white cloths that were folded over his basket.

The kettle would be whispering on the stove - the warm earthenware pot waiting as the boy clattered up the stairs to the landing. There may be more heavenly smells in the world than fresh bread and newly roasted coffee, but they haven't come my way. Soon, the heavy square table would be drawn up to the sunny window, the round bellied coffee-pot would be sitting like a fat cat in the sun, and flakes of brown crust and golden apricot jam would mingle on our plates.

More feet on the stairs - boy's feet - Henry's - "We're going to Petit Port. Are you coming too?"

Over three hundred steps down the cliffs to the cove of Petit Port - you did not go there unless you were sure the day was going to stay sunny. Today the nearby islets were hazy already, and the horizon had melted imperceptibly into the pale sky. Above, 90° across from the sun, the sky was darkly blue. No risk today of having to pack up and rush for home, up all those cliff-side sandy steps. A day to bask in the long heat that poured into the south-facing bay. A day to seek shade behind rocks, to stand in shallow water and let the big harmless waves burst breast-high over you - waves that built up in height in the narrow bay, but were soft and playful as great puppies.

Thermos flasks of tea for the grown-ups. Bottles of water for us. Tomatoes - don't forget the salt - hard-boiled eggs cooked yesterday. A lettuce in a damp cloth. Bathing costumes rolled in tight sausages of stripey towel. Everyone had a share of the load as we loped, almost out of control, down-hill to the brass and red-leather of the coast road bus, waiting at the harbour. The flat was shut up all day while the sunlight moved aslant the front windows, and after a mid-day gap, sidled in again through the win-

dows at the back. We did not return much before dusk, to sit for a while in the parlour, Father at the window touching up the water-colour he had done that day. The place never seemed quite real to me in electric light, and I went willingly to bed down the corridor, where texts on the walls blossomed with unlikely red and blue flowers, and the frames crossed their fingers at the corners. It

was a morning place, alive when the sun spilled over the breakfast table, but somehow at night no more than a stealthy refuge.

James Kirkup describes the houses he knew as a small child as having individual and recognisable smells. Though smell was an important sense to me, I remember only one house which I could say was all-pervaded by a characteristic smell. That was because the house and its inhabitants were very old, and the cottage was ancient, small, and insanitary.

One of our young daily maids - I do not remember which - took me on an afternoon walk and we called in on her great-granny, who

lived on the outskirts of a nearby village. The cottage was one of a row, set in a garden ground that sloped down to the canal. The gardens were divided between the cottagers but had no fences. They were picturesque dwellings, but seemed to me a little sinister, as they wore their battered thatch pulled down well over their eyes, like the forest cottages in Grimm's Fairy Tales. The front door opened into the living room, with a small range burning, and a kettle steaming, though it was a sultry midsummer day and outside the door bumble-bees were blundering in the scarlet runners. Once out of the triangle of sunlight by the door, the sour reek of human old age filled the cottage like a spongy fungoid growth. It clung in the fuzz of the green baize tablecloth, the cushions on the Windsor chairs, the black and grey rag rug by the hearth. It swirled like choking gas from the rusty skirts and unravelling cardigan of the old woman when she moved. It was compounded of ancient sour milk, bacon fat, smoke and unwashed stockings. Her granddaughter seemed not to notice it but I drew back nearer the open door in disgust. There I could just bear to stand and examine the room. Painted chest of drawers with a tin tea-tray propped on it. Alarm clock ticking resonantly, with a bell like half an apple. Abraham sacrificing Isaac in a bird's eye maple frame. And through a dark doorway in the opposite wall, a glimpse of an iron bed and pillows in grey striped ticking but with no pillow-slips. I was given a cup of tea and found that the tea tasted of the smell of the house. I was old enough to know about politeness and I did try to drink it, but I knew if I took more than those initial sips, I would not be able to keep it in my stomach. So when the old lady suggested I have more sugar in it, I shook my head. "I'm not thirsty, thank you".

Soon after, to my relief, the maid took me away. "I could see you didn't like the tea", she said. "Gran and Gramp get goats' milk from the farm for nothing. I don't like it either".

In the other houses I knew well, I noticed the temperature more than the smell. If they had a smell it must have been so like our own house that I thought they had none. Ursula's house, though very large, with high ceilings, was warm. A solid-fuel stove burned in the dining room most of the year. Sally's home was warm as well - fires in both rooms every day, and the tiled hall lavishly carpeted. John's family, in the next door house, was not as well-off as Sally's - and here a coolness and austerity struck you on entering - John's hall smelled of the chalky cold tessellated floor, while Sally's was several degrees warmer, and sweet with a waft of cakes baking in the kitchen. The two big private houses which made up our school smelled inevitably of polish, since they were floored almost throughout with dark green battleship lino. Sharp smells of ink, bland ones of hot milk, and flat ones of sheets in the copper, or of boiling greens, overlaid the polish smell at various times of day. The Montessori room did have an enduring, but pleasant, smell of orange juice and sweet biscuits.

Very rarely, we had to make a trembling and apprehensive call on old Miss Hipwell next door, when we had accidentally lost a ball over

her garden wall. We would be shown, subdued and anxious, into her drawing-room, which was draped and swagged and stifled in dull peacock velvet, mostly with bobbles. She sat there by her crackling fire-surrounded by ornaments, clocks, statuettes, artificial flowers, all under glass domes. Three sets of carefully draped curtains at the windows and a lace-edged blind. Rugs laid over the carpet on the floor. More draping on the mantlepiece and behind the door. Cushions in silk and velvet covers with lace covers over them. The piano was capped in velvet and crowded with photographs in silver, fretwork or curly gilt metal frames. Everything that could be covered was, mostly twice, and all of it smelled very faintly of dust and ancient desiccated lavender. After a stammered apology (in which we had been carefully drilled by a teacher or by Brown Owl) we would be given permission to fetch our ball, and go out by the back gate. Silently we followed the grey uniformed maid through the hall to the garden door, and after a quick whispered search, would thankfully seize our ball and be let out by the heavy door in the end wall. Once in the lane, a relief like being inflated with hydrogen, flooded us and we would dance and yell and hammer on the school back gate until our fellow Brownies came shouting down to let us in. Then, we felt like heroic travellers returned, we who ten minutes earlier had crept in shamed misery out to knock trembling at the forbidding portal of 'the house next door'.

I cannot recreate wholesale any house I knew before I was four years old. Of '16', and Mother's and Father's homes in Ireland, I catch only glimpses when they were part of the experiences that mattered to me. So I recall the yard and the windows of '16' when Gerald called out to Mother to beg for "stodge" from town. And I remember

squatting by the pump looking for fairies - but I have no consecutive memory - I cannot take my mind on a walk through the house as I can through '62' or the Guernsey cottage. So the cottage on Dowthers' farm where we spent a holiday when I was three, is remembered inside only by the collection of miniature jugs, some Goss china, some gold lustre, on the mantle piece. Why I was ever allowed to get near them I can not imagine. Perhaps I was not, but the lure of the miniature was too much for me, even at that early age, and I had to handle them. I loved best the fat gold lustre ones, with a broad beaded band of azure round their stout middles. Of course I broke one - or two - and of course Mrs Dowther was angry. But really, she ought to have put her collection away before renting to summer visitors. I do seem to have been a troublesome brat at that time. I copied her doling out Indian corn to her barnyard hens. I went to the bin un-noticed and scattered the grain lavishly, feeling what a kind, good girl I was to give the chookies maize. They loved it, of course, but the next day several biddies were very ill and two had died - of acute indigestion and the swelling of unlimited quantities of raw grain in their crops. There was trouble, and feeding the chookies was added to the growing list of things I saw the adults do but must never do myself.

Mrs Dowther made a little butter - I hope not very often, because I realise now with awe that the churn she used was the ancient 'dasher' churn, such as you can see in mediaeval manuscripts and Elizabethan wood cuts. It was tall and narrow, made of hooped wood, like a barrel. You made the butter by forcing up and down a perforated plunger. The long handle came through a hole in the lid, and heaving it up and down in the cream must have been unbelievably tiring, especially to a woman. The horizontally mounted barrel churn, which only required turning by a handle at the side, had long been in common use, all through the Victorian period, but the old fashioned dasher was all Mrs Dowther had. I feel I must be one of the last people alive to have seen this ancient device in daily use, and that in 1927.

Father had large feet - size eleven - and hands like half a pound of sausages - but he could make anything. Body and mind must both be developed for happiness, he said; everyone needs to have some physical skill. His were countless and he made furniture and gadgets for the new house when we left '16'. The sitting room was to be our showpiece, with everything fitting into a colour scheme. The other rooms took pot luck as did most people's rooms in those days. There was almost total indifference to incongruity and colour clashes. So a room in which we could receive 'company', and be proud of was something special in our circles. The dark blue brocade suite was the keynote, and the fawn Wilton carpet with the Paisley pattern 'went' well. The walls were to be cream (porridge, of course, but cream porridge, not brown with green and orange flecks like the dining room). The curtains were carefully chosen and lined. A large blue majolica vase was the only ornament apart from some of Father's pictures with blue tones prevailing. The vase was filled with huge dried poppy seed-heads, very fashionable at that time, and painted by Father in blues and greys. The electric light with its white bowl beneath was adequate but a standard lamp in the corner behind Father's armchair would provide a "je ne sais quoi" that would lift the room out of the ordinary. Father would make one. First he designed it. The stem was to be a slender hexagon of ash, with the cable running up through its centre. Why, oh why he was so determined to do it the hard way, I will never know, but I expect just because it was hard and he wouldn't be beat. He fashioned and planed and sanded the whole four feet of that stem and then he drilled it. It took weeks, and ruined his temper while he did it. Building the St Gothard tunnel was nothing

65

to it. After all, he had less than an inch of wood either side of his drilling in which to go off course. It was done, successfully, in the end, but as I watched on Saturday afternoons in the school woodwork shop, I learned something too. Don't make unnecessary work. Even at that age I could see that he could have taken two strips of wood, channelled them, then glued them together, and planed and shaped them into a hexagon afterwards.

When the lamp was made, we came to the lampshade. Buy one? Never. Father got to work with heavy gauge wire and fashioned the frame for a melon shaped shade - about the most difficult shape of all to make. Then he bought sheets of heavy parchment paper, cut out the sections (150% of them did not fit - it took an awful lot of parchment). Then with a leather punch, he punched eyelet holes meticulously all along the edges and sewed the parchment onto the frame with gold cord. Then, he painted each curved panel with a different flower group of blue delphiniums and triumphantly placed it on the lamp.

 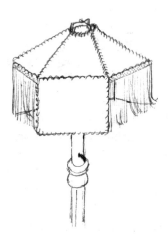

Then it wobbled.

Do what he would, that damned shade wobbled. Any vibration, a footstep on the floor, a door closing, and it jiggled and jingled about like an obese belly dancer, shaking its fringe in a highly suggestive way.

So he patiently began all over again, with a hexagonal pagoda - shaped one this time, with six inch deep gold fringe in sections round the bottom. That wobbled too, but not with such a provocative sexiness as the other, and he felt he could live with it.

The years from three to nine are probably the most aware of our whole lives. We are adjusted to the world in focus as it were, yet every experience is still a new one. We are mobile and gaining independence all the time. We examine each new thing under a microscope, and have no interest in distance or general views until much later. Take a child to the top of a hill and show it the most wonderful panorama of rolling country and blue distance, and it will crouch down and examine minutely the daisy at its feet. So each wallpaper pattern, stair rod or floor tile in '62' is sharply defined in my memory - no more so than the odd remaining details of '16', but in '62' they are related to each other. I know what lay between the three triangular steps at the foot of the stairs and the red tiles of the kitchen floor where I smashed my little tumbler. I know how long it took to get from one end of the passage to the other, and at what times of day the sun shone into each of the rooms. I have a whole, three dimensional picture of the house. But even so, in every room my mind fastens on details connected with my growing experience. The difference now is this: if I crouch under the table at '16', three years old with the butter dish, polishing off half a pound of butter in my fingers, I am under the table, dark and secret, and that is all there is. But at '62', under the same table with its red baize cloth, clasping Pussy and waiting for some boring visitor to get up and go, I am aware of the room beyond - of the far movements in the house, footsteps, taps turned on, and of the sounds outside, the clatter of wind in the laurel bush, the whisper of tyres as Father wheels his bicycle up the passage. I am still the heart and centre of the world, but it is a world with a stable pattern, that existed yesterday, and will be there tomorrow, something predictable, to be counted on, not a series of flashes, like single stills illuminated at intervals in a dark film.

Furnishings were simple and often second-hand. The little end bedroom that overlooked the coal-house roof was Gerald's at first, then later mine. It had an iron hospital bed, a tiny bookshelf, a curtained-off recess for clothes and a desk bought in an auction sale. The drawers had flower shaped glass knobs, amber gold and looked so like barley sugar that I would suck them hopefully, but they tasted of nothing. I associate them as well with the salty taste on the tongue when you lick the terminals of a torch battery (a trick I picked up from Gerald) and with the sugar caramel smell that clung in one of the drawers, where he used to store the tin plates of toffee he made from the recipes in Mother's Olio Cookery book. This smell lingered deliciously in that drawer long after Gerald had left home and the desk had become the basis of Father's work bench. Twenty years after, I could pull on the amber knob, and catch amid the oily steel chisels wrapped in hessian, the faint sugary whiff of that long devoured Everton toffee and the sunny little brown papered bedroom.

When I slept up in the attic, it was in a sloping ceilinged room with a tiny dormer window peering into a balcony hardly bigger than

a sink. Next door was a boxroom, and beyond a big empty attic where the flotsam and jetsam of family life was stored. It was the nearest I could get to a playroom, since no one else wanted to be there. It had a little square window set nearly at floor level, and I could peer out sideways and catch a glimpse of the road beyond the front garden. My chief delight was to creep up there on a wild wintry afternoon, when sleet slashed at the small panes, and splattered down the chimney into the empty black grate. In the dimness, the yellow distemper smelled dankly and the pale floorboards held a comforting mild warmth. The big trunk we took on holidays stood against the wall for ten months of the year, holding all the things we only needed in the other two. I liked secretly to raise the lid and sniff the contents. Mother's orange towel bathing wrap, bathing costumes, still with a glint or two of sandy grains caught in the fabric, floppy thin rubber bathing shoes and caps, Father's panama. These lay in the tray at the top of the trunk, and below in the dark were parcels of our christening robes, shawls and unused counterpanes. Whenever the trunk lid was opened, even on the darkest of fierce wet March days, a dry sweet scent rose out, a smell of sunbaked towels, salt sand and the hot rocks of Vazon. Guernsey and the holidays swept over me nostalgically and I sat entranced on the wooden floor, my mind filled with the green silk sea, the powder-dry white sand and the heat of the sun on my salt-encrusted skin, while the Midland dusk closed round and the grey icy cloths of rain scrubbed over the window and caught the first glitter of the gas lamp outside the gate.

There are two little houses that are dear to most children's hearts - the tent made out of the clothes horse and a dust sheet that made a secret shelter from the sun, and more exciting still, Father's big umbrella. Men's umbrellas fifty years ago were much larger than now, more like golf umbrellas. I liked to borrow Father's and crouch under it on the lawn in a rain shower. There I was, huddled in, dry and safe, except perhaps for the toes of my shoes, while the rain slashed around me and the chill in the air raised goose-pimples on my bare arms. A tiny island of security in a threatening world. What else is a home?

5. FRIENDS AND NEIGHBOURS

 he Black Saucepan was rarely used. It was too big for the needs of our family and spent most of its life on the top shelf in the scullery. But once a year it was ritually scrubbed and filled and the two Christmas puddings boiled and bumped in it for a full eight hours, their knotted white cloths peeping over the rim like rabbits' ears, as the pudding basins lurched inside. The sooty kettle simmered beside it and Mother peered anxiously to see if the saucepan needed topping up.

Those puddings were boiled in November for Christmas the following year. This year's puddings had been sitting, over-wrapped in greaseproof, on the top pantry shelf, maturing for thirteen months before they were eaten.

Dora was our maid when there was an age gap in the Darlings, who came to us one after another from Elsie through to Nellie. Dora was a Yorkshire girl, a dear but dotty, and exasperating at times to Mother. The season came for the Christmas puddings to be boiled. They had been mixed in a big enamel washing-up bowl. We had all had a stir and a wish. Dora and I had already sat at the scrubbed deal table, gouging out the pips from the sticky muscatel raisins with our thumb nails. Then we had shared the more pleasant task of chiselling cloudy white lumps of sugar candy out of the half shells of candied peel - orange, lemon and lime. I had greedily eaten as much as I could get of the hard sugar aromatic of citrus, but Gerald, home promptly from school, and Dora, had been as snatchfingered as I was. You would not believe how I resent nowadays getting my candied peel ready chopped into neat little pieces in a plastic tub, and being done out of those gobbets of hard candy, levered out of half an orange shell and divinely bitter and sweet at the same time.

When the Black Saucepan was scoured so that the puddings should  not taste of washing soda, some water found its way down the hollow iron handle. As the pan heated up on the range, these few drops of water heated too. Steam hissed up the handle, and whistled and chirped as it escaped from the tiny vent at the top. The crackled earthenware pudding basin began to bounce thoughtfully in the simmering pan. Mother was there for the first half hour, but when everything was in order, she went off to sit down, leaving Dora to watch and knit and pour a little water from the kettle if the level in the saucepan fell too low.

The silence of the afternoon closed on the house. Mother snoozed by the dining-room fire, a basket of mending at her elbow. The clock ticked, the flames whispered and flapped, and Pussy purred against her foot. All was peace and her eyelids drooped.

"Mrs Rodgers, Mrs Rodgers. Please come - I'm frightened".

Mother opened her eyes and jolted herself awake. Dora was beside her, twisting her hands together. Dora never came into the dining-room in the afternoon unless someone had come to the front door, so Mother took her interruption seriously.

"Whatever's the matter, Dora?"

"Oh, please come. I'm scared to stay in there alone".

"Why, Dora?"

"It's the Black Saucepan, Mrs Rodgers. Something's funny about it. I don't like it", Dora's voice quavered.

The puddings were at the top level of Mother's mind just then. If anything was going wrong with her expensive Christmas puddings she was going to stop it if possible, so she got up and scuttled down the dark tiled passage with a loyal but reluctant Dora sobbing in the rear.

Arrived in the kitchen Mother looked round but nothing seemed at all abnormal. She turned to Dora. "What is the trouble?", she asked. "What is bothering you?"

Dora, hovering between the passage and the kitchen door, caught her wrist. "Listen", she said, pointing dramatically at the Black Saucepan. "Listen. It's been making those funny noises. There's something in there!"

In the silence which followed, Mother turned her ear to catch whatever it was that was upsetting Dora. The saucepan made the expected rude intestinal gobblings associated with simmering puddings but above these, very faint and quiet, came chinkings and whispers as the spoonful of water at the bottom of the handle steamed its way to freedom up the confinement of the hollow tube to the tiny round hole at the top.

Mother stifled a giggle. Dora was now screwing her apron into a rope half way down the passage. Mother looked silently at the dear silly Yorkshire lass and could not resist having a bit of fun. "Whatever do you think it is, Dora? It seems to be coming from the handle."

"Do you think there's a little man in there?" Dora asked.

Naughtily, Mother played out the game. "I don't know Dora. I think we'd better wait till Mr Rodgers gets home from school".

Dora was soggy with fear and misery. "Do come away from there", she pleaded. "Come up the passage here with me. It will be safer!"

Mother was not going to let her puddings boil dry for the sake of a laugh. "Dora," she said, "you put on your coat and go home early. Mr Rodgers will be home soon and I'll be all right".

Dora was only too thankful to obey and Mother was able to have her laugh out in peace, and top up the puddings as well. But from that day until she left us, Dora could never be persuaded to stay in the kitchen if the Black Saucepan was taken down from the shelf to boil a few handkerchiefs used to mop up a bad cold.

Dora did not stay with us very long. She was engaged to be married and left us just before her wedding. Her family was not well off but her wedding was lavish. Eight bridesmaids! Mother snorted. She had no sympathy with wanton waste of money, and as she justly said eight bridesmaids was overdoing it. Even Royalty made do with six. As I saw it, Dora was welcome to eight if that was what pleased her. Why not? If I had been invited to be number nine, dressed up in ruched mauve satin like a night-dress case, I would have been delighted to carry the fag end of Dora's train, and line up with all the other assorted night-dress cases for the photographs afterwards.

Parents are obviously the people who will have the greatest influence on most children's development and childhood memoirs hardly seem possible without portraits of Mum and Dad, but mine will have to be. I am trying to rebuild the world as I saw it up to the age of ten, and before that age I was not capable of seeing either parent in perspective. I seemed to have a different parent for every passing mood. If I was in disgrace, which I often was, Mother was a cross person. If I had been promised a longed for treat, Father was a kind man. What they were really like as people I had no idea until years later, and I will not commit the injustice of misrepresenting them now. Nor will I describe my relatives, because they almost all lived in Ireland and we only saw them one summer in my memory. Mother's sister Charlotte, and her brother Hugh did stay with us once each, but not for long enough to colour my life.

I had one Auntie who did have a great influence on me, and that was Auntie Elsie from Guernsey. She was not a real relative, but the wife of a colleague of Father's from his early teaching days. She and Mother took to each other at once and Auntie Elsie's Henry and I were very close in age. When we went to the Island for holidays, we seemed to step into a familiar family circle, and a neighbourhood even more relaxed and warm than we enjoyed at home.

Elsie was the most striking woman I knew. I was not very noticing about people's looks but Elsie was nearly six feet tall, carried herself splendidly, and had the purest silver-white hair, white from her late twenties. Her gestures were extravagant, her laugh bubbled and made everyone around laugh too. As soon as she came into a room the temperature seemed to go up, I found her colourful and somewhat noisy way of life enormously attractive. She was the only grown-up, apart from our own dear daily maids, who were only teenagers, whom I could approach and say what I thought, without disguise. She could scold of course, but she never humiliated or laughed at me. She loved bright colour, flowers and fabrics. She lived with gusto, getting the greatest enjoyment out of small events. A picnic on the beach, going in swimming when the waves broke high and splashy, walking up the garden to pick a ripe fig from the knotted old tree, lovingly polishing one of the antiques she could find in heaps of gimcrack and junk, all of these she greeted with joyous cries and laughter. I used to run in and out of her house to warm my hands at her enthusiasm, and the sight of her on the quay as our boat carried us in, cramped, cold and tired after our long day's travel, was like fire on a winter's day. She had depth and substance too, because she used to appear in Rugby as well, when she would stay with us for a day or two, breaking her journeys home to Yorkshire. The older I grew the dearer she became and I cherish memories of her that sum up her glorious vigour and delight in life. When her new bathing suit shrank on her and could not be got off under a towel on the beach, Elsie put on her hat and high heeled shoes and posed saucily with the other respectably clad ladies, for a snapshot. When Gerald and I arrived on her doorstep at lunch time, having walked across the Island, she flapped her hands at us, clucked and exclaimed - whatever would our parents think? Then she telephoned them, fed us and gave us the bus fare back to Vazon. When the Germans invaded during the war, she gathered her family's needs together, embarked on the escape ship, and set up home over a greengrocer's shop in Buxton, where her warmth glowed as comfortingly as it had done in Guernsey and drew me back again and again with my Youth Hostelling friends, to bask in her warmth and admire the new collection of antiques she was building up, so that her little flat up the stairs from the cabbages soon was charming as her tall gracious house on Hauteville. When she died, a light went out that we could ill spare.

'62' was tall, narrow and semi-detached. The family in the twin house were an elderly bachelor and his two sisters, one a spinster, the other a widow. It would sound wonderful to a prospective tenant asking about the neighbours, as I don't doubt Father did - but though the facts were right, the deductions were not. A more disgracefully uproarious household would have been hard to find in a respectable residential area. The O's were dipsomaniacs! I think they were more or less fuddled every night, but once every few weeks there would be muffled thuds and slams, and bursts of tuneless song that told us that Miss O was on the gin again. Miss O was either the worst or she had the weakest head; her brother came next, and his voice was the loudest, his crashes into walls and furniture the most violent. The widow was a morose drinker, silent, but persistent even unto insensibility.

On a normal evening, no sound was heard, but if anyone called at their door, there was no response. The light might be shining through the cracks in the drawing-room curtains; smoke might curl from the chimney up to the frosty stars, but no one answered the bell. When the O's decided to make a night of it, we began to get storm signals at about seven. A body would crash into the party wall of our two kitchen passages. Doors would slam. Male growls and female yaps would rise in altercation. As they grew more quarrelsome, the shouts and squeals rose in volume, pitch and continuity. There might be a crash or two of bottles or jugs. Then silence for a while; then slowly, hardly distinguishable like the drone of a bagpipe, Mr O's singing would start. By about nine or ten, '64' was Bedlam, and Mother would long ago have insisted on all the bolts being drawn and the chains put up on our doors. Gerald thought it all rather funny, and so did I as long as Father was at home. But if it was his Lodge night, and he

would not return until ten thirty, I was as scared as Mother, and lay awake worrying in case the O's came surging out of their house with choppers and carving knives, to attack Daddy between the front gate and the door. If I had been allowed downstairs, I would have been crouched shivering in the hall, ready to rip back the bolts and drop the chain as soon as I heard his step on the path in case he was making a dash for his life, pursued by a trio of slavering octogenarians all gnashing their dentures!

The O's were uncomfortable neighbours, and Mother's very obvious disgust and fear made me feel there was something shameful here - something I did not want to recount naughtily in Recess at school- something I would rather keep dark, as though we were also blackened with their shame. I don't know how long it was before the crisis came; two years, perhaps, or even more. Father had growled at each of the disturbances and said more than once cynically to Mother, "Don't worry. The old fool will kill himself before long". It was the sort of thing you say, but never really expect to happen.

Then one stormy autumn night, as I lay in bed in the little bedroom at the end of the upstairs passage, the thumps and bangs and incoherent shouts started up. They were all over the house that night, not just downstairs as usual. Lurchings and crashings into the party wall of the corridor outside my door were so heavy they made the pictures shake, and I lay in bed, stiff with fear in case Mr O, swearing and singing alternately, should shoulder his way right through the lath and plaster division and cut me off from help from downstairs. His sisters' eldritch screeches rose from the ground floor and once there came the sound of some object hurled from the landing and bumping crazily down the dog-legged stairs. The rumpus grew so violent that Father came up to me, Mother close behind, to reassure me. "Don't be frightened - it's only Mr O - he's drunk, but he can't hurt you". Then turning to Mother as they went away, I heard him say "If they don't quieten down in half-an-hour, I'm going out to telephone the police".

Before the half-hour was over, a series of thuds as Mr O shouldered his way along the passage to the head of his stairs, climaxed dramatically in a bellow of stupid rage, and then a crash, a shout and the sound came of something heavy slithering down the stairs.

Total silence followed. I strained my ears, and every nerve in my body. Then eerily, thin and faint, from downstairs next door, came a keening, a wailing and a scream. Then babblings and gasps of hysteria followed. I heard a muttered conversation from below, Father's deep growl, and Mother's trembling, "No, Tom, don't go - don't".

Evidently Tom felt he must. I heard the front door slam, footsteps down our path. Then in half a minute the 'tang-tangle-tang' of the O's front-door bell, bouncing on its spring in their kitchen, almost directly beneath my bed.

It rang several times before I heard a voice, one of the women wailing and gobbling, but evidently communicating with Father - through the letter box I heard later. They would not open the door. Silence followed again. In a few moments, Father's key in our door, a few hasty words to Mother, and once again his steps retreating down the path.

I waited, scared of the unknown. Something was going on which I had never encountered before, and the pattern of my world was cracking.

When I could bear it no longer, I went to my door, and quaveringly called "Mummeee!"

Mother came running up. She was putting on a brave face, trying to smile and scold me rallyingly for being still awake. I came straight to the point. "Where's Daddy gone?"

"Oh, he won't be a minute". Mother's voice was cracking with tension but she kept her smile pinned to her ear-lobes. "Mr O has had an accident. He's fallen downstairs and hurt himself. Daddy's gone to the M's to use their telephone and call the doctor".

At that moment, Father came back home and I prepared to forget the whole thing and go to sleep. But the night's drama was not over. In about twenty minutes the Doctor arrived next door. The two old women must have been too drunk to be able to act reasonably at all. He rang the bell again and again. He hammered on the door. He bawled home truths through their letter box; (he was a doctor with a reputation for forcible language, anyway!). In the end, unable to get the old harridans to open up, he came round to our house. I heard him and Father laughing ruefully at the situation, but the outcome was another visit to the M's telephone (by this time it was about ten at night). Dr H went this time and called the police.

At this point, exhausted, I did fall asleep, and it was not till the next day that I heard that the police had had to break into the house, and had found Mr O on the tessellated hall floor stertorously grunting out the last few breaths of his life. He had "had a stroke", I was told, like poor Aunt Rose, fallen down the stairs and been dead before the ambulance got him to the Hospital.

After his death, life was quieter.

It was hard on Mother having a nest of alcoholics next door as she had a deep, uncontrollable fear of drunks. One night in Guernsey, when we were staying in the Hut, a drunken fisherman fell snorting and burbling on his back in the roadside ditch. Father and Auntie Elsie's husband had gone off for a fortnight's bicycle tour in Brittany, and the rest of us had packed into the Hut in the meantime for a picnic existence until they came home. It was deep dusk, almost night. Gerald, Henry and I had been sitting on the rocks out on the point, watching the sunset and gossiping. Mother and Elsie had got into nighties and dressing gowns and were cosily giggling in the lamplight of the Hut. Heavenly, happy times, when nobody had to worry if three youngsters were out alone when the adults were ready for bed.

We straggled along in the gloom, and turned through the gap in the loose stone wall that led to the Huts. A deep groan rose, as from a grave, beside our ankles! "Drunk", said Gerald with disgust. "Drunk!" said Henry, with glee. We all made for the Hut.

"There's a drunk man in the ditch outside!"

Mother's face paled. The Huts had no security locks.

"Oh, Elsie. What shall we do?" Poor Mother was no more a fool than anyone else, but this was her peculiar fear. She darted hunted glances at the uncurtained windows of the Hut. Her fear, which I shared, ran like cold water through us. Henry was enjoying the thrill. Gerald was not troubled. "He won't bother us. Let him sleep it off," he said.

At that moment, a quavering bass voice arose outside - not a song - or any recognisable tune, but you could just tell that the voice was trying to sing. Mother clutched Elsie. Her lips were pinched and white. "Oh, Elsie, can't we barricade the door? Put the table across it?".

Elsie was not at all afraid, but she lovingly accepted that Mollie was. She got up and strapped her Japanese Kimono tightly round her waist. "Nonsense", she said. "I'll send him about his business". And to the horror of poor Mother she flung open the door and stepped firmly out to the roadside ditch.

Mother - to her eternal credit - was not going to let her friend face danger alone. Nor was she going to let the children run any risk greater than hers. It does not matter at all that there was no danger - that the semi-stupefied lump of humanity on its back in the ditch could not, and would not, have hurt a mosquito. To Mother he represented danger, madness and the unpredictable. She was a heroine following Elsie down that dark grass track, because she was quelling her own deep, illogical terrors, in the name of loyalty, friendship and motherly sacrifice.

Elsie fetched up at the wall. She was a stupendous woman, nearly six feet tall, statuesque, silver-haired and indomitable.

"Who", she thundered down on the amorphous mass in the ditch, "Who are you?"

Groan.

"Speak up, man. I asked your name. Come on! Who are you?"

"Oh - her Er - jer - Oh - jer".

"That won't do. Speak properly!"

"Elsie", Mother whispered clasping her elbow, "Elsie, don't provoke him. Do come back inside".

Elsie took no notice. "Come on", she said, crisply. "Who are you?"

"Ernie --- Ogier, mum" came a mumble from the ditch.

"Ernie Ogier? Well, then, Ernie Ogier, you get up out of that ditch and take your drink-sodden carcass somewhere else! ON YOUR FEET" she bellowed.

The corpus in the ditch obeyed. Slowly it got itself to its knees and then shuffled, encouraged by authoritarian barks from Auntie Elsie, to its feet and began to lurch its way down the road towards its cottage and its long-suffering wife. Elsie watched it shambling away round the corner. Then she put an arm round Mother's shoulders. "Come along," she said, "We'll make a jug of cocoa. His wife will sort him, all right".

This little scene, with its drama and its comedy, so impressed me that when we came home I told it to all my friends, and Ursula, Sally and I acted it out over and over for many weeks that autumn, and to this day I carry a picture in my mind of Auntie Elsie, with her silver pigtail, a Valkyrie in the moonlight, sending poor sodden Ernie shambling on his way with his Friday night skinful.

Carl and Ursula were the very first friends I made for myself. All the other children I had known up to that time were the children of my parents' friends and our prams had been pushed side by side while our young mothers chatted. But when we moved to '62' I was four and beginning to hunger for other children to play with. It was early summer when we moved, and at first the strange place and the new long garden were enough. I was too timid to want to venture out alone. But the back garden ran down to a cindery service lane that gave access to the backs of about two hundred yards of houses, very large at the top end and diminishing as they came down our way. Half way down the houses, another lane, roughly surfaced with stones, crossed it from the main road to a solitary house on the edge of the fields. I could clamber up on the heavy back gate and lean over looking up and down our lane's untidy length, black cinders in the middle, weeds and grass, board fences and brick garden walls edging it. From the gates in these garden walls, now and again, a child would emerge, but not on our side of the crossroads - they all seemed to live at the top end. I observed them, day by day, but they had no interest in me. They never came beyond the intersection. There was a brown-haired girl called Joan, who had a lot of older brothers. Doreen, with corn-coloured hair, was mothered by Joan. There was a serious and shy little dark boy who rarely showed up, and a solemn and silent fair boy who tricycled down from the very far end. He looked more my age, and seemed to keep apart from Joan's group. I was being taken, by this time, to baby band classes at one of the houses beyond the cross lanes, but none of the children I saw seemed to go to it. They were too old, except the boy on the tricycle.

I grew used to the new home and I began to ask Mother "Can I go out in the lane to play?" She was still getting us settled in a new house and had not had time to get to know any of the people nearby. Still, after using the lane herself as a shortcut once or twice, she felt it was safe enough, and one morning I was told "You can go in the lane if you want, but you are not to go round the corner. You must stay in sight of the back gate".

I promised - only to forget my promise as soon as it became inconvenient, and sped down the hard gravel path to the heavy gate. I pushed up the latch, tugged against the gritty resistance of the spiked hinges, and was out in the sun on the other side. That was enough just for now. The lane was empty. The sun shone mildly, the crumbly bricks were warm and rough at my back, and the umbilical cord was cut. I was out - alone - away from home!

After a few minutes, I moved on past two gardens to the crossroads. Here I could see up to the main road where a field gate stood closed, to stop the herds of sheep and cattle on their way between pasture and market, from straying off down the lane. I leaned here, taking stock. The far arm of the lane served more prosperous homes than ours and several houses had garages. These were all built of tarred woods black and menacing. One, with a big roofed forecourt, was just opposite me. An orchard with a high board fence lay opposite the gardens of our row of houses, and extra gardens for fruit and vegetables lay opposite the richer houses. It was very quiet, so the rattle and thud of a gate right away at the top came very clearly to me on the still air. There was a trundling, and a tricycle emerged on to the black cinder track. The boy pedalled sedately but with effort down towards me. When he reached the other side of the crossroads, he stopped and we looked at each other in silence.

He was unsmiling, almost severe, with pale silky hair cut in a fringe straight across his brows. Sharp eyes looked me over. He seemed wholly self-confident and I was abashed and waited for him to speak first. At last he did

"What's your name?"

"Pat".

"I'm Carl, Where do you live?"

I pointed. He looked at our house and nodded. "Come and see my sister".

He heaved the tricycle round and trundled off again without a backward glance at me, but I followed him up the lane and when we reached the last garden gate he was holding it open for me to step in, out of sight of my gate, but I had forgotten.

His garden was twice as wide as ours - a great square of closely mown grass, with a flagstone path running all round it, and rustic arches of roses halfway down each side. He rode on up a path and at the top on an irregular patch of lawn near the house stood a girl, smaller and younger than Carl and me, but with the same straight silky cap of pale hair and the same almost frowning concentration of look. She was young enough still to be roughly barrel-shaped and wore a high-waisted smock of the kind I considered babyish (having been promoted to dresses with low slung belts and no waist at all at least two years ago).

"This is my sister, Ursula. Baby, this is Pat. She lives down there".

Fancy! He called his sister "Baby".

At that moment, a strange thing happened. A bedroom sash in the rose-covered wall of the house was flung upwards and a young woman put her head out. She called down to Carl and he answered - question, answer and so on, but all in gibberish. I couldn't understand anything the two of them were saying. The young woman nodded, the window was closed. I turned to Carl, bewildered. "Who was that?"

"That's our governess. She's Swedish. So are we. We always talk Swedish with her".

Swedish? What in the world was that? We had swedes for dinner sometimes but that did not explain how these two children could be

Swedish, or talk in funny words. Rather a lot of new impressions were crowding in on me for a first venture away from home, alone. Suddenly I had had enough and I remembered I had said I would not go out of sight. "I'll have to go back now. I promised". I began to move towards the gate.

A slightly less forbidding expression dawned on Carl's face. "Will you come back and play this afternoon?"

"Yes. If they'll let me". I was off down the lane, through our gate and on to the messy gravel path in our own comfortably ungroomed garden. Here I stopped to brood, to digest my experiences and to sort out the questions I needed to have answered.

When Father came home to dinner, my "Swedish" adventure was told and the family immediately identified. Carl, it seemed, had an older half-sister who was doing German, at an evening class Father ran. "A very clever girl", Father said. I was told I could go out in the lane again and if Carl asked me to play I could go, but I was drilled to explain, if asked, who I was - my surname (which at this stage I never thought of as mine), who Father was and that he taught Karen's German class. Protocol must have been satisfied, because life became full and rich from that day. We played together constantly, and when Carl began to move on from girls to boys, and went to his prep school, Ursula and I continued friends and companions. She was quick, humorous and full of character, and often more than a match for me though I was older by nearly two years. She could do many things better than I, and would not be sat on for very long. Altogether, Carl with his unquestioning self-confidence, and Ursula with her cool judgements of others, including grown-ups, were among the best things that ever happened to me.

In those early years I saw more of Ursula than I did even of Sally, because we lived on the same side of the road and the back lane was our safe playground.

I spent my time at school with Sally; we were the same age and in the same form. But evenings, Saturday mornings and Sunday afternoons were spent with Ursula. She had a strong, decisive character, and knew both what she wanted and how to get it. I tried to patronise her on the grounds of my being two years older, but I could never succeed for long, and I could never look down on her. She was good-natured and dryly humorous, but she somehow commanded respect. Even at six she had determined her future career. She was going to be a boy! When we made up plays to act - "Kings and Queens", naturally she had to be the Prince, never the Princess. But she was no wild tomboy as I was. She liked things done properly. Writing must be tidy and clean. Pictures coloured in painting  books must be unsmudged. When Doreen down the lane showed us proudly how to make a Dorothy bag for a doll, cutting out a circle of cotton and running a draw thread round near the edge, I thought it was wonderful and demolished the patching pieces in Mother's workbasket making a whole series of frayed and lop-sided bags for the dolls I had long discarded anyway. Ursula was not content with such unfinished work. She patiently turned in the edges of her circles and tacked them round with running stitch before she gathered them up. I was awed. Twice as much sewing as she needed, just to make it look neater! Later on, as the mother of three young children, I have known her seriously upset because she was not able to make perfectly invisible the blind hemming on her daughter's summer dress which would be outgrown in three months anyway! She had been a perfectionist from infancy and I was privately impressed. It is a comfort to me to remember, though, that she did have her weaknesses. When she came to stay with us for a few days, bringing her second baby, a boy, she explained almost despairingly, as she held Hugh out at arms' length, "I love him truly, I really do, but he leaks at both ends and he smells like a SEWER!"

My passion was for cats, but Ursula's was for horses which I found a little frightening. She took to hanging round the stable where

Amber, her next door neighbour's mare, was kept. Before long, she had wheedled Eric, the cheerful young lad who was handyman and groom, to put us both up on Amber's back, after we had watched her being groomed. Ursula's eyes shone up there above me, as she sat, her legs sticking out as flat as though she were on a table. I was eager for my turn. But when Eric put me up, I just wanted to get down quick. I was shocked to find how unsafe I felt. It was much too far from the ground and Amber would not stay still. I would have been perfectly happy astride the branch of a tree twice as high, but Amber bounced and minced and wobbled. It was like trying to sit on top of a jelly. I was lifted down and never particularly wanted to be on a horse again.

The next time I tried was five years later. I was bigger and the horse was smaller. We had been told we could ride a Dartmoor pony called Magpie, while her owner was on holiday. We had a saddle but no stirrups, so we improvised with loops of string. When Ursula was on board, I walked by the pony's head and we went through some marshy ground by a stream. Magpie objected. She whisked the bridle from my fingers, chucked Ursula off backwards and set off for dry ground with a cheeky flourish of her heels. But not alone. Ursula's foot was caught in one of those wretched loops of string, and she was dragged along like a sledge behind the frisking Magpie, while my stomach turned to water. Bump and bounce went Ursula on the back of her head with the pony's heels whirling in the air above her, all the length of the field. When the string broke at last, I caught up, panting, expecting to find her a bloody pulp. She calmly got up, dusted off the seat of her breeches and said "We'd better catch the little blighter. She mustn't be allowed to get away with that!" And catch her we did, and Ursula rode her firmly and sedately until she had time to think it over and remember her manners!

Sally was not an only child but it felt as though she were. She had an older half-sister, Gerald's age, but Mary went to boarding school. When she was at home she was kind; she took Sally and me for walks, and made us laugh with her tales of her evil doings at school. It was one of those schools which seem to go out looking for trouble by insisting that children eat up everything on their plates before they are allowed to leave the table. Mary must have suffered all the nausea brought on by rice-pudding skin, blubbery grey fat and frog-spawn pudding, but worst of all to her were pancakes. Completely outfaced by a large, rubbery pancake one day Mary had adroitly stowed it away up her knicker leg. Gym tunics had no pockets in those days, and it was, I think, a universal schoolgirl custom to keep your handkerchief, purse and half-sucked toffees in the gathering above the elastic. But elastic is untrustworthy as any of the children of men, and Mary's pancake slithered out and flopped shamefully to the floor as she was sprinting past the Headmistress's table, on her way to dispose of the disgusting object down the lavatory.

At Sally's house there was a stricter code of behaviour than at home. In some ways she risked being spoiled; her father worshipped her and she had endless toys. To offset this, her Mother insisted on Sally sharing: when little friends came to tea with their mothers, Sally had to offer them their own free choice from among her small toys, of something to take home with them. This was a firm rule. Even if the visiting child picked on some little doll or knick-nack that was painfully dear to Sally, it must be handed over with a smile and no hint of reluctance. This, I knew even then, was a very hard discipline and I admired Sally greatly for the way she carried it out. The same was true at her Christmas parties. They had a big tree, right up to the ceiling, wreathed with tinsel, jewelled with coloured lights, glass baubles and chocolate decorations. There were animals and Santas wrapped in silver paper, sugar pigs with string tails, and little gold mesh bags of chocolate coins. Every child at the party had its choice among these before Sally was allowed hers. I knew, one year, how she had set her heart on a chocolate squirrel, like Squirrel Nutkin in her book, but little Jo chose it. It was snipped off the branch and carried away by the small girl while Sally smiled unflinching, and only I knew, because she had told me, how much she wanted it herself.

Sally, being six months older than me, could just remember the two of us in our prams, scowling as our mothers pushed us out and chatted. She was always beautiful; she was never vain. When she was out of her father's sight she was a lively little devil, full of inventive mischief and well able, despite her angelic looks, to take care of herself. She joined us late at Summerlea, after two years with a nursery governess whom she tormented until even her father admitted she might be better off at school. So after being seen across the road by the maid each morning, she skipped and whirled up the pavement and through the Rec in the astonishing purple coat and hat that made her look like the Heather Fairy in her book of Flower Fairies. Goodness knows what I would have looked like in that purple tweed - the Pickled Cabbage Fairy, I shouldn't wonder.

Sally had brains, courage and humour, so much that no one ever felt jealous of her for her beauty, her pretty clothes or luxurious toys. She was too much fun to be with. They might cast her as the Angel Gabriel in the Nativity Play, with her mane of newly washed curls billowing round her like a feather bed, and all the grown-ups' would admire her beauty, but the Sally we knew was the girl who hitched up her angelic robes and delivered a swift kick to Boney the Bully who was pulling Cynthia's plaits.

I got more from Sally than a good example. She had perseverance and would work at things she did not much like until she got them right. I gave up music lessons after a year; Sally persisted until she reached the level when her music gave pleasure to others and to herself. She accepted without whining the restrictions laid down for her. I, if I had a penny to spend, could go to the little back street shops and spend it on any rubbish I fancied - a packet of sugar cigarettes in a yellow paper case, broken toffee from a tray on the counter, breathed on by customers and daintily trodden by flies, pear drops releasing the vapours of acetone in the mouth. The only thing I was forbidden was a gobstopper. Sally was not allowed to buy from these shops. She could only have sweets that were hygienically wrapped, and made by old-established firms of known probity, Parkinsons or Farrah's, Callard & Bowser's Butterscotch, or loathsome black lumps of liquorice known as 'Pontefract Cakes'. By the time we were both eight, the Wall's "Stop Me and Buy One" tricycles were roving the country, and after some thought, Sally was allowed to join me in buying an occasional "Sno-frute", a penny water ice made in a triangular bar, cased in cardboard. I accepted the double standard quite happily, and never protested that at home I was allowed to run to the Paradise Street shop for aniseed balls that changed colour as you sucked through them, or to the little off-licence where you pressed a worn brass thumb-latch and went in to an aroma of beer and vinegar, to buy Dolly Mixtures, or to the 'Handi-Spot' by the railway, where they sold delightful little tins of Phul-Nana Cachous, to disguise my beer-scented breath after a night's boozing!

6. FEARS

rsula yearned for a wristwatch. At six, perhaps part of her knew that it would be "out of the question, for a young child", but she had tried, for her birthday dropping delicate hints like flatirons all through the family. No watch materialised, but she persevered for Christmas. The afternoons after school were darkening, but she and I used to set off and walk the three-quarter mile to the shops, to allow her to gaze and gloat outside the little window of 'J. Berry, Jeweller', and sell her soul to one of the tiny round gold watches seductively sprawled on the green velvet within. Her nose flattened to a blob on the glass, she devoured with her eyes its black silk strap, its pearly dial and the sleek gold of its case. I tried, as her friend, to share her obsession, but the watch left me cold. Yet only back in the summer, I had fallen utterly,boundlessly in love with a tiny camera, not more than two inches long, lens, bellows and all, in a shop window in Guernsey. It had cost twelve shillings and sixpence (62p) and though I admitted the sum was astronomical, I asked, and pleaded and nagged and whined, but to no effect. I did not then see Ursula's longing for her watch as the twin of my hunger for the little camera.

Dusk deepened to blue, then violet. The gas flares in the fruit and vegetable shop next door blipped and fluttered in the air, and the glowing pyramids of fruit gleamed. Spicy oranges, yellow kid bananas and earthy swedes jumped out of the dusk, as the air around sank into darkness. Ursula sighed, dragged herself from the window and turned homeward.

As we trailed along the iron railings of the Rec, dreaming our way from pool to yellow pool of gaslight, a figure stepped forward with a sheaf of papers. "Read this, dearies; read this and remember it". Never averse to anything given away free, we each took a broadsheet. Under the next lamp - the one outside Ursula's house, we looked at them inquisitively. They were roughly printed in black smudgy letters, and across the top of the page ran the words, "Be warned! The World will End in Seven Years". Below that were crude woodcuts showing goat-legged devils, pitching little naked people into a bonfire, or toasting them, writhing, on the ends of wicked looking tridents. Remembering them vividly, as I do to this day, I should guess that those woodcuts dated back to the 18th century, and were part of the dusty clutter of some little family printer's workshop.

The cuts were hideous and frightening as we pored over them, but far more frightening was the threat of the end of the world. Seven years. I would be fourteen, the same age as Margery, our little maid. Never in my life before had a term of years seemed short. Last week was aeons ago, and the month from now to Christmas stretched away into the future beyond the horizon of possibility. But the ending of the world? The end of everything - so soon. I would never grow up. How would it all come about?

Shaken and silent, I left Ursula and made for home and security. But home this time failed me. Inside the door, the light and fire, the kettle steaming and butter softening in the hearth, took on an alien, sinister air, as though either they or I were not quite real. Something made me stuff the broadsheet into my pocket, and say nothing, but my subdued air and lack of appetite brought unwelcome questions and feelings of the forehead in case I was sickening for something.

The evening dragged its load of secret doom, and I watched my family, seeing them, blind victims of a Fate only I knew. I had not even the heart to play with Pussy - indeed I choked with tears as I thought of Pussy dying too, wiped out in the holocaust. Her darting paws and pricked ears only hung a burden on my heart and I was thankful to be dismissed to bed, where I did not have to hide my fear and misery any longer.

The faint street light moving in the shadows of the ceiling painted images of horror. I had visions - where did I get them? - of myriads of people fleeing helplessly from a great bellowing, pursuing force, cliff high and rolling on like a Juggernaut. It was fire-deluge, a mountain falling - inexorable, pounding onwards, with the screams of the trampled and dying thin and faint and universal, like the screaming of swifts as they reeled in the twilight air, hunting on the wing. I fell asleep at last with the sore lids and gritty eyes of exhaustion - but for once, morning brought no relief.

In the days that followed, the shadowy horror lurked alive round the corner of my mind, and would reach out a cold finger and touch me in any pause of play or lessons. Fallen- mouthed and blank- eyed I would look into the future and see Betty and Diana, Geoffrey and Jean - and always worst of all, Pussy, swept away screaming in the Apocalypse. My breath would catch, my hands grow clammy. It was coming - in seven years, and nothing would stop it.

How long all this went on I do not know but though I never told anyone, I think something must have been discovered - perhaps that abominable tract was found, (I hid it in my bedroom) for I recall hearing my father say indignantly "a wicked thing to give to a child". And his anger seemed to build a fence against the dread. Perhaps it would not happen. I was a little comforted and gradually the horror grew infrequent and faded. But it never quite went away, and crops up in bad times still, but now it is embodied more recognisably in images from the paintings of John Martin and I can rationalise it and cut it down to size.

That the threat of the end of the world should produce abysmal terror is not surprising, but looking back I am astonished at other happenings, very small and ordinary ones, which plunged me into darkness. For instance, why was I so devastated over the jam-pot? I was six; it was the summer-holidays at 'The Cottage'. We were having tea, and I had been sent, or more probably allowed to go (that may be the clue) to fetch a new jar of jam from the pantry. Carefully I had carried the two-pound glass jar through the lean-to kitchen, the length of the bedroom, and was just crossing the tiny entrance hall when unaccountably my clumsy cargo slipped and burst like a bomb on the grey stone flags. It was quite an impressive bomb too - a pint and a half of Robertson's Strawberry, and a million glass splinters showered all over the floor and quite a way up the walls as well. A domestic nuisance, a piece of clumsiness on the part of a child who ought to have taken more care. But why did it seem to me such an appalling tragedy? I can switch back in my mind now, and stand there, my feet splattered with jam and glass, gazing at the ruin where I stood, and I feel darkness engulf and blind me. Time stretches out ahead and I will never know happiness or a light heart again. All is lost, all is spoiled - anger and contempt and exile will be my lot. Despair sweeps over me and like a bereaved dog I lift up my voice and howl.

Why? I don't know. Had I possibly pestered to be allowed to prove that I was a big girl, steady, trustworthy, safe to fetch the jam, and been reluctantly given permission with many warnings? And had events betrayed me so that I stood shamed, in the wrong, humiliated? Or was it the sheer unexpectedness of the accident? For as I remember I did not trip. I was not startled. My grip did not shift. Just suddenly, the jar was slippery and fell. I was too small to put one hand under it and clasp it with the other. Shock, shame, whatever it was, I only knew at once that

I was lost forever. All my familiar and safe world had been snatched from me in that frightful second, as though a carpet had been whipped out from under my feet. The devastation was total.

So utter was my certainty that I also remember the slow bewilderment that stole across me when I found I was actually being consoled, cheered up - told not to cry. It was only a pot of jam! Only very cautiously could I bring myself to believe that they still loved me and wanted to keep me. My panic had been so heart stopping that I don't think I had any words or signs of gratitude to give - all I could do was stealthily to resume my place at table and hope 'It' would not notice, if I kept quiet. Thus I might hope, shaken though I was, to be overlooked and allowed to remain in my familiar world.

Some deep and hidden insecurity must have lain behind many of my early fears. Part of the trouble, I think now, may have been that I had a far more advanced understanding of words than my parallel powers of expression. Looking back to my earliest memories, at perhaps, 18 months, it seems to me that I understood fairly widely before I could speak more than a few syllables. I do know for sure that I overheard and understood 'grown-up talk' which even my cautious and sympathetic father must have believed to have passed clean over my head. One shattering moment I recall when the bottom dropped out of my cosy world, at least for the time being, and vast grey horizons opened out, of starvation, houselessness and suffering. I was playing on the shaggy black hearthrug and my brother, twelve years old, was boasting to Daddy of what he would do "in the next war". The year must have been 1929, and the nightmare of trench warfare not yet cold. "In the next war", snapped back my father, justly anxious to de-glamourize warfare, "you'll be lucky, my boy, if you're not out eating grass by the roadside." This was all my nightmares confirmed, and by Daddy! There was no safety net. In the twinkling of an eye all the familiar, the secure, might melt away. Years later, in my teens, when war had in reality engulfed us all, I found a poem which spoke of life as a journey where we have to:-

"Climb the stairs, knowing each step in the rear
Has crumpled beneath like tissue paper
Revealing the blue-black ink-blot of vacuity
Beneath our sinking knees..."

This re-awakened and embodied all the horror of the frail platform over chaos on which we live so precariously.

The Slump, too, played its part. Father was a schoolmaster, poorly paid, but as long as he did his job well, reasonably secure. But most of my friends' fathers were employed by the great engineering companies that were based on the town. Anxiety was the background of their lives, and every Friday's pay packet brought the dread that it might also contain the pink dismissal slip that told them not to come back on Monday. We lived near 'The Workhouse' and tramps filed down our prosperous road in dozens, hung round with tins and bags, broken-booted and huddled in old army great-coats. They had a code of signs they chalked outside our houses to let each other know who would be sympathetic and who would turn the dog on them.

It was a time of unrest; the word 'Fascist' began to be heard, and someone called 'Sir Oswald Mosley' was coming to address a meeting of 'Blackshirts' at the Cattle Market. 'Blackshirt' sounded sinister. My father and a colleague were talking as I played to myself in the dining-room. Some rival group was expected to object to the Mosley meeting. The police would be there. "I should think there'll be a riot", said my father.

Riot? I was seven. Where had I picked up my idea of a riot? I saw in my head, darkness - our road, and advancing up it a mob of yelling, wild-looking men, disfigured with fury, carrying flaring and smoky torches. They howled with savage lust and broke away in little vicious groups towards houses as they passed Ursula's house. They hammered on the doors, yelling derisively, and when the doors remained shut, they hurled stones through the plate glass windows and spilled over the sills, torches waving. Within, curtains flared and faint screams were heard. Joan's house, much closer, and Joan and all her many brothers poured white faced out at the back as the rioters smashed down the door at the front. They hid trembling in the coach house, the stables next door - the dark place behind the water butt - but the orange glare of guttering torches painted the shrubs and wooden walls and they were dragged out shrieking.

The weight of the nightmare became too great to last as it approached our house. I felt faint, though I did not know at that time what faintness was.

The painted horror stayed with me as I lay sweating with fear in my bed, waiting for the first distant animal yells of a crazed mob, and the lurid rusty flicker of torchlight on the ceiling.

The next day mercifully ended that dreadful fear. The meeting had passed off, it seems, with no more than a few humorous black eyes and bloody noses, and those only among drunks. I breathed again.

Looking back over the years, I believe I can now detect the source of at least some of my images of 'riot'. One of our maids had taken me on an afternoon walk past a farm not too far away. It had a great yard enclosed by buildings and an enormous heavy double 'porte cochère' with a small wicket gate set in it. This wicket was open as we passed, with a hurdle set across it and we could see bustle in the yard and hear a great commotion. A fire was blazing on the cobbles, a great wavering bonfire, flaring with straw and piles of brush wood. A heavy wooden table had been dragged into the open and as I watched, some farm men and boys, shouting and laughing coarsely, dragged a pig towards it. The creature was screaming like a human, and as I watched, my heart stuck like a dry stone in my throat, knives flashed in the red flickering dusk. "What are they doing?" I clutched at the maid's sleeve. She was a country girl.

"They're killing the pig for bacon. Want to watch?"

The pig's agonised pleadings beat against heaven. It fought and kicked as it was heaved up on to the table and turned on its back. Shouting, laughing, the men held its legs. The firelight flickered bronze against the dusk as the screams tore at my brain. I turned away and bolted. I ran blindly back down the road until the trees and buildings had mopped up and stopped the terrible sound. The maid came up panting and shook me. "What did you want to run like that for, you silly? It's only a pig".

For many, many years I suppressed this memory, at least in my conscious mind, but I think it lay there, unacknowledged, behind the flaring torches, the merciless shouting men with cruel unshaven faces, distorted in the glare, dragging helpless Joan and her brothers out from their hiding places, in that nightmare of 'Riot'.

There was a very early cinema in our town. Showings took place in a big room over Woolworths. There, at the age of three, I was taken by my brother - or was it <u>with</u> my brother? I don't recall. But the film was a Charlie Chaplin 'Short', and it flickered in sepia and exploding white spots, before my uncaring and uncomprehending gaze. Gerald laughed and wriggled beside me. Then came a sequence when Charlie, splayfooted and pathetic (the pathos must have reached even to me!) shuffled dejectedly past a high flight of front door steps. The housemaid who had been scrubbing them turned and shot her bucket of sudsy water downward. Passing Charlie was drenched. All at once it was too much. I was engulfed with desolation at the accident and I raised my voice and wept. Indeed I yelled "Poor man!" And wouldn't the maid get scolded? I didn't know who to be most sorry for and I was inconsolable. So embarrassingly prolonged were my shock and grief that I had to be hurried out of the place at the earnest request of the manager, who said my bawling was spoiling the show for the audience. It was the same kind of household disaster as my later experience with the two pounds of jam - and I can only think that the sudden, swift change it showed from security and normality to ludicrous devastation, released some deep fear I kept chained down, of insecurity in my own life. Perhaps for the same reasons, I hated circuses - the disasters that befell clowns sickened me, but never amused me. But this can only have been until I was about seven. I remember with shame that when I was nine, and my nice little roly-poly headmistress fell off her bike, I stood on the footpath falling about with laughter!

There were fears that we induced, and fears that we pretended - ghost stories and bogey men. For me they were not even half-believed. They were only a game to add a thrill to life. But there were fears of people which seem unbelievable now as I look back. How could I have been so afraid of Rosemary that my knees turned to water when she appeared, and I would even pretend to be ill to avoid going to school and facing her? She never laid a finger on me. She was only a sharp-tongued mocking girl a few months my senior but I lived in dread of her for all of one winter. Then suddenly, she did not matter any more. Then there was Boney, a boy who persecuted my friend John, and John feared him as I feared Rosemary. Boney used actual force. He hid in gateways to ambush John going home, and performed minor tortures on John's hair and fingers. One autumn day at playtime

he recruited the whole school (at least 35 children) into his army, to fight and annihilate John's army which consisted of John, me and Erin. I remember a lurch of real fear as we stood, three trembling brats under the chestnut trees, watching in horror as a broad line of screaming and threatening savages surged towards us like an advancing tide-race, over a hundred yards of frosty grass. There was fighting and there were casualties, but luckily for us, Boney had worked his army up to such a pitch of excitement that they had to fight - and as there were only three little Christians to share out among all those lions, several poor lions didn't get a Christian and fell to fighting each other, and we escaped when the bell went, trembling but unhurt. Brian, however, had his jacket ripped; Jean had a bleeding nose and Richard had a tooth knocked out. It was a milk tooth and wobbly anyway, but a serious scolding all round followed. Boney was kept in and all armies forbidden in future. That fear was short-lived and left no scars.

Fear of the dentist was fear of a short-tempered man, a friend of my father's, who shouted at me and slapped my face if I didn't stay still while his shuddering drill vibrated in my tooth. It was fear also of the smell of disinfectant, and of the nausea induced by a mouth suffocatingly stuffed with red wax, as impressions were taken of my teeth. My second teeth started with a gap between the front ones, but soon crowded together and overlapped. A hideous sort of expanding plate was forced into my mouth. It had a crack down the middle, and every Saturday morning I was taken to the surgery to have it screwed open a little further and crammed agonisingly back into my palate. Each week was a diminuendo from pain and strain, fading to comfortable ease, only to be. jerked up again to full pressure on Saturday morning. It never straightened my teeth, either!

One other fear, vital and horrifying, one which even yet makes my hair stand on end, but which all the same has left no shadow behind it.

When we moved to '62' I continued for a while to sleep in a cot in my parents' bedroom, but I was more than four and outgrowing it fast. Money was very short and I think there can not have been any to spare to buy me a bed. There was an empty bed in the house- a great yellow wooden double bed, part of my parents' first 'suite' when they married. It was split up now. The wardrobe stood on the landing, the chest of drawers was crammed into my brother's little end bedroom, the washstand and bed were put up on the top floor, in the only one of the three attic rooms fit for use. True, it had a sloping ceiling, but it was square, had a good window in a gable and two cubbyholes in the space under the eaves, so it was felt it would do as a spare room in case anyone came to stay. Perhaps to stave off the expense of buying me a bed, I was put to sleep up there when I was about five. It was up two flights of stairs, the only inhabited room on that floor. Next door was a box-room with the water tank which gurgled and clanked in a rather alarming way. Outside the window was a tiny lead-lined balcony, the head of the bay window of the floor below. In the front garden, a tall cedar tree partly shaded the window, and through its

100

spread hands filtered the yellow gaslight from the road beyond. These moving lights and shadows on the ceiling were rather interesting than otherwise, and did not usually alarm me. But when I had been put to bed, the light was out, and Mother's tread had faded down the haircord-covered attic stairs, and the thicker Axminster below - when the callings and door bangings had stopped and the dining-room door was shut to cherish the warmth of the coal fire, then the isolation of my eyrie swept over me. Perhaps Margery turned a tap on in the scullery, and with an unexplained hiss the ball-cock next door would drop, and water dribble into the tank. Filled, it would shut off with a dull clank. The wind would whisper through the pine-fingers and whine softly in the chimney that bypassed my room with never a fireplace.

In those days there was hardly a sound from the road after dark. I knew only four families which possessed cars, and our area was too respectable for drunks and revellers. There was no regular cinema, no evening entertainment. Even the wireless was still at the cat's whisker stage. A gramophone and a dozen records was the most advanced entertainment my family had. We were not musical and the piano stayed dumb.

Usually I just fell asleep, but some nights, the silence and the sense of being cut off by two storeys of empty darkness from my family would seize my mind and I would lie tense, afraid to move, in my huge acre of bed - fearful to call out, fearful to disturb - what?

In this attic room, the ceiling sloped, and along each side the lowest level had been partitioned off to make tunnels of storage space with rough wooden doors.

One special winter night - I must have been about six - I lay on my side, waiting for sleep and watching the changing glimmer from outside dance over the ceiling and shallow wall. The door of the cubby hole was straight in front of my nose. It was a windless night - no sighings in the chimney stack - and downstairs the family's movements had stilled and settled to a graveyard hush. I was drowsy, but still more awake than asleep.

As I lay, a hardly discernible movement signalled to my brain. My eye was not certain where it had come from. I felt my skin prickle all over as I froze into alertness. I watched like a threatened bird - even my breathing suspended.

Nothing happened.

Before I could relax again, there came the minutest creak - like a strand in a wicker chair settling. My eyes flew wide open. A movement. The bar of the old-fashioned thumb-latch that closed the door of the cubby hole was moving.

Paralysed I watched. Hesitantly it fluttered, paused, and then stealthily tilted and rose on its pivot. There was a long silence and then, along the edge of the door, where the reflected street-light made a thin line of shadow, the black line began to widen. It grew infinitesimally - as the door crawled back, and it flooded my mind with a chill like well water - that 'something' was inside and was opening the door.

At that point, a faint, heart-freezing soft moan breathed out from within.

My spirit broke. I sat bolt upright, screamed and screamed and screamed. It was a kind of defence. My screaming was like a weapon to beat back the horror. Anyway, it was loud enough to be heard below in the shrouded silence of the house. Doors were flung open, lights exploded, feet crashed up the stairs.

I remember no more. It had, of course, been my brother, who at 12, thought it very funny to hide before I went to bed and frighten me. I am certain the scoldings were loud and long and the retribution dreadful, for I must by this time have been a gibbering mess of hysteria. But it left no scar. I do not remember even feeling resentment. It had happened. It was Gerald. It was all right. I suppose that having the 'supernatural' at once uncovered and revealed to be no more than a prankish boy, took away its power to damage.

He frightened me far more on the day when he climbed out into my tiny window-box of a balcony, stood on the foot wide parapet and jumped three feet out and up over a three storey drop, from the parapet up to the valley between the gables. I did not scream that time, thank God. My guardian angel (or his) paralysed me into dumbness

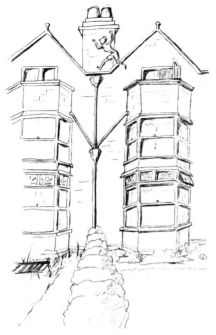

and cold shock. But those few seconds engraved my mind, and changed me for life. I have a fear of heights so acute that I can not even think about standing on a tower. I can't watch comedy films about people clinging to the hands of Big Ben, or kicking frantically from a bush on a cliff face. Some of my worst dreams are of high places. I begin to shake if I think about having to go up the Empire State Building, and I almost faint if I picture going up our local wireless masts by lift. On the Eiffel Tower my legs were jelly on the first great platform, and even a 'see through' staircase up one floor in my school makes me feel insecure. I have to sit on the aisle of an aircraft, and I have regular nightmares of being on top of the six-storey staircase well of my old University buildings, and having to reach my destined lecture room, by crossing a cat-walk over a cathedral-like hall below me. This fear, born that morning my brother showed off to me, forty feet up, with goatlike confidence, has crippled a part of my mind.

Father was necessary to my security and comfort, and it was purely, selfish fear motivated me on the day when, as a four year old, I turned into the sitting room to find a policeman, ten feet high in his helmet and boots, standing on the carpet under the light. "Daddy hasn't renewed his gun-licence. They've come to take him off to prison", some idiot

tried out on me. Quick as a cat, I picked up a stool and hurled it viciously at the poor unoffending Bobby! He must have had more understanding of kids than whoever it was that teased me. He didn't march me off to the jug!

Fears come on a young child so inexplicably there is no need for any shock to bring them on. My best friend Sally, at six, was quite happy to look at pictures of witches and goblins and ghosts in her picture books, but a perfectly inoffensive coloured plate of a hot-air balloon and two intrepid travellers in the basket, terrified her so overpoweringly that, long before the picture was due, she would clasp a wad of pages together between the flat of her hands, with the fearsome picture safely flattened in the middle, unable to escape, and carefully lay the whole wad down to the left and weight it down, before she felt safe to go on through the book.

The half mile of road between '62' and school could be as empty as Siberia. Now it has two sets of traffic lights in that stretch, but then, any normally sensible child could cross alone. The stretch outside the Rec seemed the loneliest. It was barely two hundred yards long but behind the looped iron railings, the round or diamond shaped flower beds and the row of conker trees, grass stretched quietly out and became the pasture and copse of open country, and on the other side of the road, not even the two great houses were visible. They withdrew behind brick walls and sheltering pollarded limes. Except at 'Works times' the road (it was the main road to Northampton) could be silent and blank and I the only moving speck on it.

One such morning I was idling up towards town at about eleven o'clock, and I had reached to the railings of the Rec. As I came abreast of them the emptiness of the Rec seemed to gush out like water between the bars, with the flavour of open country - nectar scented limes, cut grass, the unremarked hum of insects. I watched my feet as I bounced on and off the low brick plinth that supported the railings. The road was silent; the sun shone. I was content.

Some movement on the edge of my vision brought my head up, and beyond me, perhaps twenty yards away, was a creature, a monster, of such sickening horror that I felt the skin shrivelling round my lips

104

as blood drained coldly away. The thing was huge, walking towards me with a ponderous rolling gait, and I was utterly alone. There was no one in sight.

It was half human and half caterpillar. It had arms and legs, swinging clumsily at wide angles from its body. Its head was a dome and it had huge, blank shining insect's eyes that stared at me, but sightlessly. Its whole shape was flabby, white concentric rings like the bloated sections of a caterpillar, and they bounced and sagged as it waded clumsily towards me, its tiny feet and hands like suckers on the end of its swollen limbs. Its head like an old fashioned bee-skep bobbed seven feet high and it came remorselessly nearer with every rubbery lurch.

For a few seconds I must have been actually paralysed with terror. Then I whimpered, spun round and fled back down the pavement - my breath tearing my chest in cruel gasps. I raced past Ursula's house, and Joan's, across the mouth of the lane, fought for a sickening moment with our own clumsy gate latch, and stumbled, by this time blind with fear, down the passage to hurl myself through the back door and fall sobbing hysterically on Margery peeling potatoes.

I was incoherent, but the noise I made brought Mother and Father running. I remember the awfulness of not having a name to describe this terrifying monster, and the choking urgency with which I had to make them realise they must lock and bolt all the doors as it was getting closer every second. Some gibberish about a caterpillar and the road must have come out and roused Father's curiosity for he went to the front door and began to open it. This was worst of all - far worse than the possibility of a train going off and leaving him stranded. He MUST NOT GO OUT! I shrieked and fought and had to be held back forcibly to let him go and see what was outside. My heroism did not amount to much. I did not dash out to protect him. Only, as soon as I could slip my jailers, I raced to the sitting room window, compelled to witness the hideous fate of my Father. I think a picture postcard he had in our magic lantern collection, of that fearful sculpture of Laocöon and his sons being carried off by the sea-monster must have taken over my imagination at this point, as I clung to the window sill and saw Father outside the gate looking puzzled, gazing first down the road, and then turning and looking back up towards the Rec. I saw a change in his attitude, then he turned and ran jauntily up the front path, and - he was laughing. My gasps fell silent as I waited. He came to the window and thrust it up.

"It's all right", he said. "Nothing to be afraid of. It's just a man dressed up in a rubber suit, and he's advertising motor-tyres. I expect he's going to the garage over the bridge. Look, he's coming now, and you can see 'Michelin Tyres' painted across his chest."

Sure enough, the hideous head was bobbing between the neighbour's shrubs, and in a moment his blubbery white segments were seen outside our gate, loosely bouncing as he walked, like the coils of a slack spring. 'Michelin Tyres', I read on his back as he passed on into the distance, and the horizon steadied itself as the day resumed something like normality.

Not quite normal though - the shock and horror had been too great for that. I would not say that, like Wordsworth, "unknown modes of being" had been suggested to me. But certainly some ancient fears had been darkly revived and were "a trouble to my dreams".

'The Michelin Man', built up of tyres, still appears in advertisements and as a drawing he is innocuous. But my meeting with him, half beast, half human, in the uncanny solitude of that summer morning, still makes me shudder. Many years after, I was reminded of the experience, which I had thrust firmly into the limbo of the mind, where we tuck away the flotsam we can not bear to contemplate. One morning, during the petrol rationing period just after the war, when there was hardly any traffic on the roads, I had stepped outside a shop in High Street, and found that the street was completely empty. The sky overhead had that intensely clear greeny blue that suggests the superconcentrated light of a dream. No shoppers moved, no doors opened or shut, no sound broke the spell. All this was uncommon enough to be noticed and I stood for a moment, relishing the unusual stillness. As I watched, a shape swung round the corner a few yards away - a large grey shape that moved step by step, in total silence. All on its own, a quiet elephant padded down the middle of the empty road. I retreated cautiously into the shop again and the girls who sold the bread joined me to gaze, giggling nervously, at the inexplicable happening. However, in a few minutes, the elephant's keeper strolled along, hands in pockets and cigarette glued to his lip. A circus was on the move and the odd vision was explained, but called out of the darkness my meeting with the Michelin Man, which I had deliberately forgotten for years.

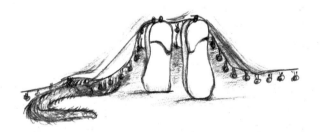

7. TRAVEL

 think the two things which have changed most in my lifetime are transport and entertainment. Boxes. We get into our personal box on wheels to go to work and come back, and as soon as we are inside our front doors we are asking "What's on the Box?". When I was small, one hand could count up the number of people we knew who had cars. The Headmaster had a big brown six-seater touring car. Sally's father had a well- polished blue bull-nosed Morris, and John's father, who was a builder, had its twin, but brown and mud-spattered. Sally's father cleaned and polished his car every weekend and if it rained on Monday he went to work in a taxi. Ursula's father had an Armstrong-Siddeley saloon, with a small cut-glass vase as an ornament on the radiator cap, and the car was so sedately driven that the button-hole rose or carnation set in it never fell out ! An elderly and enchanting bachelor colleague of Father's had an erratic vehicle which was rumoured to require tempting forwards with a dangled carrot, like a donkey. Certainly it was subject to mysterious sulks, followed by surges of inexplicable energy that took it careering round the Clock Tower and skating from side to side up Clifton Road. But it is just possible that dear "Colly's" mechanical ineptitude was responsible for that. But cars were kittle cattle in those days. Not many years after, one of my teachers had an elderly Riley which stopped dead frequently and could only be restarted if you stood up and stamped on the floor-boards. It was one of the endearing local sights. You would come on an open car in the middle of the road, with a handsome grey-haired lady standing up in the front, with an expression of deep concentration and stamping earnestly. After a while the car would cough, and the engine whir into life. She would sit down, engage the gears and motor away quite indifferent to any eccentricity in the proceedings.

We took it for granted that we got ourselves about. At '62', my walk to school was only a quarter of a mile, though it used to take about half an hour to cover, allowing for detours into the Rec and lingerings to giggle in Ursula's gateway. But when we moved to '106', there was a mile and a half to go, on quiet back roads. The first part of this walk was up an unadopted lane where the Catholic children went to their school in the convent. It was rather scarey. First you had to pass the Convent door, with a little square grille as a peephole. Diana and I went together for mutual protection and we always scurried past that door with a thrill of fear that it might fly open and we would be snatched inside. A more palpable danger lay in the row of cottages further up the lane, where Theresa lived. Theresa was a wild-haired, leggy Irish girl, who despised the smug and coddled children who had to pass her house to get to their posh little private school. She lurked in the Seminary gate and leaped out at us with heathen yells, and chased us ignominiously right up on to the main road. I can't think why we never turned and confronted her - we were well nourished and two to one. But she must have had more personality than Diana and me united, and every day we hung back, and spied out the land, and schemed to be able to pass up or down the lane at a time when we could dodge Theresa.

The children who came to the school from outlying farms used to be brought in, mostly by pony-trap, on a Monday morning, and boarded at the school till they could be fetched on Friday. They might live no more than three miles out, but time could not be spared on a busy farm to take the trap out and drive six miles every day to get them to and from school. One family, to be sure, came daily in a chauffeur-driven Rolls Royce, but their grandfather was an oil millionaire.

Buses did run to the ring of villages close to the town, (villages which now are merely the names of suburbs, with houses all the way) but I hardly ever rode in one. If we went to tea at the farms of friends a mile or two out we would be given a lift in the baker's delivery cart or in the milk float as it went back home to collect the milk and cream for sale at the dairy in town. The cart would put us down at the end of the narrow track that led half a dawdling mile across open harvest fields and between hedges draped in honeysuckle or whiskered with hay or barley snatched from passing wagons. The track was unsurfaced and a line of grass grew down the middle. At first the fields stretched, unfenced on either hand with poppies and ox-eye daisies and rusty sorrel to be picked. Then the track made a bend: the hedges shut out the horizon, and the poppies gave way to blackberries and the great limp umbrellas of the white bindweed. A trickle of water wove its shallow way over the silt of the ditch, and had to be crossed by a single plank to get to the house the near way through the orchard. Overhead, larks would unreel endless threads of song in June, and later the swifts would curve and scream as they hunted in packs for the high-flying insects. Only one field away lay the railway line and in the lazy afternoon air the rhythmic clank and rumble of a goods train would beat as rural a sound in its way as the cuckoo, or the chuckling of hens as they foraged in the orchard grass.

Basil and Alison's father farmed about four miles out. The children boarded at school all week and Basil and I got on very well together. One morning in the summer term Miss Margaret announced that the whole school was invited to a hay party at their farm, and that, provided our parents agreed, we would all be taken there the next afternoon and brought back again about six. Basil and I, Sally, Geoffrey, Betty and the Dianas were all in the Upper First and about eight years old.

We were all taken there in cars. Miss Margaret had lately bought her first car, a green Austin Seven with elastic sides, that could be persuaded to accommodate as many as ten children if suitably packed!

111

I wonder she didn't put a net over us for safety, like pigs going to market! Ruth's mother got another clutch into their big tourer, and Beaky got a good number into the dickey of her Morris. Basil's father brought his lorry.

The afternoon was idyllic. We pulled the hay about and made great nests in it. Basil's father organised a hay battle - and led one of the armies! The object was to snatch as much of your enemies' hay-castle walls as possible, and the hay in that meadow certainly got a tossing and drying that afternoon, Then we were given tea, all among the sweet smelling grasses. Raspberries and cream, and sticky buns, well decorated with grass seeds. Then, replete, tired and tickly, back to town to trudge our short walks home, at an unfamiliar hour that somehow made the familiar roads look alien and rather exciting.

Sometimes, in Guernsey, we would go by the local bus in to St Peter Port to visit our friends and shop, and when we did, we had to be early at the stop as the driver was his own timetable. We would walk half a mile to Cobo Post Office, a squat whitewashed granite cottage, sunk below road level, and with a typical Guernsey wall round its garden built of rough boulders, and broader than it was high. It made a perfect seat and did all it needed to in the way of keeping the little soft-eyed cows from straying. We sat in a row on the sunwarmed stones, with sheep's bit scabious and the little pink bells of bindweed round our ankles. Lichens and grasses had lodged and grown between the stones of the wall. Meadowsweet creamed the damp ditch behind us, and, untraceable, but close at hand, came the rackety chirr of the great green grasshoppers as big as your finger, that leaped like mechanical toys if you were lucky enough to spot them in the warm flowery banks. Otherwise it was silent. Even sea-gulls were rare in this part of the island. They thronged round the fishing boats and the passenger port, but here they had to dive for their own living and not many bothered. Even the pulse of the sea was unheard here, a bare quarter mile inland. The lush green grass and the lines of glasshouses mopped it up. So we would wait, swinging our legs through the wild flowers, in contentment, unless I restlessly got up to hunt for the goggle-eyed grasshopper.

The bus would be heard, turning the corner from the coast road, and we would jump down and be ready, Father with the change for our fares in his hand. There was no conductor. The bus was hardly more than a very large open touring car. It had bench seats right across to seat three - the whole bus did not carry more than twenty passengers. Its metal work was all brass; its 'headlamps' were carriage lamps mounted at either side of the front windscreen. A folded hood on a sort of extending trellis could be drawn forward in wet weather, and every seat had its individual door with a brass handle. Father paid the driver and Gerald and I made for the back seat. Why do children always go for the back seat? In all my years as a teacher I have grown used to parties, even of eighteen-year-old sixth formers on a theatre trip, making a rush to pack themselves far too tightly on to the long back seat of the coach. They would rather squash seven in a row, jammed like sausages than be comfortable in pairs in the seats further forward. It must be one of those things, like longing for snow, that marks the dividing line between childhood and grownupness.

The cushions of the bench seats were loose, and stuffed hard with horsehair. The leather was hot, cracked by sunshine, and the duckboard floor was filled in the crevices with sand. We could turn our backs on the bus and lean, our arms on the mackintosh of the folded hood, to watch the narrow, steep-banked lane spin away behind us. Half way across the island was a huge road junction - three lanes joined! Here there was another little cottage-shop with a white painted board over the low door, saying that A.S. Cumber was licensed to sell tobacco. It was one of the repeated annoyances of my life that A.S. Cumber's mum and dad had not had the foresight to christen their offspring Quentin - or Queenie, so that the signboard could have read A.Q. Cumber.

It was only five miles across the island, and soon the bus would be climbing steadily up the long slow slope that brought it to the head of the steep hillface that was St Peter Port. The houses were more frequent; they were bigger. Their granite blocks were carefully squared, and huge billowy bushes of hydrangeas lolled and pouted like Edwardian beauties in the gardens. Tall trees had been planted - (too many monkey-puzzles). The rolling lawns of the Candie Gardens swept by. A whiff of vile odour from the fish glue factory - stuccoed houses with porches and striped awnings - then the bus would turn its nose downwards through narrowing steepening streets and the glittering blue of the sea stood like a sheer wall ahead of us dotted with boats and flags and islets of rock. The tiny islands of Herm and Jethou lay a couple of miles off, and Sark beyond. The sea-mist blurring the horizon would usually hide Jersey, and Alderney to the north lay so low in the water that I never recall seeing it in my life.

Travel was by rail and sea. The air age had not begun. At five or six we used to rush out into the garden to gaze upwards in wonder if an aeroplane passed overhead. And one day, a cry went up from house to house; people rushed out, then turned and called their children. Mother ran with us down the lane to where open pasture allowed us the greatest and longest-lasting view of the wonder, and for once

the two cross maiden ladies, John's aunts, did not chase us away but came out of their fortress to gaze as well. What was the strange sight?

High above us floated slowly, like a long silver bubble, a ghost shape, one I had never imagined before. It gleamed like metal, and yet looked frail and airy. It drifted in silence in the pale morning, high and strange, but not so high that we could not read on its fish-like flank its black identity - R. 101.

It crashed in flames so shortly after, that the sighting was fixed in my memory, and left me for ever with a mistrust of flying. When I do have to fly, the other passengers on board have no idea what a lot they owe to me. I am the person who is holding the aeroplane up by sheer will-power!

The railway journey for Guernsey was not eventful. We ran through endless placid green hills, with the trees getting a little sparser as we drew further south. The grass looked thinner and the roads whiter as chalk replaced the Midland clay. Then came a point when Father, who had a map, would take us over to the corridor window to look out for the great White Horse, cut in the turf of the hillside. Not long afterwards came the climax of excitement as we reached Weymouth. Here we were allowed to have the carriage window open and lean out, because the train slowed down to a crawl. The

115

astonishing thing here was that the railway ran right down the middle of the street. There were no fences. You looked out of the window and saw the people going in and out of shops with baskets, children sitting on the kerb dabbling their feet in the gutter, little boys racing alongside the train waving, and we waved back. The train towered above them all. You did not realise at a station platform how high above ground the carriages really were. You only felt this when you peeped out and found yourself looking vertically down on the top of some shopping woman's decent felt hat, and saw directly into her basket with its load of potatoes, carrots and brown bar soap.

You could smell the sea. Over the hot metal and sulphurous smoke came a flat and nauseating odour which belongs only to passenger sea-ports. Rightly or wrongly, I have always explained it as the smell of too many people being sea-sick, since it is always worse on a choppy day. This smell would now waft over the line of grey sheds at the waterfront. The train would crawl into the echoing dark of the covered platform, and we would climb down, hung about again with all the coats and bundles we had lugged up the road only a few hours ago. A moment of panic for me as Father got back into the train to check that we had not left anything behind. Suppose it suddenly started off and whisked him away back to Rugby? I never trusted trains.

All well. He rejoined us and we started with the rest of the crowd along the dark platform, and out on to the tarred timbers of the dock, until we came abreast of the black and white paint and orange funnel of the St Patrick and the St Julian. Up the steep ridged gangway and into a totally new world, where sailors in rough navy jerseys and bell-bottomed trousers nipped around the scuppers, and seagulls flew low, screaming angrily when a stream of potato peelings shot out from a deck below.

Here we were allowed no freedom. We had to stay strictly with Father and Mother, camped on a hard slatted seat, with macs and coats to soften it a little. Father would work out the best place to be, sheltered from the wind when we got out into the open sea, and there we would stay. Other parties would gleefully settle in sunny corners, while we sat stolidly in the shade, but we had the last laugh when the ship steamed out of harbour and pointed south. The shade slid away from us, the breeze was no more than pleasant in our nook, and at last we were allowed to walk about a little, sedately, and watch the line of flat-fronted houses of Weymouth fade, honey-coloured, into the distance, their pretty wrought-iron balconies diminishing to finger smudges, as the boat throbbed and pulsed her way out to sea.

It was a daytime journey by Weymouth, but a long one, and it was always rough round the Casquets. There was no way you could approach Guernsey and avoid this dangerous reef, lying at cross tides off the coast of Normandy. By this time, all novelty had worn off the journey. I was tired and gritty-eyed. My stomach heaved and protested as the boat began to slither, pitch and wallow. This was the one miserable part of the day. The sun would be setting by now and sea-chill clung round us, but it had to be endured. "It was always choppy round the Casquets". That was a fact of life. Many years after, making the journey at night with the luxury of a berth, I watched the Casquets light shoot from top to bottom of the porthole glass and disappear at both ends, and realised that twenty five years makes no difference to a Channel tide race, and the big 'Princess' only pitched a fraction less frivolously than the bobbing little St Julian used to do.

As it grew dark and we felt our way cautiously in through the rock-strewn approaches to the island, a sheet of twinkling lights would be hung like a curtain against the afterglow. St Peter Port clings by its claws to the steep hillside, and when the boat glided in past Castle Cornet, sleeping like a curled-up cat on the still water, and the lights of the White Rock beckoned us in to the pier, to the rumble and clank of the gangway run out, and the surge of passengers, white faced in the electric light, Auntie Elsie would have run down from her tall French house on the hillside, and be waiting, six foot of silvery haired magnificence to call, and greet, and laugh and hug us, and - we had arrived!

The journey to Northern Ireland was more intense - emotionally more wearing. For one thing we had about ten hours on the train, with a night crossing to Larne at the end. The journey took us up through a great industrial belt - huge clanging stations like Crewe, and there was bustle, a throng of strangers, and my deep-rooted fear when Father was out of sight. The long weary hours would begin strangely with breakfast by yellowish electric light as daylight eased its way out of the night clouds. Then, a taxi would come and we would creep out of the house, hushed by Mother, while all the neighbours' bedroom curtains were tightly drawn. Father would check the locks on the doors, the keys, and all the tickets before joining us in the taxi, and the motor would grind into action and the hard wheels lurch forward. It was the only time we went in a taxi and I would wait rather anxiously, secretly worried that as taxis were 'very expensive', Father might not have enough money to pay.

Everything about this great station was odd and alien - pierced iron pillars and a square wooden canopy, with fretwork eaves. We had a long climb up the ramp to platform level - through closed-in corridors of white tile - branching away into unexplored glooms where, Gerald whispered, they had found a man's body, hacked to death, not many years ago.

On the platform it was better. The station was immensely long but had only one island. If the great London express had just thundered through, the air would be filled with the disturbing smell of November 5th - gunpowder and sulphur. Our train rumbled in to the North Platform and my tension grew. What I wanted was for all of us to go aboard at once, sit down and stay still until the train was safely on its way. But it was not due out for twenty minutes. Mail bags had to be taken off and new ones loaded. Luggage must be packed in the van, Hampers of burbling pigeons on the porter's barrow would be taken aboard for release far North in some great race. The crates of peevish hens, grumbling in their confinement, would not go on our train. They were for local services, where they could be unloaded at villages or farm sidings. "We've plenty of Time", said Father, as we moved up the platform, reading the long white boards slotted above the carriage doors. "Crewe only". "Carlisle and Glasgow". "Stranraer Boat Train" - that was our bit. You had to get in the right section or you might be shunted off at Crewe and end up in Glasgow!

We found an empty carriage and put all our belongings in the racks or on the seats. The doors all down the train swung loosely, their window straps lolling like tongues. Far away, at the rear, a clutter of

118

trolleys hemmed in the Guard's van, and more were being dragged there with an iron roar, freighted high with reddish brown mail sacks, like Father Christmas' load.

"I'll go and get some papers", said Father, for whom the journey without the Crossword would have been unbearable. My nightmare began. "Don't go, Daddy. The train might go without you".

"Nonsense. We've got more than ten minutes still. You stay with your Mother. I won't be long". And he would stride off across the platform, past the ticket office, and DISAPPEAR!

This was the dreadful thing. The Smith's Bookstall was on the

other platform, out of sight. I hung in the open doorway, one foot waving out over the wooden running board, my voice squeaky with fear. "Daddy, come back, come back, <u>please</u> don't go" It was no good. Father took no notice. Why should he indeed? I was going to have to learn to cope with facts, and not expect everyone to pander to my pet nightmares. Poor Mother was the one who had to face the embarrassment of a five-year old, white-faced and desperate, wailing in panic, while people glanced curiously and contemptuously at my exhibition. The only small advantage it may have had was that a screaming devil of a brat effectively put other travellers off joining our carriage, so we could count on having it to ourselves at least as far as Crewe!

My fear was so real, and so uncontrollable that as years went on, even Father agreed that it was better to buy his papers on the way to the train than to start off a full day's hard travelling with me sick with anxiety - and resentment. But in those early years - when it mattered most - the mounting fear that began when we entered the station would grow and master me, and leave me wrung out, exhausted, my faith in the security of my world shaken, and myself a jumpy, sulky tear-sodden mess at the very start of our long run North. It was purely selfish. The root of my fear was that as a family we could not survive without Father, and as I regarded trains as creatures of chance and impulse, which might decide to set off willy-nilly at any moment when their impatience overcame them, it was clearly foolhardy of Father to go sauntering away out of my sight, with a savage railway engine hissing out steam angrily between its teeth up at the front end!

At last Father would come back and my whimpering would die away. I would not be pacified, though, until he shut the carriage doors when all the others were still open with passengers strolling about on the platform. I did not mind if they got left behind. That was their own lookout. But over my own possessions I was going to keep a close watch and this was easier done with the door shut!

At last, from far down the train would come the sound of doors slamming, growing louder as the porter walking up got nearer. The engine would spout and hiss at all its crevices. The Station Master would suddenly be there outside, walking about with a whistle and a green flag. "Watch him". Father would divert me from my sorrows. "When he waves his flag, we'll be off".

The last door slammed. Silence on the platform, save for the gentle rumble of mail-trolleys being drawn away. The Guard would wave and jump aboard. The Station master's glance traversed the great train, checking. Then, his whistle between his teeth and his right arm raised, he blasted his signal. The green flag flapped, the engine sucked in its breath and with the same huge initial effort as a dray-horse getting its load rolling from stand-still, it would put its shoulders into it and with a jerk, a clatter and then a glide we would move forwards. The platform and people swam backwards out of sight, the sky would grow light, the shuff-ha-shuff-ha-shuff would change to a cheerful chuffa-chuffa-chuffa-chuffa, and before long even that would die away and we would be chattering along the lines with only the five stroke resonance of the wheels over the joints to be heard - 'ti-trang-ti-ti-ti', always with a stumble on the second beat of the phrase.

I suppose every child who ever travelled by train has asked its parents, "Why do the telegraph wires jump up and down?" and been no more enlightened by the answer than I was. But there were other mysteries. This rhythm of the wheels over the joints in the line for instance. Why did you never hear more than one approaching beat before the very loud one, but you heard three or four diminishing ones as the wheels behind passed over? And the physics of motion puzzled me silently for years. The train was moving at a certain speed. Telegraph poles, fences and trees just outside flashed past almost too quick for the eye to catch them. But further away, farms and cows and barns idled slowly by and you had plenty of time to examine them; out in the far distance, though, the blue hills stayed motionless for half-an-hour at a time. Yet the train was racing past all of them at exactly the same speed There was no accounting for it!

When Father had finished his Crossword, and read all of the paper that he wanted, he would sometimes take a dull page (usually the

Stock Exchange one) and amuse me by making a palm tree. For some reason this was only a railway treat. He rolled up the double page tightly, then with his penknife, made four or five long slits at one end of the tube. Then he pulled the tube out gently as you do when making a spill, gave it a shake and the slit paper would spread out and flop, like the leaves of a date palm on the end of its long trunk, or if you were not feeling so romantic, like a housemaid's trundle-mop.

There were other diversions, especially at the great stations where the train drew up for perhaps fifteen minutes, and we could lean out and watch a greasy man in overalls work all the way up and down the carriages, banging the wheels resoundingly with a great hammer "to see if they are cracked". Sometimes the train would halt and hiss quietly to itself while it took in gulps of water through a great leather hose as thick as a tree trunk, from a round iron tank perched like a mushroom beside the track.

There were little black huts beside the line where I imagined the signal-man lived. Then we would dive into a clanging tunnel, and Father would leap to close the windows, for cinders and soot poured down the slipstream and the carriage would be filled with choking fumes. No lights were put on for tunnels then, and I would screw my fingers into a painful bunch, trying to control my fear that the hillside above us might vibrate and collapse, burying us for ever. The faint pallor that flickered on the walls outside meant we were coming to the end. The walls would begin to gleam, wet and shiny; the ribs of rock would stand out in the sideways light; then with a whoop of triumph the train would burst out of the coffin darkness into a cutting, and soon the side walls of that would dwindle away, and we would be trundling out across open country again.

The journey was punctuated with events. Crewe station - still quite early in the day - seethed with energy, its wide span ringing with noise. Then lunch, out of paper packets. By this time the guard or his mate would have gone the length of the train, and if you wanted it a table with one leg would have been hitched into slots under the window. Four people could sit at it comfortably and draw or read or play games on its green leather top. It made eating more civilised too, and we could spread napkins as plates and enjoy our ham sandwiches and tomatoes, while the fields reeled past the window, cows and horses munching incuriously, and now and again a group of urchins on a stile, yelling, waving, and sometimes thumbing their noses as we sped by. Oranges, neatly peeled by Father, and a boiled sweet would finish our meal. By now I was contented, felt safe, and enjoyed this gritty picnic in a flying box more than I enjoyed any I ever had on damp grass with ants and wasps to pester me. The only drawback was thirst. We brought Thermos flasks of coffee or orangeade with us. We would need them on holiday anyway, but they held so little relative to their bulk. However, even that little soon demanded a trip down the corridor with Mother to a corner closet, where a pivoted brass latch inside the door would, I knew, miraculously make the word "Engaged" replace "Vacant" on the outside.

Mother would not let me 'go' alone in case I locked myself in and could not get out again. It was quite embarrassing enough to have had me screaming myself into a fit at the carriage door on Rugby station without facing the humiliation of fetching the guard and having me rescued by ladder out of the loo window at the next stop. So she came in with me though there was scarcely room to turn round. I could have had much more fun on my own. There was a little circular basin with mysterious taps that you had to clout to make any water come. As often as not, the cistern was empty, but sometimes a well aimed clout would produce a snarling gush that ricocheted off the sloping basin and drenched your socks. There was a railway towel with LMS on a red stripe down the middle - a cardboard towel that would not dry anything. But best was the juddering, jumping lavatory pan with its hard round seat, that lurched and shuddered under you as you tried cautiously to sit down, and seemed to want to catapult you out of the window with your knickers at half-mast. It was nearly as good as a fairground!

Soon we would be gliding into another great station. I have forgotten the exact route. Could it have been Lancaster, or Carlisle "the Gateway to the North", as the railway poster called it? Carlisle sounded romantic and the poster showed a knight in full armour on a white charger and a streaming scarlet pennon, riding boldly through a portcullis raised to welcome him. Gerald loved that poster and tried to copy it. Father, seeing the botch he was making, sat down and gave him a lesson in how to paint silver armour. He showed the gleam of the high-lights, the reflections, and the distortions in the curved shining plates. Gerald stood by, admiring the way the silver-clad knight began to grow out of the paper. But secretly he was bored by the lesson. Many years after, he described it all to me, and revealed in a few bald words what Father quite often forgot about the mind of a young child. "I <u>knew</u>". said Gerald sourly, "how to paint silver armour. You used SILVER PAINT".

The Restaurant Car was too expensive for a family travelling on a schoolmaster's pay. We took our own food. But at the big stations, boys pushed heavy trolleys up and down the platform by the waiting trains, and for a penny or two you could buy a cup of tea from their urns. This was the answer to our thirst. Mother was dying for a cup of tea. Father would lean out of the window (not opening the door, out of deference to me) as the boy came near. Money was passed, and four heavy white cups and saucers full of bright brown tea, almost the colour of tomato soup, were handed carefully in and placed on the table. The cups were straightsided and thick - surely the thickest china that ever came out of a kiln. You could drop them on the platform and they only bounced and rolled. There was a tin spoon, and two lumps of sugar in each saucer. Just lumps - none of that hygienic nonsense about having them wrapped in paper. We dropped them in and stirred, clinking as the bustle of the station went on outside. "Drink a little now, then it won't all splash in the saucer when the train goes", said Mother. Most of the children I knew were not allowed at my age to drink tea at all. Milk and hot water was all they got. But my Irish family liked their tea so strong you could stand the spoon up in it, and saw no reason to deny me tea if I wanted it too. As long as there was plenty of sugar I did want it. (I never found out what tea really tasted like until I gave up sugar for ever in the War). So I drank a little, and then waited, in order to enjoy the full flavour of the treat, by sipping delicately as a cat, while watching the countryside fly by, from a Railway Train, going North, to Ireland on a Sunny Afternoon, Glory Hallelujah! All's Well with the World.

Drinking tea elegantly under difficulties had long seemed to me the epitome of grownupness. When I was no more than two-and-a-half one of the Staff wives had brought her brand-new baby daughter to show off to Mother, and she sat on the sofa, with Léonie propped goggling on a cushion beside her, to sip her cup of tea. The fire was warm and the sun shone through the window. Her hat of course, was immovable. Hats never came off on visits in those days. But her coat, with its low slung button and its bolster of fur round the neck, could be discarded. I watched entranced while she balanced her cup and saucer on her knee, and slipped out of her coat. Maybe it was only draped over her shoulders anyway but I had a distinct impression that she shrugged her arms out of the sleeves and let the coat fall with elegant nonchalance behind her all without spilling a drop of the tea balanced on her lap. It was amazing and I silently resolved that I too would display such poise and aplomb as soon as I got the chance.

The opportunity did not come for quite a while but I cherished my ambition secretly. When I was four, Gerald took me along with him to pay a call on two delightful old ladies who had taken a fancy to him. (Even at ten he was marvellous with old ladies). They were the daughters of a famous Victorian cricketer and he had come to know them when they spoke to him, walking home with his bat from a School cricket game. They lived in a charming Art-Nouveau house, and had Persian rugs on the floor and Persian cats in all the best chairs. I was accommodated on a footstool and given a cup of sweet milky coffee. I purred with satisfaction. At last the time, the place, and the chance to show off had all come together.

My black velours hat was anchored safely under my chin with elastic. But my little double-breasted coat of hunting pink with a black

velvet collar was removable. I put the full cup on my lap and cautiously undid my buttons. Then I began to wriggle out of the sleeves. Oh dear! What went wrong? Was my lap too small and jelly-like? Had I put the saucer on the skirts of my coat? Or was the feat just impossible anyway, and a figment of my imagination? There was a yowl, a crash, and my coffee was shared about equally between my best red coat, the exquisite rug and a cream coloured Persian cat. My humiliation was terrible, but Gerald's was even worse. He couldn't take me anywhere. What would the Misses Buchanan think? Why couldn't he have a sister who could be civilised? What on earth was I thinking of, putting my coffee on my knee and starting to do acrobatics. What did I think I was, a monkey or something?

So, my ambitions cut down to size, I was glad to have a table before me as I sipped my strong sweet railway tea, and watched the hypnotic dance of the swag of telephone wires outside, leap and subside, leap and subside, until I drowsed off in the afternoon sunshine.

The countryside began to change. The train had to stop and have a second engine attached for the long slow grind up Shap Fell. The brown moor with ragged grasses cut featureless across the horizon. Up on the top, you could look out of the window and see the twin engines far ahead, leading the curving train as it crawled round the long bends of the track. Then came a point when Father told us we were in Scotland. I looked for some radical change in the countryside, but there was none - or none at first. Gradually, the heather and mountains of Galloway drew alongside us, and distant crags and hills changed from powder blue in the sun to damson purple when the cloud shadows swept over them. Father was standing in the corridor gazing entranced, and turning this spectacular landscape into water colours in his mind.

Dusk would be falling before the lights of Stranraer bloomed against the pale sea. My parents came from Larne and knew many of the officers on the boats. We would go aboard straight away. Stranraer was a small port, easy and informal, even more than Weymouth, and we would hardly have time to feel the evening chill off the sea before we were snugly settled on padded benches for the night, Mother and me in the Ladies saloon, Father and Gerald elsewhere. I remember none of these crossings, so I must have slept and they must have been calm. Coming back in daylight at the end of the holiday, I found that two thirds of the journey was in shelter of the land, in water so shallow that the propellors churned up a curly khaki wake from the mud at the bottom, and Ireland was barely out of sight before the Coconut Pyramid of Ailsa Craig nosed out of the sea mist.

When we berthed alongside the pier, with its great straddling timber struts, even Larne Harbour was not quite the end of our journey. We had to cross the loch to Island Magee, my Mother's home. There were two ferries, and the nearest was the smallest. Bob's ancient open motor boat with a wheezy engine you wound up with string, took us bucking over the neck of water where the loch opened to the sea. We always got across safely, but at times Bob's old engine would die in mid-channel, and the boat would drift gently with the wind and tide (and a few resigned passengers) until he could tickle it into life again. One famous winter night, it refused to re-start and Bob

126

and his boat were swept right away from land. Everyone feared he was lost for ever, but his oily little tub kept stubbornly afloat, and drifted right across the Irish sea to Scotland to make a safe landfall two days later on the Mull of Galloway.

Bob's ferry would put us down at a tiny jetty, where sand and shingle from the shore got in our towny shoes. Then came the very last leg, and leg was the word. With our bundles and coats and umbrellas, we had to climb The Hill, a long, long, steep climb, heading east, then turning south at "Bal'lumford" - a simple corner of the road with one whitewashed house. Now it is unrecognisable as 'Ballylumford Power Station'. Out on the hilltop at last the wind would strike us, and the honeysuckle in the low hedges drift its perfume sweetly along the morning. Past the great exposed dolmen in a front garden, past McGowan's farm where the turkey-cocks gobbled, and in at the fuchsia draped gate, where geraniums spread spice on the air in the coloured glass porch, and Auntie Charlotte and, in the early days, my one-legged Grannie, waited to greet us.

8. PARTIES AND FESTIVALS

he year's festivals were celebrated quietly. My birthday was the high spot for me. I really do not remember any of Gerald's September birthdays, though I do recall him having a party once, when he was leaving Father's school and going on to Rugby. It was an evening party for boys only, but I was allowed to stay up for it and boasted boringly to the other seven year olds at school that I had not gone to bed until eleven! Father's August birthday came when we were on holiday. Mother's was three days after Christmas, and was marked year after year with one present only - a big box of chocolates with a picture and a glorious bow on the lid. These ribbons fascinated me. So did the chocolates of course, but it was a SIN to help yourself. What I loved was to stroke the satin or velvet and feel the convolutions and hollows in the knots and loops and see the variations of colour in the shadows and highlights. The insides of the boxes were opulent, too. Round the edge was gold paperlace. Each chocolate sat in a little crinkled cup and was decorated - wrapped in silver paper, or topped with a crystallized violet, or rose petal, a chip of pineapple or a piped swirl of chocolate. Sometimes there were gold cardboard trays for each layer, with ribbon loops, and the bottom layer would be filled out with shredded paper like straw, which could be used to make birds' nests and propped hopefully in the crook of the plum tree, while I waited for a grateful pair of birds to come along and claim my highly desirable residence, and get busy with eggs while the other birds were still staggering about with bundles of dead grass, or fluff from the carpet sweeper.

Our children's parties were for birthdays, but rarely for Christmas. This was a good idea as the parties got spread out over the year.

Little girls would be brought well wrapped in fuzzy Shetland shawls under their overcoats, and had to be peeled out of layers of leggings and coats, sitting on the bottom step of the stairs. They all wore taffeta or crêpe-de-chine, or panne velvet, and Erin always carried a little Dorothy bag on her wrist, for her hankie. My close friends and daily playmates looked strange in their party clothes, an alien Carl in black velvet shorts, buckled shoes and a white shirt with a lace jabot instead of the Harris tweed and jersey in which he played in the lane; Giulia, dark and Latin, always had something arresting like crimson velvet, and Christopher wore a kilt and sporran.

Mother would have made a big birthday cake for the centre of the tea table. The business of lighting the candles and blowing them all out in one puff was fun, because the light was switched off while the candles burned. But the plain truth was nobody liked the cake much - they picked at the icing, but the rich dark fruit cake was not attractive to children. One small boy used to refer to his Grandmother's fruit cakes as 'Granny's dirty cake'. No savouries were ever offered in our day; sandwiches were jam, honey or banana, and glowing towers of jelly, clear ruby or amber, with blobs of whipped cream on them were piled on our plates. Chocolate biscuits were the most desirable of all. These were wrapped in gloriously coloured silver paper, to be smoothed out carefully on the cloth, and compared for pattern, scarlet and blue ribbons entwined on silver, purple bubbles, interlaced, azure and viridian peacock's feathers. We collected silver paper for charity at school, and brought it rolled up into balls small as a marble or large as a cricket ball. The biscuits were luscious - crumbly shortbread, heavily coated in milk chocolate that ran in thick ripples down its back; Cadbury's fingers, that were more chocolate than biscuit and, best of all, long sturdy wafers, many-layered with pink sugar, and a top layer of toffee, with chocolate coating so thick that it flaked off as you bit, and lay on your plate with the waffle design of the wafer imprinted on its under surface.

Tea was certainly a high spot at the parties, and gave the mothers a lot of trouble. It is easier now, when sausages on sticks, crisps and a can of fizzy drink seem to be all the guests require before they get back to the business of stunning themselves with Pop music.

Games before tea meant all old favourites. Musical Bumps would be followed by a quiet game like 'Pass the Parcel', 'General Post', 'Turn the Trencher', or 'I sent a letter to my love'. All these games with their rituals and patterns, were controlled by the hostess. There was none of the encouraging of screaming and unruliness, no goading to over-excitement that seems to be automatic nowadays. We were there to enjoy ourselves, but with decorum, and the hostess's drawing room was not expected to suffer. Though I admit Mother used, very wisely, to put away any vases or photograph frames in case of accidents, and the old fireguard was brought down from the attic for the afternoon.

After tea, some sort of novelty would have been arranged. Father would set up our big tin magic lantern and show a collection of funny postcards on it. Some families had the more sophisticated models that showed transparent slides, telling a story in stages like a comic strip.

131

These were usually a good generation out of date and we got to know the tales, year by year, of the misfortunes of oddly dressed students in gowns and mortar-boards, or naughty Victorian boys in Norfolk suits, who threw snowballs at old gentlemen in top hats. Once, at a very grand party, a conjurer was engaged and he produced streamers from the air and ping-pong balls out of our ears and the backs of our necks. Erin's parties were my favourite because we always played 'Family Coach'. Erin's father would come in and tell a marvellous story, full of detail, about the Brown family going off for a holiday in the family coach. Each of us would be a member of the family, Mr Brown, Baby, Nurse, Master Brown, or the Coachman, the horses, the whip, the brakes, the trunks. Whenever our role was mentioned, we had to get up, spin round and sit down again, and on the words 'Family Coach', everybody spun round. It was a wonderful game because Erin's father told such a gripping story that you all too easily forgot your cue, waiting open-mouthed for whatever would happen next, while your neighbours nudged you and called "Harness, harness - get up, harness!" The tale would gather speed, the items be named, three or four in a sentence, and the Family Coach, racing out of control down a hill towards the sea, would overturn in a welter of lamps, trunks and harness, Nurse, Baby and family, coachman, footman and Rover the dog, and everyone would be spinning madly and sitting down, when Mr S would wind up and that was the end of the FAMILY COACH! " And up we would all spring for a last, exhausted twirl. We got a game and a story both together, and it was non-competitive, so the party would end on a friendly note, and the waiting maids and mothers could parcel up their good-humoured charges again in the tickly shawls, the leggings and woolly gloves, and we would all solemnly go to our hostess and say "Thank you very much for having me", before going out into the night, where black damp air slapped at our hot cheeks. Our breath would condense in little droplets on the hairy shawls, pulled up well over our mouths. The gold fuzzy balls of the gas lamps would float above us in the dark, and the grind of a taxi motor, or the occasional clop of distant hooves on the road would echo through the ringing night as we were hurried homeward, clutching the little parcel we had been given and told not to open until we got home. With this to look forward to, the parties did not collapse into flatness as the front doors closed behind us, but were carried along on a bubble of anticipation and pleasure that would get us safely through to bedtime without tears.

Sally had a summer birthday, and so did Peggy. Peggy lived with her Granny, who was too old to cope with a children's party, but in a village only two miles from the town she had aunts and a family of cousins, who lived on a farm that supplied its own dairy business in town. The aunts used to give Peggy a party nearly every summer, and Sally and I both loved them and also in a way feared them because they had so many strange features. We would be among the youngest there and did not always understand what was going on. We were asked to go in ordinary summer dresses, not party dresses, as we would be playing in the fields and the stackyard. One year, the cousins, who were older than Peggy, had organised a paper chase. Philip was something called "The Hare" and I watched uncomprehendingly, as he slung a full satchel over his shoulder, waved us goodbye, and trotted off down the lime avenue that led from the back of the farm to the fields that bordered the canal. We stood about waiting, and after a long time Janet said, "Now we can go". We moved away in straggling bunches and Sally and I clung together, not knowing what we were supposed to do. A cousin seized our hands and ran us to a field gate where a little scatter of torn paper lay. It seemed we were to find more torn paper and we cast about hopefully - but before we had found any, bigger boys and girls were calling us from the far side of the field - "Come on, you two, this way". So we plodded unenthusiastically in the wake of the crowd of young teenagers, until we found them sitting panting on the grass in the field just across the road from the farm. Philip was there too and they were all talking excitedly at once. When I got home after that party and Mother asked me if I had had a nice time and what had we all done, I dredged up and delivered myself of the only event I had understood in the whole puzzling afternoon. "Janet sat in a cow-pat!"

That was the last and biggest of Peggy's parties. She was about to join her widowed father in South Africa, and she seemed already to have passed far beyond our reach, an 'almost grown-up' who played tennis and was busy learning a strange language called "Afrikaans". When she was younger, and seemed more one of us, the parties had been cosily domestic, but with enough oddness about the farmhouse to give them a special charm. First, it was a strange house and garden, not Peggy's home. The farm was at the top of a short steep hill. The village street ran up it and near the top, between church and farm, the road had to be carved into the hillside. So the farm garden was six feet above the road, and a great retaining wall sloped backwards from the footpath, buttressed every few feet, and topped with round coping stones. When you were in the garden, you could creep to the edge,

behind the shrubs, and peer over the low fender of the coping, down to the road below, and the hats of passersby. Behind you the flat lawns embraced a low, haphazard dwelling of the softest, most crumbly rose-red brick, with windows set very low in the walls, so it was like a cat sprawled in the sun. Round the north wing it was shady with shrubbery and great trees, and round the south you came to the farm yard, and a field beyond, through which, unbelievably, a canal ran, nearly at the top of the hill. Lower down the hill, across the road, lay a disused arm of the canal, and a mysterious blocked off tunnel that had once joined the two. The old arm was a romantic, still, silted up basin where waxy white and gold waterlilies grew, and a little white footbridge led you over their unwinking eyes, to a tangle of thorn, and great dry hollows in the ground, which must once have been reservoirs for the locks. They were overgrown with ferns and brambles, secret places where violets grew in spring. The old arm stretched for about a mile beyond this lovely end basin, before it petered out into mud, pocked with hoof marks of cattle. It was shallow and exposed, and usually the first place to freeze over safely in skating weather. But in summer, heavy with honeysuckle and the big, white flowered convolvulus, sweet with Ladies' Bedstraw, and acrid with nettles and docks, the whole area was enticing, rarely visited and delicious, so that in the dark of winter I used to wonder if it really existed, or if it was only one of those vivid and beautiful places I visited in recurrent dreams.

Very rarely, a daring parent would send out invitations for one of our parties, announcing it as "Fancy Dress - Optional". I remember three, but the middle one was the best, because it gave me the chance to wear the most delightful dress I had throughout my childhood. I forget who gave the party, but it caused enormous excitement in the Lower First as we all pictured ourselves in dazzling, romantic or swashbuckling disguises. Sally had a special costume beautifully made at the dressmaker's. She went as a Fairy, in a white ballet dress, with gauze butterfly wings, looped on to her middle finger, and a wand with a silver star. Sally was beautiful, and the rest of the little girls regarded her with resignation rather than envy; we all knew we could not have carried off that white and silver miracle, as she did.

John, whose family had no money to spare, but plenty of imagination and fun, went as a tramp, in his father's old flat cap, a collarless shirt and one of his front teeth blacked out. He had ancient, rolled up torn trousers, and a red handkerchief bundle on a stick, and his costume did not cost a penny.

What was I to wear? <u>Please</u> could I be a Queen, with a gold paper crown and a velvet cloak? Or an Elf with a tunic cut in points? Or a clown? Or a witch with a tall hat? No. All too expensive for one afternoon's pleasure. It must not cost much. It began to look as though I might have to be "optional". Then Father produced a stunning idea. I would go as a Pierrette from a Concert Party.

My aunt in America, who sent me strange transatlantic clothes, had sent a dress that I knew was perfect. I loved it passionately on sight. Little girls wore pink, or blue, or pale green. Never scarlet, black, purple or mauve (mauve was 'vulgar'). A few, like Giulia, with her dark beauty, had strange dresses, but her mother was Italian. English mothers dressed their daughters conventionally, so when Aunt Annie's parcel was opened, and we found a party dress in navy blue taffeta, Mother could only lament that her sister's gift was so unsuitable. But why was it unsuitable? The dress was lovely. It was distinguished, it would make me envied and I would feel right in it. Its paper crisp silk was edged with scallops at the hem and bound with scarlet. But its striking feature was a fichu of scarlet georgette with a ruffled edge. No neat little Peter Pan collar, but a great curving petal of brilliant red, and the dark taffeta to set it off. I recognised style when I saw it and I wanted to wear that dress. I wanted to feel well dressed, for once, with my full skirt like a flower and my dark silk making all the pinks and blues look washed-out and babyish.

But it was put away in a drawer, and I was told that I could not possibly be seen in it at a party. Everyone would stare. Good. I would have enjoyed that. But it was not to be.

Now Father saved me. They could buy a few red pom-poms and sew them down the bodice, and he would make me a pointed hat, with pom-poms all down that as well, and we could stitch them on the toes of my dancing slippers too. I had no idea what a Pierette was meant to be, but I was fully satisfied, as at last, I was going to wear my American dress.

It was a glorious success. The dress itself was so beautiful, and was admired so sincerely by the other mothers, who fingered the scarlet fichu, and speculated on their own little girls in glowing dramatic colours, that Mother was won over, and I was allowed my navy and red for next winter's parties. Never in all my life have I felt better dressed and more confident. Unhappily when I outgrew it, I was timidly restored to the ranks of the conventional, and went back to harebell blue or salmon pink (a terrible colour in which to dress a fair complexioned child).

Christmas was quiet. Relatives sent us presents, and our parents added a few small toys, but there was no pressure on us to go on believing in Father Christmas. We hung up pillow cases, and all the parcels were put into them. There was a dolls' tea service once-metal, coated in thick blue enamel. Once, a pastry set with a tea-cup sized mixing bowl, a wooden rolling pin, and tin spoon and flour dredger. Gerald had more than one model aeroplane, covered in oiled silk and elastic powered. Then there were sparklers, not the exciting kind like a big grey match on a wire that you lighted and it spat and fizzed and could be whirled round the head to make rings of light. These sparklers were metal wheels that could be spun at speed by a lever you pressed up and down with your thumb. The sparks flew out from a flint the wheel caught as it whirled. I remember one humming top, its pattern blurring inexplicably to iridescent rings as it spun and hummed nasally to itself.

Church on Christmas morning and my bare legs sticking to the toffee varnish of the pews. The sermon was boring, the prayers extempore and too long, and there was nothing to look at except the pink and green lozenges of the glass in the windows - same old lozenge, hundreds of 'em, in every window in the church.

Dinner was always roast chicken. It was the only time we had poultry in the year, and I would eat a little, because it was white and did not really look like meat. Plum pudding I refused, but not the sixpence, or the little silvery favours concealed in it - the ring, the bachelor's button, the bell and the horseshoe. The iced Christmas cake at tea was more to my liking, with the icing hard and crackly, and ruffled up with a fork "to look like snow". But snow doesn't look like that. It is one of the conventions we accept unquestioned, like burglars always wearing flat caps, striped football jerseys, and carrying bags called "SWAG".

We stopped having Christmas trees, even tiny ones, when I was very young, so I grew up with an unsatisfied hunger for them, and love still their tinsel peacock colours through December. But before January arrives, I feel they look tawdry and want to clear them away. Gaudy baubles and glittering chains shine bravely through the December gloom, but the first of January must smell of the cool sappiness of daffodil buds, and their modest lime green heads stand austerely in the hall.

The other festivals of the year tended to be disappointing and this was largely the fault of the children's sections of the newspaper and of the coloured 'comic' called "Tiny Tots" that I was allowed weekly. They exaggerated the thrill of each feast day and none but Christmas could ever match their build-up. Pancake Day would have a picture for a colouring competition, showing a child wearing a tall chef's hat, tossing a pancake the size of a doormat. The Tiny Tots (a chubby brother and sister aged about seven) were allowed into the kitchen by themselves, to mix and fry a stack of pancakes, and bear them triumphantly into the dining room where astonished and beaming Daddy and Mummy greeted them admiringly. If I had so much as put my nose in the kitchen at such a time, I would have been chased out of doors, smartly, not offered a chef's hat and the freedom of the frying pan! It was the same with April Fools' Day. The pictures

showed a naughty boy, successfully pinning a notice saying "Kick Me" on the teacher's back as he wrote on the blackboard, and followed the teacher through the day, as the poor bewildered man received kicks from his colleagues and passing errand boys. He taught in a gown and mortar-board, which no teacher I have ever met in my life has done, and as well as being blind, deaf and half-witted, he was obviously born very late yesterday evening. Beaky, Maggy and the other teachers at my school, were all far too alert to be taken advantage of like this, and if I had succeeded in pinning anything to their respectable lacy jumpers, I knew it would have been treated as a piece of monumental rudeness, boring and babyish. So our April fooleries were confined to the usual old chestnuts - "Your shoelace is undone"; "You've got ink on your nose", and it took a fairly dozy child to be caught by those. Fireworks Night ought to have been splendid but never was. It fizzled out like a damp squib. For one thing, all too often it <u>was</u> damp. The Tiny Tots had a bonfire - a glorious crackling blaze with whole logs burning on it. They danced round it, scarves dangerously flirting with the flames and Daddy and Mummy, who had clearly given birth to asbestos children, beamed stupidly from a safe distance. One Tot - the boy - would be carrying a bundle of fireworks as big as a Fun Fair - fat gaudy rockets, Catherine wheels like dinner plates, and huge zig-zag Jumping Crackers that chased cross Auntie Gertrude round the garden with an unerring sense of direction and timing. Life did not live up to Art.

We had no bonfire. The only place it would have been safe to have one was right in the middle of the Brussels Sprouts. If we did have a few fireworks - a very few, because they were quite literally money going up in smoke - they were all over in about five minutes. The jumping crackers were thin white worms that went "Phut-spzzz-zack" and then lay panting in the flower border, trying to heave themselves out of the tangled wet leaves of the red-hot pokers. Sally's father adored fireworks and roused our awe by spending a whole ten shillings on them every November. (Ten shillings - 50p - was the weekly wage for a full time general maid then). They lasted a little longer than our display, and the white stuffed worms of crackers and Catherine wheels were plumper and longer than ours, costing two or

three pence each, rather than one penny. The squibs, marked "May be held in the hand", jetted out tinsel pink and acid green, cold fire like phosphorescence, and the rockets, set off from a milk bottle, burst with a handful of red and green stars, instead of simply rushing heavenward in a trail of shining bronze dust, as ours did. But something was missing: an opulence, a spontaneity. We were all only pretending to be enthusiastic and amazed. I would surreptitiously blow on my fingers, and stamp my feet on the damp grass and long for the moment when we could all go indoors where the coal fire glowed and the long red velvet curtains shut out the depressing chill of the damp November wind, and Pussy was curled up in the best chair.

Once, Sally and I made a Guy. We had all the proper things - old trousers and jacket, a muffler and hat, plenty of newspaper and a sack for a body. We stuffed it with fallen ash leaves, filled the jacket sleeves tightly with rolled paper, made a head of a newspaper ball tied around with string, and put on it a crudely modelled pink mask and the oily hat Sally's father had at last demoted from 'going under the car'. This was at Sally's new house with a huge garden, and we hoisted him on top of the well built bonfire with a good wigwam of broken up packing cases left over from removal day.

Dark came and we were marshalled out and placed at a safe distance by Sally's father, who took charge of the fire-works. This time, I told myself, it was going to be the real thing. We even had potatoes ready planted at the edge of the fire to roast in the ashes.

The Roman Candles, the Silver Rain and the humble squibs and sparklers scintillated in the dark. Sally was not fond of 'bangers' and I feared them intensely. I could not even bear to have balloons bursting near me. When the firework box was empty, Sally's father struck Swan Vestas out of the flat yellow box in his pocket, and lit the crumpled paper on the skirts of the pyre. It flared smoky yellow, then with whispering crackles and little red eyes of sparks that ran about

141

like gossip mongers in a crowd, the wood shavings caught and flared. Then twigs burned and split board, and finally the pile was well alight, building up heat and a good updraught. Sparks whisked upwards, paused, hung on the wood-scented air, then sauntered off sideways on a puff of breeze to die in the cabbages. On top, a dark shape in the smokey orange, our Guy waited. At last he caught - the rolled paper of his arms and legs was alight. The clothes smouldered, and as I watched, he began sickeningly to writhe and twist. His torso jerked as the heat rushed through the damp ash-leaves in the sack. Spurts of smoke and steam broke from him. His head lolled and twisted. My stomach turned right over. He was surely alive, there on the blazing heap. Why had I never thought what it would be like to burn alive? Joan of Arc, her eyes on the cross held up before her. And Latimer - "Be of good courage, Master Ridley. We have lit this day in England such a candle as by God's Grace will never be put out!"

It was too much for me. I wanted to put <u>that</u> candle out quick, now. But I was a guest, and could only screw my eyes shut and turn away in the darkness and try to pretend that awful travesty of human torture was not happening. It was far too like the real thing. I never wanted a Guy again, and afterwards Sally said, looking a bit white around the lips, that she had not much enjoyed it either. But we did not talk about it. For a moment, a door had opened into the secret world of cruelty, and at nine years old, I could only cope with it by slamming it shut again and pretending it was not there. It had made its impression, though, and stalked, a spectre, through my sleep in the form of a recurrent dream in which I had murdered Sally's father and tried to burn his body in a furnace, but instead of burning away, the

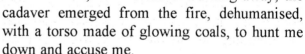

cadaver emerged from the fire, dehumanised, with a torso made of glowing coals, to hunt me down and accuse me.

The potatoes did not cook, either.

November was a black month. A bare week after Bonfire Night came Armistice Day, 11th November. The Rec, fifty yards down the road from school, had great wrought-iron Memorial Gates on which from end to end of the year, the wreaths of poppies hung. Names were carved in a close tapestry on the huge stone pillars. Every school day, we ran through the little side gates to play at Recess, but now we were in the proper school, and we would all attend the Remembrance Day Service held around the gates. It was explained to us quietly, soberly, what it was all about and what we were expected to do. It meant very little as death meant very little to me. I had turned over a dead bird I found in the lane, and underneath it was a seething tangle of white worms. But what had that to do with people who had their names on the gate pillars?

In the grey chill, earlier than ordinary Recess time, we were coated and hatted, and led along to the Rec, where a crowd of grown-ups had gathered outside, clogging the big road-junction, and inside, filling the broad asphalt walks in both directions. The Rector was there in scarlet and white, and black-clad men stood at the front of the crowd holding circles and ovals of silk poppies. We were led inside and stood in a subdued little group under the chestnuts where we usually played. They were nearly bare now, and their yellow leaves, damp and smelling of cellars, smothered my shoes and chilled my ankles. The service was short, and then far down the hill the factory sirens sounded, unbearably melancholy, like great lonely animals, signalling the two minutes silence.

It was a profound experience. It seemed as though the whole world stopped breathing. No traffic moved. I believed even the trains drew to a halt on the railway lines. Errand boys got off their bicycles and stood staring uncomfortably at their shoes. I was lost, low down among the tall grown-ups, and my eyes flickered uneasily about, noting the impossible, the incredible evidence of grown men and women in tears. Many of the women who attended wore again their full mourning on this day, black from head to toe, and veils that hid their faces. The shuddering jerks of their shoulders and an occasional gasping sob, quickly stifled for decorum, betrayed their memories. Most of the men gazed downwards, their faces folded into stony blankness, but I saw an occasional surreptitious handkerchief dabbed across mouth or eyes. The silence was a huge soft cloud pressing down on us all, until a foot shuffling or a late piping bird seemed like an insult. It was a strange ceremony. I was aware both of not understanding it, and of feeling its colossal importance to the silent people around me. Looking back now on my uncomprehending little seven-year old self, I am shaken to realise that it had been only twelve years since the signing of the Armistice, and in only nine more years the whole filthy disintegration was to begin again.

Two minutes - 120 seconds - is not very long to mourn your dead, but the whole country stopped. All work was put away. Men stood at their office desks with bowed heads. Yard-sticks and order books were laid down in shops and customer and clerks stood silent. Doctors' rounds were arrested in hospitals. Cars drew to a halt and engines were allowed to die. Folks walking about the streets stood still, and the thoughts of a whole nation concentrated, all on one resolve. Never again!

At last a suppressed sigh and stir of movement breathed across the crowd. They came back out of their private memories, and, faintly embarrassed, moved, coughed, craned to hear the Rector's Blessing, and quietly as water, slipped away. When the Rec was nearly empty, we were gathered up again, and walked subdued down the footpath to school, where we now had Recess, and a session of dancing Sir Roger de Coverley to warm us up again after our vigil in the cold November wind.

I had no knowledge of Hallowe'en, and it was not celebrated at all in our area, nor was New Year. There was a small Scottish Society that kept Burns' Night, and Hogmanay, but it was American influence that popularised many of these events - Mother's Day, Halloween, and the re-emergence of St Valentine. At school, we were told, as they came round, of the customs of Plough Monday, Ash Wednesday, Oak-apple Day, Trafalgar Day, and Empire Day. For this last we copied out in our best writing, Kipling's Children's Hymn, "Land of our Birth", and were allowed to decorate it with crayon flags, while the pink areas on the map (so huge and imposing on Mercator's Projection) were pointed out. "The Sun never sets on the British Empire".

Our churches took care of Easter and Whitsun but in our family, Easter was only a matter of a chocolate egg with a crackled surface, and Whitsun hardly seemed to exist. We did not go to Sunday School; we did not sport our new summer clothes; we did not even eat a tart of the first gooseberries. Pancakes we did have, and Shrove Tuesday was the day when you burst in through the door at mid-day and sniffed the sugary lemon tang that drifted

from the kitchen where a pile of steaming pancakes was being kept hot in the oven, and cut lemons, sugar and butter waited on a tray to anoint and bless them. Some time in late October we would be invited to the kitchen to give a good luck stir to the Christmas pudding mixture and the mincemeat. In Ursula's house, the Swedish Ladies made dozens of little biscuits the colour and thickness of cardboard, but spicy, and cut in marvellous shapes - stars and hearts, angels, animals and Santa Claus. These were piped with icing to give them features and hung on a high Christmas tree that tickled the ceiling.

The festival that moved me most deeply was not religious at all and was not even local. It happened in Guernsey in August when we were on holiday there, and it had a magic for me that was every bit as good as Christmas, if not better, because it was not a present-giving occasion. There were no expectations involved and therefore no disappointment. It was the Grandes Rocques Show.

I was not sure about Carnivals. The apprentices had a "Rag" to get money for the hospital at home. They decorated lorries as liners, Cannibal Islands, pirate ships, circuses. They dressed up, played and sang, jumped up and down from the floats and ran among the crowd shaking collecting tins under their noses. The procession began down near the Railway and wound its way slowly, craftily, through the town to cover as many streets as possible, before going to the Sports Club for races and athletics. I was rather frightened of these dressed up people, fiercely shaking tins at me for pennies I hadn't got, and I really only liked watching it all from the front bedroom window. If we went out and leaned over the front garden wall, a cannibal or a skeleton or a comic Scotsman with a doormat of red whiskers, might come and harshly demand my pennies - and if I had to shake my head because I had none left to give, might they not grab hold of me and drag me off to those strange, slowly moving structures, populated by shouting groups exchanging insults with the crowd? If I disappeared into the maw of the ginger-brown Loch Ness Monster, would Mother ever be able to find me and get me back?

The Grandes Rocques show had a little carnival procession, but it was mostly a fancy-dress competition for children, with decorated bicycles and pony carts, or even ordinary wheel-barrows and prams. It was quite cosy, and not at all frightening, and I was happy to sit on the loose stone wall with the dry summer grasses tickling my legs while the vehicles rolled slowly past and hospital tins were proffered courteously. This was only the prelude anyway, to the real event of the day.

The Show came late in August, when I was feeling that I had lived in Guernsey for ever and that grey and mud-coloured Rugby did not really exist. I had always been on the Island and always would be, on this flat shore with the hard ridges of wet sand pressing painfully into my bare instep. Then turning my back on low sea and great dome of pearly sky I would run barefoot into the hot dry sand of the dunes, where slippery cords of dune grass caught in my toes, and the slopes collapsed like flour as I tried to run up them. At the top I could see across the narrow road to where, in a little field, the marquee was pitched with its straddled guy ropes all round. Down the shady side of the dunes, feet plunging into the chill of shadowed hollows, where the sand felt icy on the hot bare skin. Over the flat sea-side grass as fine as hair. Pick your way daintily through the granite chippings of the road, and the gap in the low wall to the field where a Silver Band was blaring uncertainly, and half the population of the island had gathered to talk, compare entries, drink tea and eat fish paste sandwiches and Jersey Wonders.

The little carnival procession came slowly down the road and circled the field before the judges. The prizes would be awarded later. I watched and was amused, but it was really only a device to put off, a little longer, the real joy of the afternoon - to prolong the pleasure of anticipation. For what I was waiting for was the moment when the grown-ups would have wandered off together, and I could slip alone into the marquee and go silently round the exhibits, gazing, sniffing, filling my whole self with their essence and character and richness. From year's end to year's end, my mind would slip back to this hour, in the twilight before sleep, and I would go round the tent again, smelling the bruised grass underfoot, and satisfying my soul with the perfect pyramids of sealing-wax red tomatoes, each with its perky curl of green on top, and wafting a perfume as cool and fresh as chrysanthemums, or the fans of carrots, copper-pink as a new minted penny, the vast, unbelievable marrows, striped green and cream, or peach coloured squashes, like round fluted bowls with lids. I wanted no more than to creep round, gaze and smell, but it must be alone. There must be no grown-ups to say, "Come along, Pat, come and look at the Donkey Race".

Total absorption, total fulfilment for all my hungry senses. That was the attraction. As you stepped in through the triangular opening, the light changed from blue-white to amber, filtering gently through the canvas. The breeze vanished and all the varied perfumes, so light and subtle yet all so different, were cherished in this gold bubble of still air. I could steal along the rows of trestle tables, from the fresh earthy tang of potatoes and pea-pods, to the sunrise of colour where

147

the prize gladioli stood to attention in green painted tin cones, and the powdery scent of sweet peas ravished the nose. On the next aisle, a group of local ladies, with brown, work-knotted hands, crowded about the produce, discussing the red and blue prize winners' cards. Their chatter was about equally English and patois, and I peeped under their muscular arms to see the dark spicy fruitcakes, the crystal-topped Victoria sponges, the garnet glow of the sparkling jars of jam, the tortoiseshell pickles and the varnished plaited loaves. Farther down the line the aroma changed again to the musty smell of straw, where baskets were filled with twelve perfect deep brown eggs, dark as coffee; where thick gold cream lay in china basins, so rich that the ripples of its pouring-in remained in faint rings on the surface. Pats of butter, slightly glazed from the afternoon warmth, sat on vine leaves, arranged on the owners' most cherished china plates, turquoise rimmed or flower-wreathed. The butter held me for a long time as I scrutinized the patterns printed by the wooden moulds. Swans, cows and wheatears stood proud of the surface in meticulous sculpture. But even the fine crisscross lines made on a block of butter by the "Scotch hands" used to knock it into shape, were pleasing, and the mixed scent of cream and the rough vine leaves intoxicated me.

Crafts would be on show in another part of the tent, and the air would be filled with the smell of plasticine from the lanoline-heavy wool of beautifully knitted seamen's Guernseys. There would be doyleys in hairpin lace, children's dresses smocked high up, like Ursula used to wear, quilted tea cosies and crocheted babies' shawls fine as thistledown. Then a tableful of jampots of wild flowers, children's collections, one of everything they could find - honeysuckle, sheep's bit scabious, sea-lavender and ling, poppy and hawkweed, and ox-eye daisies. Here I came to love the entrancing yellow toad-flax with its satisfying spire of snapdragon flowers each with a slender pigtail, and to recognise that the delicious, frail pink convolvulus resented being picked, and would furl its umbrella and twirl its skirt round its knees in disgust if taken indoors.

All this time, as I stole round from item to item I was silently absorbing into myself the essential qualities of each. Potatoes, washed and graded, were jewels of beauty. You could hardly believe they were even related to the dull brown lumps, crusted with dry mud, that I was sent to fish out of the sack in the garden shed for the maid to peel. Here, they were oval like goose eggs, their flawless skins rose coloured and thin as silk, so that the cream flesh shone out through them like light from a lantern. Here a pea-pod, cracked open by the judges, held a row of blue-green pearls, dewy and graduated, and the little kidney beans were creamy pink as moss-roses. Everything, all the commonplace stuff of living, was presented with pride, and its perfection, its 'selfness', called to me. The curd of a cauliflower with a white card saying "First Prize" on it, was not arranged haphazard. You could see the florets were set in great spiral swirls, like the seeds of the giant sunflowers, or the scales on a rarely found, and jealously cherished fir-cone.

The last experience left, the one I carefully avoided until I had seen all the rest, was the honey. Black grapes frosted with sea-mist grey, striped gun-metal figs, velvet raspberries, each with its special perfume, enticed me at last to the climax of my joy - the honey. Wherever it was in the tent, I dodged past and kept it to the last. I wanted it, its ravishing colour and scent, to be the strongest impression I would carry away with me, to be dwelt on, wide-eyed in the darkness, on winter nights when I lay in bed in my Midland attic, and watched the feathering of street light through the pine tree on my ceiling. I never wanted to go all round the tent again. Something warned me not to blunt my sensibility. So I would turn at last to where the soft gold light filled the honey pots, glowing bubbles of clear amber, deep bronze, or pale cream, when the crystallization was complete. The polished glass jars had waxed paper lids. Beside them sat the honeycomb, collared in squares of white wood, shaded from heavy waxy white to pale amber, running with oily drips where the judge's knife had uncapped the cells, and perfuming the air with a scent so delicate yet sweet that it made my head swim. New honey, like new milk, has a perfume so fleeting that only those who actually produce it have the chance of smelling it nowadays. New honey smells of flowers, fresh warm milk of woodruff, and a new laid egg, boiled on its first day, has a white that parts in feathery layers and has no resemblance even in colour, to the porcelain rubberiness we find in our shop-bought eggs, 'fresh' only from weeks in a cold-store.

Sated with honey-comb at last, I would emerge into the blinding white afternoon. The blare of the silver band would hit me like a bursting wave. The crowds would jostle and push above my head and I would turn out and cross the road to the shore, my feet sinking into the cold sand where the afternoon sun had dropped too low to warm it, to sit a while and brood, and lock up my treasure safely in my mind, to be gloated over later.

9. BIRTH, LIFE AND DEATH

he period of my life I have been looking back on goes from intermittent recollecting at about two years old up to fairly connected memories at about ten - a span of eight years - which sees more change in the human being than any other decade of life. When you think about it, the changes are so swift and so huge as to be almost unbelievable. How can the new-born baby, hardly more than a struggling blob of jelly, become in twenty-four months, a personality, able to walk, solve problems, converse and think constructively? And that two-year-old, goggle-eyed at every moment of the day, since almost every sight and sound will be a new experience, becomes in four more years, a member of a social group, able to share toys, treats and attention (even if reluctantly), developing a moral sense and a standard of justice? And the nine or ten-year-old whose one idea is to escape adult domination, and whose perfect world would be one in which all the grown-ups had been wiped out, was, only three years previously, a shrinking newcomer, venturing into the maelstrom of school, anxious for the approval of its teachers, and racing back blindly to mummy if anything hurt it. Looking back, I find this one of the saddest aspects of childhood. We were very lucky indeed in our little school. The teachers were able, imaginative, and above all, kind. We had one fierce little Welsh woman who lost her temper and shouted at me for my disgraceful arithmetic, but apart from that, no tyranny, no mocking, no pleasure in making us look foolish, and only such gentle teasing as we were used to from our parents when we did something more than usually dotty. I was occasionally afraid to go to

151

school, but it was the sharp tongue and tormenting ways of another child that scared me, never the teachers. These ladies were in many ways more like stimulating and approving aunts than AUTHORITY. They encouraged us, brought out our best points, made sure that each one of us was given the chance to shine at something. We should have loved them. In fact, at first we did, but as we grew from seven to eight to nine we felt our increasing need of freedom. We turned more and more to each other and away from grown-ups, and above all, we absorbed from ignorant and badly written school stories and comics, the idea that all teachers by definition, were tyrants and fools, to be mocked, despised, and if possible hurt, by the clever children they strove in vain to dominate. I can not help feeling, now, that Beaky, Maggy, Mademoiselle, and sweet, quiet, grey Miss Savery, must have felt hurt at their hearts when they watched, year after year, the friendly little seven-year-olds they encouraged and cherished, turning into sneering monsters of ingratitude, who repaid all this loving effort and forbearance with stony-faced contempt or open mockery.

At some time during this first decade, children normally become aware of the differences between the sexes, and begin to ask questions on the mighty subjects of birth and death. I learned about death suddenly and shockingly when Smutty was killed, but I never learned anything about birth. I do think, now, that I was abnormally lacking in curiosity about it. Of course, I asked the question all children ask - "Where do babies come from?" but the only answer I ever got was "The doctor brings them in his little black bag".

Mother was excessively shy on the subject, and being also given to feeling socially insecure, she was specially anxious that her little girl should never do or say anything that other mothers might criticise. I think they were really a great deal more broad-minded than she realised, but she was shrinkingly afraid of her children letting the family down. There was that flea, at the Guernsey cottage, about which we must never speak.

Mother was definitely not the pioneering sort to tell her little daughter that babies came from inside mummy's tummy! She was enchanted with all new babies, but otherwise I believe she felt the

152

whole natural process of pregnancy and birth to be messy, inartistic and better ignored.

So my questions got the doctor's bag for an answer. And I was quite satisfied. Until I was ten I really was not interested enough to pursue the matter any further. At ten, I was as dirty-minded as all the rest of us, and like the others of my group, had to glean distorted information from school friends who had mostly gleaned it from housemaids. But at seven, that little squashy Gladstone bag Dr Waugh carried when he called to listen to my chest or flip his knuckles up the knobs on my spine, seemed a perfectly logical place to produce babies from. Meanwhile, the world was bursting with more interesting things to wonder about and it never occurred to me to ask where the doctor got the babies from in the first place.

This absence of curiosity was largely because there was nothing to stimulate it. It happened that I and all my close friends were either only children or the youngest in our small families. No babies followed us until I was ten, when John's mother had a second child. By this time, John had moved on to the Grammar School and I no longer played at his house on a Saturday morning. Ladies were reticent then about pregnancy, and John's mother did not go out much in the last months. I probably never saw her until a few weeks after baby Anne had arrived, when she invited Sally and me to watch the ceremony of Anne's bath, which we found interesting but also mildly embarrassing, and were happy to escape afterwards, asking no questions.

There was a question much more intriguing to self-centred me than "Where do babies come from?" When some tale was told about the family before I was born, I wanted urgently to know, "Where was I then?"

"You weren't born yet".

"I know, but where was I?"

"Nowhere. You didn't exist".

No. That was not possible. Somehow I was able to accept that there had been a time when there was no body that contained me. After all, I could remember my infancy and even babyhood, when my body was small and unrecognisable, and I had seen very new babies in their prams. I was prepared to agree that those small pink animals, with no hair or teeth, would grow and change and become proper children. I could just understand that there was a time when their families did not have them - they had not appeared yet.

But in my case, (and so why not in theirs?) my sense of my Self was so strong, that though I could accept that my body "began" at some point and was popped into the doctor's bag to be brought to my lucky family, I existed before that, I must always have been somewhere. But where? Before I was sealed into that little bag of jelly, bones and pink skin, WHERE WAS I? I persisted in my futile questioning, meeting incomprehension and exasperation, but however often I was told I did not exist before my "birth", I simply did not believe it. The me that was ME, and the me that was my body were not indissolubly united, and the puzzle of where and how I had existed and why I could not remember it was far more compelling when I was under ten than the merely physical question of where my body came from.

The only time we spent in the country was the summer holidays, and August is not Nature's birth time. We lived close to the country; we were never far from fields and woods. We enjoyed watching early lambs and calves; birds nested in the garden, and in fact, Pussy once had kittens - three of them, on my bed. But the actual processes of mating and birth were not evident. I can remember, when the flocks and herds were driven to and from the market, that occasionally as they ambled along, the odd bullock or ram would try to mount, but I was not aware of the sexual features of farm animals, and as far as I was concerned, it was one lazy cow trying to hitch a lift on another cow's back, bad

154

cess to her! The only piece of real information I collected in those first ten years came, when I was eight, from another eight-year-old I met on holiday.

It was the summer that Ursula's two grown-up sisters were to be married - a double wedding, and Ursula and Carl were to be attendants. The grown-ups were all wise enough not to try to dress Carl up as a page in satin knee-breeches. I wonder what he would have done if they had tried? Gone quietly but grimly away and stuffed the lot down the loo, I shouldn't wonder. But he had an unexceptionable Eton suit, and the long trousers reconciled him to the collar and bumfreezer. Ursula, however, was to have a long, pale blue satin dress, and a wreath of rosebuds for her hair, and I was consumed with envy and talked a good deal about this wedding which was to take place at home while I was in Seascale on holiday. Jane listened doubtfully to all I had to say, and when I had finished, she shook her head gravely. "I'm never going to get married " she said.

"Why not?"

"When you get married, you have babies; they grow inside you and when they come out, it hurts most <u>dreadfully</u>".

I did not like the sound of this at all. I really preferred the doctor's bag, although I fancy by that time, it was beginning to go the way of Father Christmas. So I filed away Jane's information and simply resolved not to think about it. I certainly never considered approaching Mother on the subject. By this time, I had had it drummed into me that intimate matters like this were RUDE, and NASTY, and I would get into serious trouble if I were known to be even thinking about them, let alone asking questions. So I folded my mind over them and left them to hatch in their own way. I can't say it did any harm. I did not grow up warped or paranoic, and I found in the end all the information I needed between grubby whispers behind hands and the diagrammatic openness of "Reproductive Systems" in teenage Biology lessons at school. I think I would prefer to see a more open attitude than I met myself, but I do not think it is always necessary, or wise, to give clinically detailed information to very young children, as seems to be the fashion now. Many children simply forget it all again. Others sense that their Grannies don't like that sort of talk, and take a rather unpleasing delight in recounting the facts of life loudly in public places, for the pleasure of seeing Granny upset. Somewhere, it must be possible to find a balance between hypocrisy and a decent reticence.

The idea of the death of other human beings comes gradually and did not affect me greatly. Mother's mother died, far away in Ireland when I was five. I scarcely knew her ; she was more of a picture than a person. Father's grandmother, an ancient blanket-wrapped bundle, muttering to herself, followed in her nineties, two years later. She was even less real to me and all her death ever meant was that a crate of lovely cut flowers arrived from The Nursery.

Dead. What was dead? It meant they had gone away and would never be coming back. But for me, they had hardly been there anyway. They were two shadowy old figures glimpsed rarely when we were in Ireland on early holidays. I was four the last time we went there and my memory limited and short. I knew slightly some children of Gerald's age who only had mothers. Their fathers had been "killed in the War", but that too was only a phrase - words with no real meaning. The dead blackbird I found in the nettles down the lane was a seething, heaving tangle of white worms when I turned it over with a stick. I recoiled from it with disgust, but made no connection between the dead bird and the dead body of a person, buried in the ground.

One summer morning at school, we were all lined up round the Big Room for prayers, when Miss Margaret came in looking more rheumy-eyed and cherry-nosed even than usual. It was a Monday. We sang our hymn and our psalm, and recited the Collect for the week. Then Miss Margaret spoke, and as she did, began quietly to cry. I was young enough to be awed by this and not to giggle, as I would have done two years later.

"Children, I have to tell you something very sad. Bill Leigh won't be coming back to school any more. He was knocked down and killed by a car on Saturday afternoon".

Bill, a boy I only knew vaguely, was in the Transition still. I looked along their rank, in front of the big Mercator's map of the world with the British Empire in pink. Sure enough, he was not there. Roderick and Desmond, fierce boys in white roll-neck jerseys, and Patrick, and Roger, but no fair sturdy Bill.

He had been leaning over the parapet of a narrow bridge, watching the river below, and had stepped back in front of one of the rare cars on the country roads then. He was unconscious when they picked him up and died soon afterwards. We felt a moment's solemnity, and whispered a little as we filed off to our lessons, but by Recess, it was forgotten, and Bill was just a name.

Death did not touch me for a further year, but when it did come, it was close, personal and so shattering that there is a certain sense in which I may say I have never got over it. Fifty-three years have passed and I can not yet bear to take the memory out of its closed box and look at it squarely.

My kitten, Smutty, my little black kitten, grew to a lively, pretty young creature, full of fun and energy. Mother did not really like cats, and it was quite an effort for her to consent to my having one. That made it all the more dreadful for her when it happened.

I slept in the attic and the second flight of stairs was lit only by a dim bulb on the top landing. There was no two-way switch. It could only be put on and off up there. Smutty used to wait until I had gone to bed and then race off up to the top of the house to me for a final romp. Somebody, usually Mother, had to come upstairs to see I was all right for the night and shoo Smutty down again. One night, on the dark stairs, she trod on Smutty and broke his back. He did not die quickly or easily. The Vet had to be fetched to put him out of his pain. I was asleep when it happened and knew nothing about it until the next morning when I had to be told that Smutty was gone - dead. He had played with me on the counterpane and then I had slept, and would never see him again.

If I had been able to see his body, I think I might have been able to accept the fact and adjust to it, but the poor little thing was too mangled and crushed for them to let me see him. One evening he was there - a joyous, bounding, precious part of myself. The next day he was gone. The great black vacancy of the unalterable obscured the sun for me. It was not possible - Smutty could not have gone. But he had. Never - never - never. The days that followed were dreadful. I threshed and flailed about in my mind, battering myself against the bars; there had to be an escape - it must be changed - he must come back. I was trapped by the unbearable. Then I learned what death is - the inescapable, the unchangeable - in whose grasp we are totally helpless. Smutty - come back, come back!

They had to get me another kitten, quickly. I was not even crying. I was just dumb, rigid with grief. Father asked desperately at School for a kitten to spare, and the only one to be had, in this emergency, was a half-grown female, born in a barn, and pretty wild. Father brought her home to me about a week after Smutty's death and as soon as she was released from her cardboard box she went straight up the dining-room chimney, where she cowered for eight hours. Father coaxed her down at last, after I had gone, uninterested, to bed. By next morning, her paws had been buttered and she was warily prepared to look over the premises. I was warned to speak quietly and move gently, and for the first few days, she did not seem to be anything to do with me. She was not house-trained either, which made it all more

 difficult for Mother. Little by little, though, she grew more settled and I learned to care for her. The lure of a cat was irresistible, and her white tummy and socks and the lopsided black moustache on her white daisy-petal face enchanted me. She throve on love, and shared my meals, my games, my dolls' house, and my bed. I was moved down from the attic to the little end bedroom where she soon found a way to my window up the fir tree and over the roof. Before very long, she was the dearest thing on earth to me. It was not that Smutty was forgotten; it was more that I had put him away and would not remember. The shock of losing him made me anxious and painfully sensitive about Pussy. I feared for her and I could not endure that she should be hurt. If Pussy was punished by being slapped and put out for pinching a herring off the kitchen table

(what cat would not?) I bled inside. When she made a mess on the floor, and Mother, exasperated, rubbed her nose in it and shut her out, she came to the French window and mewed pathetically to me through the glass, her funny little face all smeared and dirtied. "Let me in - let me in". I was forbidden to let her in until she had cleaned herself. "She must learn", said Mother. But it was me she was punishing more than Pussy. I could not bear to see her on the other side of the glass, asking me for comfort. I waited until no one was watching and then sneaked out with the damp floor cloth. I cleaned off her face as best I could and we sat in the cold October dusk on the step of the summer-house, out of sight - until I was missed at tea-time and we were both allowed back in. But if Pussy had been banished from the house, I swear I would have put my belongings in a knotted handkerchief and set off on my travels with her. If she was going to suffer, so was I. Plainly, I loved her a great deal better than I loved my family or friends. I even loved her better than I loved myself. And that was one step forward!

 izzie was my earliest doll and the only one who ever seemed to me to be alive. There was Jane as well - a rag doll, but she hardly counted. For a short while there was a small baby doll called Rusty, but Rusty had a china head, and an unlucky fall smashed it in like an eggshell and revealed a grisly and rather obscene mechanism of wire and weights that controlled her eyes. Dolly eyeballs seen from the inside are as repulsive as raw oysters and I did not mourn when Rusty went to her grave in the dustbin. I was not really a <u>caring</u> mother. Later, when I was six and had really grown out of dolls, a great cardboard package arrived from America, from my gener-

ous Aunt Annie. Opened, it revealed the largest doll I had ever seen. She was a "little girl" doll with bobbed brown hair and a gauzy pink dress. She was as large as a real baby, had open-and-shut eyes with thick eye-lashes, an open-mouthed simper, two tiny teeth, and a body stiff enough to stand, though it was only stuffed. I was proud. I showed her off, and I called her Gwenny after a ten year old I much admired who lived nearby. But I didn't really love her. Her hair soon became a gungey tangle and came off, revealing glue, and the standard moulded hair usual on composition dolls' heads. She spent most of her existence in the dress tray of the great travelling trunk, with an occasional winter sortie to be the infant Jesus in the Nativity play, since she was the right size. But Lizzie was the only true doll-companion I had. She was the person-to-talk-to we all need when we are too young to be able to talk easily with grown-ups. Lizzie and I did it by thought transference.

About the time of my infancy and Gerald's, everyone had a Teddy Bear. Pooh was only a year or two old and had set a fashion. But I had no bear. Gerald was given a jointed monkey called Pongo and he was the only "soft toy" I remember apart from the cat that lived on the dining room clock. He was a work of minor genius. His head with its lidded glass eyes was intelligent, lively, humorous. He regarded the strange world of people with love and amusement, but also some contempt. He had a stumpy tail that controlled his head and would make him shake it from side to side with a happy grin, or nod it up and down slowly and sagely. He very nearly talked.

When Gerald was four he had scarlet fever, and was allowed to take Pongo to the hospital for the six weeks' isolation necessary. Afterwards, Pongo had either to be burned, or, if he was to come home, fumigated in a sort of oven. Unthinkable to burn him, so he was sulphur baked instead, and Gerald brought him home, still bright-eyed and quizzical, but turned grey all over, instead of the rich, youthful ginger-brown he had gone in. He stayed with us most of our lives, not so much because he had been companionable - he was not - but because he was so very much alive. There he sat for forty-five years, eyeing us all in amazement, and storing away his own private thoughts about us. Dear Pongo. I'm sure he was much wiser than we are.

A little girl then who still played with dolls at nine was thought rather sweet. I - so often a failed girl - was a disappointment. I demanded and got, a superb doll's pram for my fifth birthday, and had lost interest in it by five thirty. But a boy was not supposed to play with dolls at all. Teddy bears were acceptable but only up to a

162

certain age limit. Even Christopher Robin was ready to abandon his beloved Pooh when he got to the lessons-in-the-morning stage, and Pooh and Piglet were to be left to the wistfulness of a life without purpose as Christopher Robin came more and more rarely. And so it was with Gerald.

The summer before I was born, the family went to Ireland and were to be away for several weeks. Small Gerald wanted to take his family too - a teddy, I am told and one or two other stuffed creatures. Father was not willing to have his son, going on six, carrying such toys about. It wasn't manly. So, after a good deal of persuading, tears, and finally a peremptory order, Gerald was made to range them on the windowsill, looking outward to await his safe return, and was promised that they would be much happier there than being dragged all the way to Ireland.

Father cheated. I must try to believe that he did not really understand how appallingly cruel it was, but he left orders that the toys were to be thrown away. He judged it was time his great boy of six should turn his back on such babyish things, and banked on Gerald forgetting all about them before they all came home. But Gerald did not forget. Long before the taxi put them down at the gate, his heart was beating fast at the thought of gathering up his woolly family again, and he leaped out and ran straight to the window. They had all disappeared. A frenzied search up and down the house and urgent questioning of an embarrassed maid failed to discover them. Fear and frustration led to tears, and in the end in exasperation, Father told him the blunt truth. They had been destroyed. It was time he gave up dolls.

Gerald speaks of it now with a smile, but a rueful smile. It seems unbelievable to me that Father, who was not insensitive, could have committed an act which to the little boy who loved them must have seemed like mass murder. If a child clings to toys it is because he needs them - because the grown-ups in his life are not adequate. It was an action as bad as taking away a child's pet dog and having it put to sleep. Was Father jealous? Or was his pride stronger than his sympathy, that it mattered so much to him that his son should measure up to the conventional standard, even at the cost of heartbreak? I remember - because I found it out at seven - the helpless threshing about in the mind, the blackness, un-belief, insane belabouring of the inescapable, when the fact of mortality has to be faced. My first kitten was accidentally killed - and for Gerald the rape of his toys must have been the same, with the added agony that Father had deliberately lied, betrayed him and done this dreadful thing.

The toy that influenced me most and shaped a part of my future life for me was not mine at all. It belonged to Sally. By the time we were both seven, we were "best friends". Our mothers were friendly acquaintances and I am told that Sally and I used early on to pull hideous faces at each other over the edges of our prams. A few years of armed truce followed babyhood. This meant that we played together nicely when we went to tea at each other's houses, but if we met on neutral territory like the Rec or the back lanes, or the side passage at school when Sally came for dancing class, there was Hell to pay. Sally had long hair in ringlets and I pulled it. So did John. So did Bill. Sally was a cherished only child, but she had personality and spunk. She never ran to Mummy to complain. Instead she set grimly about the job of defending herself and teaching us that in spite of her angelic appearance, her swift right-left with doubled fists hurt, and so did the toes of her sturdy little walking shoes. Sally was different. She did not come to school but had lessons with a governess. Clearly she must be made to suffer for the crime of not being like the others. I joined happily in the hooting mob that pursued her, flying curls and purple tweed coat, through the treetrunks of the Rec. I can't recall feeling the smallest shame or any sense of being two-faced, when the next day we were happily playing on the carpet of her nursery, reading 'Little Black Sambo', or making the German tin miller climb a pole, by winding a handle at the bottom, accept a bag of flour on his head at the top and climb down again, or spinning the beautiful Zoetrope her father had made out of a biscuit tin, and watching the kangaroo that leaped smoothly up and down, through the whirling slits.

Sally had a kaleidoscope her Daddy had made, triangular and fascinating, where scraps of broken glass in jewel colours slipped and combined to make flowers and crystals of inexhaustible beauty. She had a tin egg, gloriously painted, with a snake inside. A set of scarlet lacquered babushka dolls, primitive earth mother shape, unscrewed to

164

reveal even smaller dolls inside, right down to a fingernail sized baby. She had a bookshelf, full of her own books - all the Beatrix Potters, and the Flower-Fairies of the four seasons, which I preferred. But grandest, best and most breathtaking of all, she had a dolls' house.

I had a dolls' house too, and from an early age, but mine had been a disappointment - one of those lapses in imagination that occasionally overtook Father. He was an expert craftsman and he made me a doll's house. Gerald and I can be seen in a photograph standing smugly beside it, hand in hand, in the garden of '16'. So it must have been very new then, recorded with pride on a half-plate when I was not quite four. We are in our best clothes - mine a rosebud printed cotton which I can see and smell still. Gerald in his smart new grey flannel, coat and shorts, both a good bit too big to allow for growing - so the coat sleeves come down over his knuckles and the legs of the shorts engulf his knees and rub noses with the top of his socks.

The house was large, with a red painted roof, two chimneys and a green front door with a satisfying brass ring knocker. But two things were wrong - it had no furniture, and it didn't open properly!. Instead, the roof lifted off. You could get into the bedrooms all right, but the really interesting part, the living room and kitchen, were sealed off permanently. You could only get at them through the wide hinged windows - with real glass - but who wants to play with a room that can only be arranged and re-arranged by a fist through the window? Who can enjoy making cakes of sand and dirt mixed, in a patty pan on the kitchen table, when it has to be done through the window?

A little simple furniture was bought for it, but money was very, very short in 1928, and I had to be content with matchboxes nested together for cradles, conkers, pins and wool to make chairs (Elsie the maid did those) and for dolls, strange shock-headed little creatures made from a hank of coloured wool, or a clothes peg with a scrap of cotton tied round its neck.

Children's imaginations are usually quite able to ignore such deficiencies, and so would mine have been it had not been for Sally's dolls' house. From the moment I saw it on visits to tea, I knew it was the perfect, the ultimate dolls' house, and mine, beautifully though

Father carpentered it, remained a hollow disappointment, no entice-
ment to play, and ended up under the laurel bush at '62', where Pussy
slept in the upstairs bedroom on inclement nights.

Sally's house opened at the front. It had brick-papered walls, a
door with a porch and six windows. A hook at the side held it closed,
and when the front was swung back with door and muslin curtained
windows, Paradise was revealed.

It had electric light, from a torch battery, and installed by Sally's
father. It had a whole family of properly dressed dolls, including a
cook and a nursemaid. The kitchen had a battery of saucepans, and a
kettle on a tin range. There was a dresser with jugs and cups and
bowls, there were brooms and buckets, mixing bowls and plaster food
on plates - a ham, a Christmas pudding, a jam tart with a slice out of
it, a fish. There was a silver eggstand with egg-cups as tall as reading
lamps, each with an egg as big as a Rugby football, and a spoon the
inhabitants could have rowed a boat with. The dining room, next door,
had carved Jacobean furniture in dark oak, a table and chairs with
bulgy turned legs, and a sideboard with cupboard doors that opened
and revealed the most amazing miracle of all - a complete silver tea
service. The lid took off the teapot (no matter that it would have been
the size of a dustbin to the dolls - scale did not seem important). The
tea cups and saucers, the knives as long as cutlasses, the forks and
spoons, were a joy to handle, and we were utterly content to lay places
at the table for dinner, and then for tea, with the boiled eggs, the
immense salt and pepper pots, and the plaster jam tart for afters.

Then the family could go upstairs (real stairs with red paper
carpet) to bed, where there were sheets and little bran-stuffed pillows
and an eiderdown, flat and hard as a biscuit, that slithered sideways
off the bed as soon as the dolls were put into it. It was rather shocking
that Mr had to go to bed in his black felt coat and trousers and Mrs in
her long-skirted print dress, and shoes! But such minor imperfections
did not dull our bliss. I would quite cheerfully have saved time and
trouble by going to bed in my shoes if they had let me.

Equipping and improving the furnishing of this dolls' house had
obviously been a conscious pleasure to all Sally's family. Tiny vanity

bag mirrors had been added, and little glass vases, ornaments out of Christmas crackers, miniature photograph frames and old brooches for pictures on the walls. Cushions and rugs had been neatly stitched. There was a row of tiny wooden books on a shelf. The coal scuttle had real little lumps of coal in it, and there was a hearthbrush, shovel and poker in the dining room grate. The electric light was only four torch bulbs and really did nothing to light the rooms, but what a joy to switch them on from the switch on the side wall of the house, close up the front and see the faint yellow glow shining out in the November dusk, behind the lace edged muslin curtains.

I suppose that all children are fascinated by little houses, but I was so enraptured by the miniature perfection of Sally's that in my forties I began to create my own - No 1 Wellington Walk - a six roomed house in a glass-fronted bookshelf, where the date is 1860, and the scale so strictly right for my truly life-like dolls, that a set of teacups and saucers I made are only one eighth of an inch high! Most of the items in it I have made myself, but once placed in the house I have to handle them with tweezers. I am so hooked on this tiny house that nothing passes through my hands from the mechanism of a derelict clock to the springs and plastic mouldings of a worn out Biro, without my scrutinising them to see what they would be if they were scaled up to Wellington Walk size.

Most of my friends' fathers, like my own, left the management of the children to their mothers, but Sally's father not only doted on his only child, but had a streak of the child left in himself that made him take more part than many fathers in her pleasures. When I had a birthday party, my father's part in it was to come in at tea time to demonstrate his "parlour trick" - he could wiggle his ears - and to press all the little boys and girls to have another plate of trifle, "or we'll have to have it fried for breakfast".

Sally's father's hours of work did not allow even this but he made up for it on other festival occasions during the year. He adored fireworks and spent lavishly on Roman Candles, Silver Rain and Jumping Jacks that crackled at our heels and chased us squealing about the garden. At Christmas, he earnestly assured Sally that Father Christmas would be coming with his sleigh, long after Sally had been

167

privately told by the rest of us that it was your own father and mother. At Sally's bedtime he would sneak into the back garden with the little silver table bell and shake it gently in his cupped hands. Then he would rush in and call to her up the stairs to hurry up and go to sleep. He had heard the reindeers' bells in the distance, and if Father Christmas found her awake, he wouldn't leave any presents. Sally and I laughed over this together, but she respected his illusions and played along with him, at least until she was nine!

Sometimes, on a Saturday, I was invited to tea with Sally, and in

the summer this occasionally meant the thrill of a motor car ride. Sally's father was one of the only five people we knew who had cars, and his was a Morris Cowley tourer - what they used to call the "bull-nosed Morris". It had a round radiator, leather seats and an open top. In bad weather mica side windows had to be erected and plugged firmly into place with wedges cut from india rubber. Then a folding hood like a pram canopy was pulled forward, and the car became a dark, little tent, snug from the weather, a yellowish light filtering in through the side windows. But it was more fun in hot sunshine, when the dark blue leather burned our legs as we romped all over the back seat.

Sometimes on a Saturday this Morris would take us on a picnic to Cottesbrooke, where there was a meadow for play, a little wood to explore fearfully, and a shallow stream to paddle. Or we might be driven over to Leamington Spa, past the oak which was "the centre of England" (one of many) and be given tea in the Pump Rooms, where Sally's father always made us giggle uncontrollably by his saucy remarks about the half naked statues of simpering Greek goddesses in the alcoves. On other days it might be tea at the Bedford Stores, a big shop on the fashionable Parade. One day, bloodhounding over the toy counter there, both Sally and I were smitten with love for tiny jointed

168

plush monkeys, pink or blue, with tin faces like Pongo's younger brothers. They cost a shilling, and were only to be admired. (Sally's father was rich by our circle's standards, but Sally, I must say, was not spoiled). Suddenly, to the astonishment of both of us, he exclaimed, "Pink or Blue? Which do you want?" I was dumbfounded, but Sally retained her wits, and in a moment said, "Pink, please". Two shillings were passed over, and a pink monkey, two inches high, was put into each of our hands.

I hope, I do hope, I said "thank you" as nicely and sincerely as I should, but I know my thanks could never have been adequate, for what Sally's father had given us was not two charming toys, but a new world of entrancing and ever spreading horizons that amused us, woke our minds to question, opened the doors of the imagination and the fancy - became the pivot of our friendship for many years, and when we finally abandoned "Mickey and Minnie" in our early teens, we had behind us such a shared world of laughter and fantasy as bound us in friendship for a lifetime.

They were the right size for the dolls' house and visited there, but they lived with us, in coat pockets, pencil boxes and in little cave-like dwellings in the gnarled roots of the chestnuts in the Rec. As soon as we came together each school day, idling up the broad safe pavement to school "The Story" moved on to its next chapter. What had my Micky and Sally's Minnie done since we parted at four o'clock yesterday? Minnie's exploits reflected Sally's personality and were always more imaginatively humorous than Micky's. But through each we explored the world beyond us, embodying our own fears in them, giving shape to our own longings, loves and hates, testing the water of the real world with the toes of our imagination. They travelled, they fought bandits, encountered ghosts, won world records, got married, went to parties, and had wonderful clothes. Dorothy at school, a brown clever girl with skilled fingers, became their 'dressmaker'. Sally's mother had a 'piece bag' full of glamorous scraps of delicate, filmy fabrics, glittering gauze, cobweb tulle, crisp silk, and we were allowed to rummage. On the hearthrug, in front of the gas fire with its bowl of water gently steaming, we plundered the sweet-smelling fabrics, and planned the fairy-tale details of the Royal Ball, where

169

Minnie (dear squat little Minnie with her wicked monkey grin) would sweep down a wide curving staircase wearing a crinoline of that silvery silk - no, this pleated chiffon. The incongruity never struck us. Romance and fairy tale and adventure were all fulfilled in our eight year old hearts. When, at twelve, we were separated for a term as I preceded Sally to our secondary schools the pain of being lopped off from my other half was almost equalled by the knowledge that Micky and Minnie were deprived of each other's company. Minnie would still be in her old surroundings while Micky lurked bewildered in the pocket of my new navy gymslip, in a seething community of three hundred girls, with as many in my year alone as in the whole of the cosy little school we had enjoyed so far.

It is hard to say what is a toy and what is not. Crazes came and went like the craze for Yo-yos. At one point all the children playing in the lane had bright celluloid windmills. It must have been a Saturday, or the school holidays. I had watched the others running into the wind, their windmills whirling, clacking and jamming, and I ran home.

"Daddy, can I have a windmill, PLEASE?"

Father glanced out of the study window to see Stewart and Joan and Ursula dashing past the open gate with their glittering toys. "Of course", he said. "Wait here".

He lifted up the loose top of his writing table to reveal the recess where he kept his store of drawing-paper. He selected a sheet of crimson. Then out came steel edged ruler, setsquare, pencil, and a selection of razor sharp craft knives he used for cutting mounts for his paintings. He went down to the cellar and rummaged in the drawers of his workbench, while I hopped impatiently from foot to foot and craned my head in his way as he carefully sorted through the miscellany of odd bits he kept. What <u>was</u> he looking for? Why all this waste of time? A stick for a handle and the red paper -

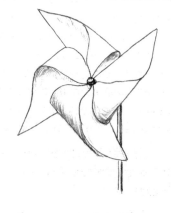

that was all that was needed for a windmill. I told him so, but imperturbably he went on sorting through tins and dropping this and that into his pockets. A pair of pliers, a bradawl, three inches of wire, two or three old beads and finally a length of dowel rod. At last we were ready to go upstairs, but not before he had reprimanded my impatience with the quelling statement I heard so often - "Children and fools should not see half-done work".

Back in the study he spread out an old newspaper on the table and got to work, patiently, slowly, accurately. Nothing was ever slapdash when Father did a job, and nothing ever seemed to go wrong. But you had to wait. How long I had to wait! Stewart and the others were called in to dinner. We had to go down ourselves and eat shepherd's pie and stewed plums. Then back to the careful boring, and threading of beads and gumming of paper so two layers were stuck together and measured and cut into an accurate square. Still I could not see that it looked anything like a windmill. I was scared to ask any more questions. Father was on the verge of impatience. But now - he was cutting diagonals in the paper square. He was lifting corners and folding them in to the centre - he was piercing a hole. And miraculously, under his hand, there was a windmill - but twice as large as any of my friends' - twice as firm and a richer colour.

Soon the windmill on its wire shank, with a few beads to ensure that it ran free, was fastened to its stick, and presented to me. Father had enough pride in his skill to come down with me to the lane, where Ursula and Joan were running again indefatigably with their shiny pink and blue celluloid vanes jamming and wobbling against the green sticks. We watched their faces as I held up my mill to the wind. It began to turn slowly of its own accord, but when I ran, it gathered speed, and with a regular, purring whirr, it spun steady and powerful, never varying, but throbbing sturdily, unchecked. A splendid windmill. "Did your daddy make it? I wish mine could do that."

It was lovely to bask in the reflected glow of superiority, and to know oneself envied, even for the short day when windmills were the craze!

Was a cocoa-tin a toy? Or was the dangerous disc of tin that had to be cut out of the top of the Symington's Custard Powder, before it could be used? Both were pressed into service, though the latter was so lethal that I am amazed it was not forbidden. The disc of thin glittering tin sealed the powder from damp and could be cut with scissors. Gerald would snip the edges with little slanting snips, then bend each section slightly, so that it looked much like the sails of a Guernsey windmill. He made two holes in the middle with the scissor points, threaded a long loop of string through them and knotted it. You hooked the string over your thumbs, with the disc midway along, and whirled it to twist the double string. When it was twisted enough, you began gently pulling. This made the disc revolve, overrun and wind itself in the opposite direction with a whirring noise. You increased the speed and strength of the pull and the whirling disc became a whining devil that spun like the unguarded blade of a circular saw and would have sliced through an artery in a split second. Did anyone see us playing with these, or was it only done out of the grown-ups' sight? Like the dare Gerald and the big boys accepted, to balance walk across the parapet of the railway bridge when the Royal Scot was roaring underneath. My fear of heights kept me clear of that one!

The cocoa tins were not dangerous. You pierced two and connected them with a length of twine anchored by buttons. If the twine was taut, theoretically the device became a telephone and Gerald and I could talk to each other from top to bottom of the garden with the string stretched hard between us. Gerald maintained that it worked, and so did I when boasting to Carl or John. But privately I thought that what I was hearing was Gerald's voice direct from the yard, not Gerald's voice emerging from my cocoa-tin.

We made "caterpillar tractors" from a cotton reel, a pencil stub, rubber band and slice of candle for lubrication. There was a bought red and green box kite flown successfully by Gerald, and innumerable flat kites, wobbly with inadequate frames, made by me hopefully, covered in tissue

paper and stinking of that most vile-smelling of all fish glues - Secotine. None of mine ever got any higher in the air than I could hold it up, and most of them disintegrated stickily even below that altitude. The thing was, I was so impatient. I could never endure the waiting needed for the glue to dry. Tomorrow would never come. I had to have everything today. This desire for quick results has cursed me all my life, and led to countless half-finished cobbled dresses with unravelling inner seams. Impatience, and the boredom of doing the same job more than once, have led me through a path littered with crafts and hobbies taken up and discarded as I found I could not get perfect results without practice, and I would have been too bored to persevere.

It was always fun to go to tea with Erin. She had an attic nursery and a rocking horse on carved rockers. Energetically used, it not only rocked but moved round the wooden-floored room. Being Dick Turpin or riding the winner in a race was much more convincing if you travelled from the fireplace to the dormer window while doing it. Jane and Evelyn, across the road, had a rocking-horse too, much bigger than Erin's, with a bolting eye and scarlet harness, but it was built on a kind

of square frame, and could not move from place to place. On the other hand, the big black lacquered rocking chair in Ursula and Carl's nursery could also be rocked so that it waltzed about the room. Thrilling sea voyages were made across the polished green lino to the island of the table in the middle and the continents of big iron beds against the wall. But once again, it was Sally who had the best. She had a swing, a really satisfactory one with double ropes and a broad seat on which two little girls could swing together standing up. It hung on a timber framework as solid as a church. Other children had rather thin, loopy swings slung from an overhanging branch, and one family had a trapeze indoors. But Sally's swing felt secure. You could go high on it, but not dizzily high. And when you did go high, you could see over the tall back fence, across the lane and into the allotments, where crazy little henhouses and crooked huts punctuated the gardens. One garden was worked by an inoffensive little old man who pushed a flat handcart with his tools and the vegetables he grew back and forth to his home, but we credited him with living in the henroost and having an evil eye. I don't know which of us began it, but we shuddered deliciously and crouched down on the swing if we saw him at work, and fed each other thrilling horrors that he would perform if he saw us. To be secure and imagine danger is one of the joys of childhood. In "Peter Pan" one of the best moments is the security of the house under the tree, when the ticking crocodile goes by outside.

Hoops, whips and tops, conkers, came and went with the seasons. We never played marbles and did not know how, but hopscotch was

chalked out on the broad asphalt paths of the Rec. White clay bubble pipes cost a penny, and I remember the joy the great rainbow bubbles brought me, drifting away into the spring sunshine, especially after Father had shown the secret of making stronger and bigger bubbles when you put a few drops of glycerine into the water. I see children nowadays, with a tin tube of solution, dipping and waving a silly wire loop, and getting a stream of small uncontrollable bubbles that drift a few feet and burst. Our way was much better. It had a ritual that built up the excitement. A pudding basin had to be borrowed. The maid filled it from the kettle. Then we took the wire soap holder used for washing up, and swished it endlessly back and forth in the hot water while a froth of glittering hemispheres formed on top. The drop of glycerine was added, a few more swishes, and the bowl could be carried out to the top of the garden. You dipped the pipe and blew, very gently. The bubble grew, egg size, apple size, orange, then grapefruit size. Would it get any bigger? Often it burst with a soapy splatter in your face, but if you took the pipe away from your mouth and gave it the gentlest of sideways shakes, the beautiful bubble, flabby for a moment, would lurch loose from its moorings, catch the light breeze, and float, a taut miracle of rainbow delicacy, away into the sunshine. With luck it might sail all down the garden, its surface a running film of colour, and its globe weighted by the tiny drop of soapy water that hung below. I held my breath as I watched until it tangled in the branches of next door's pear tree and burst amid the foam of white blossom. A lovely death! And I could dip the white clay pipe, so dry it stuck to my lips, and try all over again.

I never cared for organised games so much as the plays we made up for ourselves, acting out the stories I invented. I was the story-teller of the group, and more than once Ursula's mother came round to complain because Ursula was having nightmares caused by the ghost stories I told. I honestly did not see why - I didn't believe them myself. But Ursula was two years younger, and for a short while I would try to temper the wind to the shorn lamb.

Some games, like "Happy Families" with its strange Victorian

grotesques, rather frightened me, and I was soon bored by the toys that came in cardboard boxes. "The Little Weaver" showed on the lid two rosy children

175

running in the wind, with streaming scarves which they had, presumably, woven themselves on the kit inside. But no way could that have been true. The cardboard frames with holes pierced for a wool warp were not large enough for a kettle holder, let alone a scarf. And the soft loosely wound little balls of purple and shocking pink wool were too short even to thread the frame properly. The "Natty Nitter", a round scarlet frame with brass pegs, allowed you to go on making an endless snaky tube, as long as your wool held out or you could beg the left-overs of her knitting from mother. But what could you do with six and a half yards of hollow woollen tube? The only use I made of the weaving cards was to thread the holes back and forth with string and pluck hopefully at them, in a desperate desire to manufacture a "lyre", like Orpheus carried in the picture in my wonderful book of myths. The string made no sound, the cardboard buckled, and the whole silly contraption was chucked disgustedly in the wastepaper basket. It was much more fun to make woolly balls on a little cardboard ring. They taught us that at Brownies, and you could trim the balls, and stitch them together, and even a quite ham-fisted child could add a felt tail, ears, or beak, and make a chicken, or a rabbit or a mouse. If you weren't that inventive, the balls could be strung in bunches from a ribbon, and given to the newest baby as a pram toy. Most of us were only, or youngest, children, but John had a little sister when he was eight, and baby Anne came in for quite a lot of woolly goodwill this way.

Recorders for children were not popular then, but you could buy a remarkably good tin whistle for sixpence. I was given one and soon became quite acceptably proficient. The thing about a tin whistle was you could carry it about with you and have a blow when you felt like it. "Learning the piano" meant the agony of sitting half an hour (a precious half hour - lost for ever) each day in a cold sitting room, numbly thumbing five finger exercises, while Stewart and Gordon, Ursula and Joan, Gwen and Doreen called and laughed outside. You couldn't use a piano to biff Ursula over the head if she got too cheeky. And why should I have to waste precious Saturday mornings going for a music lesson? I hated Monkey Russell anyway!

Father made us some splendid toys. My dolls' house was a failure, but it was beautifully made. I wish I had it now. The toboggan was an immediate success and was still in good shape in the bitter winter of 1940, when seven of us large teenagers or young grown-ups crammed into Geoffrey Thomas' little Morris Minor, with a Labrador sitting in the gear change, and two sledges and our toboggan roped across the back, to spend a long glorious afternoon on the mile-long Napton Hill, where they tested motor bikes. The toboggan's maiden voyage was rather different and had stuck in my memory because it was my first conscious experience of snow.

The winter of 1927 was long and hard. The snow fell early and was obviously going to lie. So Father got busy in the woodwork shop at his school and made a large, solid, heavy toboggan with polished steel runners. He brought it home one Saturday ('16' was only across the road from the School) pulling it with a bumpy roar along the pavement behind him. The snow had been trodden by then to ice and the toboggan skittered about on the end of its lead. Soon after lunch we set out for the Golf Course, where a steep short hill ran down to the flat by the Canal. I was sat on the toboggan, a globular bundle of leggings and mufflers, and told to hold on tight while Father and Gerald trudged ahead pulling me. The world was changed - everywhere grey and white with the rutted road too slippery for horses. When we reached the Golf Course, the dazzle of pure untrodden snow on the fields made you blink, and the romantic and smelly cottages across the water glowed in the afternoon light like a Christmas card. Big boys of eight and nine were spinning down the glassy slope, with very little idea of steering, and being halted short of the canal by the snowbanks and drifts they ran into. I was left in the charge of a Staff wife at the top while Father indulged himself with a run or two "to show Gerald how to do it". Then he was allowed to go alone, or with his friends. The afternoon sky paled, the sun dropped behind the Club House, and the chilly air began to bite through my woollies. In spite of the novelty of it all, I started to grizzle. It was time to go home.

At that point, the activity was halted anyway. Geoffrey, racing downhill on a nippy little sleigh, overshot the snowbank and crashed into a fence post that wired off the towpath. He was catapulted off and cut his face so badly on the wire that he had to be rescued, wrapped up hastily in all the spare coats, and rushed, on a sledge as fast as possible back to his doctor father's surgery to be stitched up. Gerald and I plodded wearily home along the Irish mile to '16', dusk falling round us, yellow light wavering and blossoming in the houses as we passed, and my feet and fingers clumsy and wooden with cold. I expect I whined and snivelled all the way. I was not one to be reticent about my discomfort, and Gerald must have been very glad to hand me over to Mother to be unpeeled from my onion layers of clothes and set down by the fire.

1927 was followed by winter after winter of green mildness, but no longed for snow. The runners of the toboggan were kept greased, it was upended in the garden shed, and we lived in hope, but it was many years before we were able to take it out again to the slopes of Crowpie Hill, where Tom Brown in his Schooldays, went poaching.

A circus came to town when I was seven. It frightened more than pleased me, but it also started a craze for stilts. Ursula's father made a

pair for her and Carl, and Father a splendid pair for me. They were sturdy with rock solid foot rests. The poles were good straightgrained two-by-two, with the sharp corners shaved off and the tops shaped into comfortable hand grips. In a day or two I really hardly knew whether I was on them or not. I could run and jump on them, and the power of seeing over gates and walls was exciting. I had them for years, and could use them to pick apples that were out of reach, or look for birds' nests. I could go up and down the back garden steps on them, and I certainly never had a serious fall or they would have been forbidden. Along with my Fairy Cycle, they extended my horizons at just the right time.

A couple of years later came "The Bogey". This **must** have been Father's work. It was too well made to have been cobbled up by me though other children made their own. Two pairs of pram wheels were fixed below a well sanded length of board. The front wheels swivelled

178

and a strong rope steered them. Sitting astride this bogey and hurtling down the hill with Peter and John and Diana was dangerous, exciting and hard on the shoes, since the only brake was a foot on the tarmac. It was pretty hard on clothes too.

The wheels were unprotected, and in one long afternoon I managed to ruin a new shepherd's plaid kilt, wearing holes through the cloth where it chafed on the rubber tyres. Mother was justly furious, since I was quite old enough by then to realise for myself that such violent activity required a change from Sunday best to something darned and faded, and set aside for playing in the garden.

I think my zither must have been the most beautiful toy Father ever made. It was hardly even a toy. It was a real miniature musical

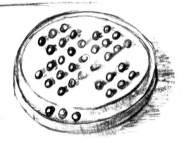

instrument. The smooth and polished triangular sound box had graded piano wires strung on the square metal pegs used in a piano. Father had an artistic friend who kept a music shop. The strings were tuned with a proper key, and though there were only two octaves, the tone was sweet. You plucked with the fingers, and fragile melodies were formed. There was none of the embarrassment of most juvenile music making, that you couldn't hit the right note. It was like my tin whistle - tune it properly with the piano, and the right note was there. All I had to do was pluck the proper string.

The zither came because I was so ravished by the pictures in my Greek myths book that I yearned for a lyre. When Father said lyres weren't made any more, I switched to a guitar. I did not actually know what a guitar looked like, but it sounded right. Father always tried to fulfil desires that would extend our minds, and he resolved

179

to make the zither. Secret evenings in his cellar workshop over a good part of the winter produced this plain but lovely little instrument, easy to play, and a tremendous excuse for bragging, as no one else had anything like it. A mouth organ was the height of luxury. Sally had a musical box but most of our home-made music was performed on a comb with a sheet of lavatory paper folded over the teeth. It produced a strange buzzing note that made your lips zing, and was only as tuneful as its performer. Ursula's elder half sister played the mandolin, but I was the only possessor among the small fry of a real musical instrument of my own - two indeed, for I remained faithful to my sixpenny tin whistle.

Forgotten friends! They have come back crowding out of the shadows, bringing with them all sorts of unimportant toys, fragile, easily broken, but satisfying for a day. There were books of thin gaudy card, cut out in the shape of a child or a puppy. Paper dolls with whole wardrobes of hats and dresses to be hooked over their shoulders on white tabs. There was an expanding dolls' cradle, with rough, splintery trellis work sides. We had the game of "Fishponds" where you fished over the edge of a cardboard box painted on the outside with gaudy fish and weeds. On the inside lay flattened fish with rings through their noses to be caught on lengths of limp thread and wire hooks. Father carved me a "Folly" for a dancing display - a sardonic jester with bells on his Fool's head-dress. The other children had smug, fat celluloid dolls' heads on sticks. A fortune-telling game brought us a many sided crystal as big as a walnut. I kept it for years. You rolled it and read off the number on its uppermost facet, then looked up your "Fortune" in a little book. There was a blue-tit made of woolly balls, with wire legs and a felt tail and beak. Someone gave me a green stone pig half an inch long, with a lens as small as a pencil point through its belly, but when you squinted through, miraculously four different postcard views appeared of places in Ireland Short clay bubble pipes came and went; so did homemade 'crawlers', made from cotton reels. I had the makings of a farmyard with metal animals, and an occasional penny-to-spend would open for me the delights of lingering as long as Mother or Gerald could be persuaded to stay, in the poky little toy-shop on High Street, with its slantways entrance between the china shop and the drapers. Here I could tantalise myself, choosing between a black and white pig, a turkey with its tail spread like a fan, a pump with a delicious bucket as small as an acorn cup, a man with a scythe and an arm that went up and down on a ball joint at the shoulder, a pair of lambs, a tree ... "Oh, <u>do</u> come on", Gerald would sigh. "Here". He picked up the black and white pig "She'll take this, please." Satisfied now that my mind had been made up for me, I would hand over my penny. Next time, perhaps, a leggy goat, or a milkmaid on a three legged stool ...

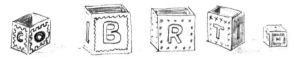

hen we moved to '62' and I was four and a half, I was enrolled in a babies' band class run by a girl who taught music a few houses up the road. It was as good a way as any to introduce me to the idea of school, a teacher and being in a group with other children. An hour, twice a week, was enough for a start. I was overawed.

For one thing, I had no idea what was going on. I was taken into a room that seemed so crowded with people you could not move. The mothers all knew each other and were chatting while the children raced in and out amongst them or besieged the young teacher who was handing down strange looking toys from a high cupboard. A boy

I recognised called Peter had a bright coloured drum and two knobbed sticks. The drum was not tin all over like the ones in the toy shops; it had leathery coverings stretched over the ends. I stood silently until the teacher handed me two short lengths of wooden rod, with sleigh-bells fixed to either end. "You have the bells, Pat" she said, "and when you hear me call 'Bells', you shake them like this". She waggled the rods and made a shivery treble like the jingle of harness. We all had to sit on the floor, round the piano. Peter and his drum were just opposite, and next to me was a little girl with a triangle on a string and the key of a sardine tin ready to strike it. Triangles were what most children seemed to have, some large, some small. The piano began. "Drums" called Miss D. "Tambourines".

A shivery sound began so I shook my bells too. The tune went on and sometimes the teacher would call someone's name instead of the instrument and then a child would strike a triangle. I was growing bored as well as bewildered and the pleasure of making a noise overcame me. I began to shake my bells vigorously. When I was

younger and had walked with Mother to nearby shops, I had worn reins with bells sewn to them, and when I pranced they had rung like these. I shook away, utterly oblivious of anyone else, or of the teacher's exasperation. Mother had to stop me in the end, and before I went to the class again she explained to me that the teacher only wanted me to shake my bells when she told me to. It seemed fairly dull and as often as not I would either ignore her because I was staring round at all the strange faces, or I would go on shaking long after she wanted me to stop. "No, dear, not so long. Only while I count four. Er-ONE, a-two, a-three, a-four". But I could not count and had no idea when to expect "Four" after "Er ONE". That was another thing they had to teach me quickly, before I went to school. Then, sometimes, we had to clap and chant "Tar-tar, tattay tar". I had no idea why.

I got used to it in the end, and was promoted to a triangle. I found that my triangle made a note different from the others, and that only certain triangles were to be struck at a given time. This was to sound pretty and fit in with the music whatever that meant. Gerald had 'music' lessons. He didn't like them much because he had to 'practise'. He would shut the sitting-room door, prop a book on the music stand, and get on with his story while mechanically repeating the one tune he had learned by heart for this purpose. We had a wireless, made by Father, but it played chiefly whistles and electric cracklings. The one or two records we had with our sale-room gramophone were all songs: Harry Lauder and a few Gilbert and Sullivan. Music without words meant nothing to me, so I was too inattentive to be anything but a liability to the little band. I was released from it and taken to Dancing Class instead.

Peter was here as well, and Sally, who made faces at me because she lived near to Peter and did not approve of him or anyone who associated with him. I had only said shyly "Hallo, Peter" being glad to see a familiar face in this vast, empty echoing Hall.

The floor was of dusty, unpolished wood blocks. The walls were distempered plaster and the air was chilly. The mothers sat on a row of bent wood chairs at one end. I had been peeled out of my red coat and my bunny-wool cardigan and was shivering in my pale blue party dress with the crystal pleated frills. We were lined up in front of a tall thin lady in a long dress, who held her hem a dainty six inches off the ground so that we could see her feet and we marched on the spot, trying to keep time with the music. The pianist thumped the first beat of every bar, and eventually most of us got the idea. It was hard for those of us who still didn't know their right from their left, but I did, so apart from a self-consciousness that made me feel that my feet had suddenly inflated to the size of footballs, I did not make myself conspicuous.

185

We made a circle and marched round in time, then we skipped and several small persons fell over and began to cry. I rather scorned them, but of course I was a six months older child than the one who had sat bewildered on the floor with my bells at the music class. Those of us who survived the skipping were rewarded with an action dance. We mimed while the tall lady said some words loudly to a tune

John had great big waterproof boots on
John had a great big waterproof hat .....

We 'pretended' putting on the wellies (that puzzled me - I had never had wellies), the sou'wester, and mackintosh, and then splashed out boldly into the puddles on the dusty dry floor of the Central Hall.

As the winter advanced, we learned the basic steps of the waltz "FORward-side-together, FORward-side-together", and the Polka, "one-two-three-hop, one-two-three-hop", but we only danced these on the spot, singly, our skirts held daintily out in a fan, and the little boys with one hand on the hip. In pairs we did the Gallop, round the hall, swirling to the tune bounced out on the swaying piano. By Christmas we were learning the series of movements in a dance called - amazingly - "Sir Roger de Coverley". I was proprietory about this dance. My name was Rodgers and I thought the dance belonged in some special way to me, just as John Y, who was my age, thought that the "Waterproof Boots" routine was written specially for him.

Mother bought a gramophone record - His Master's Voice - with Giula's smooth-haired terrier, Rags, gazing down a tin trumpet on the red disc in the middle. It had "Sir Roger" played by a band, on one side, and the Post Horn Gallop on the other, so I could practise these in the sitting room at home. Mother put the record on and danced them with me, reminding me of the movements. Down the middle and right arm swing with the boy from the bottom - wait for your partner to do the same - then left arm swing, then back to back. Lead your line out and down, make an Oranges and Lemons arch until they are all through, and then behold - you are at the bottom and dance with the top couple. It was better at home with Mother because we could dance all the time. At the classes, you had a long tiresome wait with little to do except jig up and down, as you worked your way up the set from the bottom to the top again. When I went to school, we used to dance "Sir Roger" in the Big Room on wet days in Recess, and I have never forgotten it. Then, when I went on to Grammar School, I discovered to my amazement that there was a whole book about Sir Roger and his doings as an eighteenth century country gentleman, and it was like finding a long lost relative.

We had no records for me to practise the waltz and the polka, but Mother would sing the popular tunes of her dancing youth (when dances did not end until five o'clock and morning milking time). For the waltz, we always had her favourite, The Merry Widow, but as she only knew one line of words she repeated these for all the lines of the tune. "Come and dance the Merry Widow - Waltz with Me - Come and dance ....."

For the Polka, with its heavily accented rhythm, we had a choice. There was

> "I have a bonnet trimmed with blue
> Why don't you wear it?   So I do.
> I will wear it when I can,
> Going to the fair with my young man".

But I preferred the intoxicating bounce as she sang and clapped to-

> "You should SEE me dance the Polka,
> You should SEE me swing around.
> You should SEE my flounces flying
> As my FEET lift off the ground".

The dust would be shaken in the carpet. The poker and shovel would rattle in the hearth and the glasses jingle in the sideboard cupboards, as I pranced from side to side, touching my knee with my toe and bending my leg neatly on every 'Hop'. The polka was my favourite dance.

The ash tree that grew at the top of the garden had swelling roots that ran out into the lawn, and made comfortable grassy mounds to sit on. The sun was gently warm, the sky pale blue and the green trunk of the tree was rough and reassuring to the touch. Voices above my head

- Gerald's saying "Miss Margaret says Pat can start school next week"; Mother saying "There now - you'll be able to go to school. Aren't you growing up!"

What did 'school' mean? It was where Daddy taught; where Gerald went every day with thick grey woollen socks and a striped cap. A boys' world, a man's world. What was it going to be for me?

I must have begun school in the summer, and I must have been five-and-a-half. Certainly long months had passed when I was largely alone, and had come to feel the new garden like a second skin. There was the cave twenty inches high, under the Japanese anemones; the angles in the brick wall where snails piled up like clusters of grapes and little triangular hammocks of spiders' web collected dust; the tarmac of the front path, the patchy yellow gravel of the back, different textures and temperatures of all the various steps, measured by infant behind, baking heat and sawtoothed edges, scraping the bare thighs, of the blue brick steps down from the yard to the back garden; chill of the roundnosed front-door step where the sun never shone; the mild warmth in the morning of the stone step halfway up the front path, and the muddy, splintery threshold of the garden shed where the smells of tarred twine and bicycles seeped out on to the silent afternoon air.

There is no transition time in my memory. Suddenly I was one of the Babies' Montessori class and I had always been one. The world had dark green lino and low tables and chairs. It smelled sweetly of milk and orange juice and dimpled Lincoln biscuits. It was quiet and reassuring as tall Miss Savery moved gently among us. Its sensations were of squeezing a washing-up mop in boneless fingers, over a shallow bowl of luke-warm water set in a low green table, as we "washed-up" our milk mugs before going out of doors to sit under the trees for a story. It was a hushed, dreaming world and it only existed in summer-time. By the autumn I must have learned the alphabet and the numbers up to ten and been ready to pass on to the big Transition where nearly twenty children accumulated. Like leaves and rubbish on the surface of a pool, some spun slowly round for months, and others picked up reading and writing fast and were swept on down the stream like twigs on a spate. In the Transition, with the conker trees in the

188

garden turning orange, I caught up with Carl, and John; clever little Christopher followed me up and swept out ahead of me, an infant prodigy!

But meantime, for a few placid weeks, our little band, in pinafores or linen suits with buttoned-on trousers and cotton sun-hats, held hands as we tip-toed down the garden and out of the sunblistered green door by the coach house. The back lane was black like coal dust, and cindery where housemaids carried the ashes down to fill potholes. It was shut in between the high walls of the empty coach houses. Horses had gone in the Great War, and the middle classes did not yet keep cars. Tall walls and trees shut out the light, but at the end of the lane, where we turned left for Caldecott's Piece, all was open and flooded with sun. The loose gravel underfoot was gold and crunchy, with chalky fossil shells and bits of broken flint like toffee that we sucked hopefully until Miss Savery, clucking softly, held a cupped hand under our chins and commanded us to "spit it out."

The Big School Vivarium was here, heated glasshouses where slow tortoises hobbled about on painful feet and withdrew their old men's leathery necks when we poked dandelion leaves at them. Tropical birds fluted in a big aviary and a white cockatoo swelled slowly as he eyed us in anger, and raised and curled his lemon crest. Damp earth and warm moss scented the air except where the smell of urine defiled it round the spider monkey. We were kept away from him. He was too fascinating, and we would probably have worried him into biting.

Mowing a games field, one of about six, was a slow, infrequent business in those days. Only the cricket pitches were kept closely cut. So where we sat under the tarnished pink hawthorns and the crude mauve rhododendrons, the grass was inches long and full of daisies, speedwell and sorrel. We sprawled on the big fringed rug, carefully unfolded for us, and picked little bunches of blossom. The gaudy rhododendron trumpets were a cheat, for they had no stalks, and the long springy anthers fell out as we picked the blooms up off the grass. The speedwell, too, dropped its little plates of sky blue and left bare, threadlike stems. But the double red hawthorn, where we were able to reach them, were perfect miniatures of the great flat-faced roses that

grew on the back wall of Carl and Ursula's house, quartered flowers, a muddle of petals and drenched with perfume. Roses were grown-ups' flowers only, and the joy of having perfect tiny copies of them, just my size, sent me searching in the long grass for fallen blooms with stems, but they were hard to come by. Daisies were the next best, and even a baby thumbnail could slit the juicy stalks and thread one through another to make crowns and bracelets for everyone.

Soon, we would be told to sit quiet and still, while a story was read to us, five or ten minutes only, and the cuckoos in the far lime trees mirrored each others' voices, and little brown grasshoppers chirred unseen around our feet.

Then it was twelve o'clock. We folded the rug, and went back into the dark lane, through the heavy door and up the garden, to where our mothers would be waiting in a comfortably chatting group by the gate to take us home. Our school day ended at dinner time and in the long afternoons I slid back into the private bubble of my own world, school expunged from my memory. Only the immediate present existed at that time, and I can not recall ever looking forward to tomorrow, or regretting or remembering yesterday.

190

The Transition was a rougher world altogether, though still very safe and watched over. We had more children - twenty or more - from five to nearly seven. The older boys were developing their aggressiveness and the older girls their quicker wits and power of hurting with taunt and pinch and tweak. There were tears in the Transition, and squabbles and victimisation. Rivals squared up and took measure of each other and the foundations were laid for antipathies that have in some cases lasted a lifetime. Here Carl and John became enemies, and could probably be no more than superficially polite were they to meet now. Here Rosemary emerged as dominant, and reduced me, and Ursula and Erin to a shaking and reasonless panic. Here too, we had to learn at last. The recitation of the alphabet was changed into a confusing set of sounds. A B C D E made a, ber, k, der and ... well E was unpredictable - often it had no sound at all.

We sat at little tables with large pink shiny cards in front of us. Stuck on these were letters cut out of sandpaper, and the teacher's hand held ours and guided our forefingers over the letter, in the motion of writing it, while she said its name and its sound. Then we had to recognise the same shapes in the print of our readers, and make the shapes in pencil between double ruled lines on paper. We were taught to write "script" because the letters were as like as possible to the letters of print, and one unnecessary muddle was avoided, though the curly 'a' of printed books puzzled me for a long time, after being taught to recognise the 'α' and finding it in our specially produced (and very expensive) readers.

These readers had very large print, and printing in colour as well. The pages had small drawings in corners and margins, and looked cheerful and attractive. Certainly I found no difficulty in learning to read or write, but when it came to Arithmetic, I was in trouble from the start! The only thing I enjoyed about arithmetic was the little cloth bags of beads on wires. We had sets, one bead up to nine, each on a scrap of wire, and by putting say 3 and 4 together you could match them with a 7. But even here, I only enjoyed it if I could get one particular set. These beads were peach pink and slightly iridescent like the sweets called 'satin cushions' and it was their colour that made me love them. If I had to have the ordinary flat blues or dull greens, I did not want to play.

We had winter in the Transition. The old double drawing-room of the house was our room. It was divided by an arch, and had a fireplace 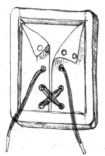 in each room, but though there were great high mesh fireguards with brass rails, I never remember fires there. The walls were thick and the panelled shutters folded back into the embrasures. The tables had their tops engraved in two inch squares, and we were allowed to do sums in chalk in the squares. We still had to learn some skills, and would sit with frames of eyeletted linen, learning lacing up for our shoes, 'criss cross', or the much more difficult 'straight across'. Other frames had matched pairs of laces and ribbons, for learning to tie bows. We had sets of blocks that fitted in order inside each other, and 'counting frames'  with ten beads of different colours in rows, for something unexplained called units, tens and hundreds. These never made any sense to me, any more than later on I could fathom the mysteries of 'borrowing', and 'carry one' in sums. Arithmetic was a bog in which I sank struggling ever deeper, and no one seemed able to pull me out. By the time I was seven, Friday, Saturday and Sunday were a black fog of misery, because of the only homework we had - SUMS. Father used to try to help me, but I floundered in despair as he didn't do them the same way as we did at school. He could not see why I was not able to follow the logic instead of demanding a blind formula. Soon he would be shouting and I snivelling. Another miserable Sunday, and I slid one step further into the morass from which I was only released on leaving school. Even as a student, doing teacher-training, I dreaded being sent to an elementary school to do teaching practice, and being expected to teach even the most juvenile arithmetic. I knew too well that as soon as I and figures confronted each other, my mind would go into a whirl and I would make stupid mistakes that seven-year-olds would sneer at. I remember the light-headed relief with which I heard from my tutor that "As I was obviously never going to teach anywhere except a grammar school, it would be a waste of time to send me to an elementary school". The horrible truth was that I just <u>was not good enough</u> for primary teaching!

There was a figured walnut piano with yellowed keys like an old woman's teeth. Its fussy fretwork front was backed by faded silk. If you poked behind the fretting and uncovered the hidden silk you found it had once been glowing ruby, but now it showed only dusty fawn. Two brass candle stands swivelled on wobbly hinges either side of the music rack, and the loud pedal was bent, slippery and shining brass, getting much more abuse than the soft one, as the teacher bounced "Sir Roger de Coverley" for us to dance in wet playtimes. We learned easy hymns, and singing games like "Pat-a-cake" and "The Farmer's in his Den". I had mixed feelings about being the last chosen to go in the circle. "The child wants a dog" and the child chose one from the ring of chanting children. "The dog wants a bone" and the dog chose one. But then, the Farmer, his wife, his child and the dog all ran away and rejoined the circle, to chant the haunting melancholy of "The bone's all alone". If I was the bone, I would feel the tears pricking at my eyes as the long sad vowels tore at my feelings. But then - the lonely bone had the privilege of becoming the Farmer and starting off the next round.

The school was in an old family house, and the three sisters who ran it had bought the next door house as well. It was a terraced row, and only an outside passage had separated them at ground level. A door had been made from our room into this covered passage so that the kitchens in both houses could have contact. Now and again, in our morning's lessons, the door would open and Miss Hetty who kept house, would shuffle across the room on a visit to 'the other house', or an aproned maid would slip through with a basket of potatoes.

The house had been furnished two generations before my own home, and at school I examined with the intensity of the very young all the objects that were strange to me. There was a huge green glass door stopper, filled with bubbles. A cuckoo-clock on the wall was carved like a Swiss chalet and had weights like pine-cones. The window-shutters had white china knobs and curved brass latches. The

193

white marble mantel-pieces had huge arched over-mantel mirrors sitting above them. Their gilt frames were moulded like ropes, tied at the apex with plaster tassels. The front bay window had terracotta serge curtains, edged with fascinating woolly bobbles, which greedy little fingers twiddled and twitched in the hopes of abstracting one. All over the house it was the same. Any furniture other than the regulation school-room stuff was in the style I would have known in my great-grandmother's house if it had been in the Midlands and not away in Ireland. At home a 'sofa' was dark blue brocade, low, with soft stuffing. In the school it was a strangely shaped, hard stuffed object with only one end and half a curly back. A bookcase at home was a simple set of open shelves. At school it was carved, with glass doors, and fancy edgings of gilt stamped leather along the fronts of the shelves. Elaborate and dusty gilt picture frames held huge steel engravings of people with their clothes improbably bunched up, their heads tilted backwards with mouths half open. Whether they were the infant Samuel in the temple, Iphigenia about to be sacrificed, or Europa run off with by Zeus, they all went to the same couturier, and all had the same half-baked expressions! In our house, there were no pictures of people. We had some of my Father's watercolours, an etching by a friend, and two hideous blurred daubs of cottages and muddy roads, bought for the broad gold frames and hung up in the sitting room 'for the time being', which lasted fifty-two years.

The Transition was where we learned to read and write. As soon as we could do this, we went up to the Lower First and joined the real school. We went to Prayers every morning in the Big Room. This was a back bedroom of the house which had been extended on iron pillars out over the garden to make one long light room with windows all round. It could be divided into two by a pull-down screen like the slatted top of a roll-top desk. It was assembly room, concert room and gym, as well as dining room each day for the Staff and Dayboarders. It was the centre of my daily life for most of the years from seven to twelve, and I can shut my eyes still and take a leisurely walk all round it, touching, feeling and smelling as well as seeing.

Once a week, strange faces appeared among us when the beloved Mr Aspey came for the afternoon - a naval Petty Officer who gave us

Physical Training. He was a springy, round little man like a sorbo ball, and he made every exercise into a game. Children who had governesses at home would be brought to join in the P.T., and so warm and delightful was he that one small boy who began P.T. and Sunday School in the same week came home from the latter and asked his mother wistfully, "Is Jesus as nice as Mr Aspey?"

We had very little apparatus - two long low benches, a balancing-beam which could be let down from the ceiling across the middle of the room, and a horse over which we used to flounder and flop, hauled like little sacks by the muscles of Mr Aspey. The Big Room floor was of unstained boards, varnished pale gold, but growing splintery in my day, and the only painful part of P.T. was the way long splinters would run themselves into our serge bloomers and remain prickling cruelly all afternoon until we could modestly remove them at home after splinter hunts.

Being a bouncing ball, a windmill, or a fish was much more fun for me than the activities of the other afternoon that brought little strangers into the school. That was Friday afternoon dancing class. At first, Dancing Class was in the Central Hall - a great barren cold box of a room in town - but so many of her pupils attended it that Miss Margaret decided it would be worth having a class at school. It was tradition that Mothers came to the class and sat round the room with shawls while we pranced through the Polka and the Waltz. In the Central Hall days, nothing would have kept the mothers away, because the dancing mistress was a perpetual source of wonder. Week by week, she came <u>every time</u> in a different full length evening dress. As John and Sally and I shuffled and skipped home behind our Mothers, through the foggy November dusk, they would compare notes on the dress. One week it was black pleated chiffon with a skirt that spread into a great fan, when she curtsied. Another, it was a ruby silk with a handkerchief-pointed skirt - emerald georgette, flame taffeta, peacock shantung, grey voile. Week by week the show went on, and still the mothers puzzled. How <u>could</u> she afford it? Teaching dancing could not possibly pay all that well! So sheltered were the dear ladies' lives from all that was at all 'fast' or 'tasteless' that they never even thought of theatrical costumiers and Moss Bros!

Miss White's dresses were long responsible for my attending th
dancing classes with Mother looking on. When we had them at school, sh
stopped coming. Partly I was getting coltish and clumsy and did not shov
up very well against graceful Giulia, fairy-like Stephanie or lively Barri
who learned tap-dancing, and partly, Miss Barnan danced in thick red tigh
and a plum coloured tunic. There was no glamour in <u>her</u> wardrobe!

Two years after I had stopped going to dancing class, I was roped in t
make up the numbers in a Concert the Staff arranged. When I was abou
seven, I had reached the stage most little girls go through of havin
enormous teeth and feet, and two wooden legs. Mother, having watched m
flump grumpily through pretty little arranged dances like "Robins in th
Snow" and "Spring in the Forest", decided it was not worth wasting
guinea a term on me any longer. Sally, Joanna, Barrie and Betty were lik
thistledown or nodding bluebells, but I was a deadweight, always half a ba
behind, mute and resistant as a dragging anchor. I was withdrawn from th
Friday afternoon class, and along with the boys and a handful of othe
failed girls like myself, gladly got on with my weekend prep. It was a joy t
get that beastly arithmetic out of the way, instead of having to take it home
and cry miserably over it on a Sunday evening when Father looked over m
shoulder and found every sum wrong. If I did it at school and left it there, i
was still all wrong, but I was spared the patient correction, the growin
exasperation, and the final shouting that always paralysed me. And if Mis
W threw my book at my head on Monday afternoon and danced with rag
at my stupidity, at least it was only one row, not two. I was learnin
worldly wisdom.

However, this Concert came along. The school needed advertisement. There was to be a play, "The Young Visiters". The teachers kept laughing at the words in that, but I could not see that they were funny. My friend John was Mr Salteena, and his eight year old pompous self-confidence gained a lot of applause. I was only a maidservant - a non-speaking part. So when I was told that I could be in the dancing group "because you were doing dancing until last spring", I was pleased. Sally and Giulia were in it by natural right. We were to do a "Hoop Dance". We had two big wooden hoops, four feet across, twined round with yards of Alexandra roses, twisted on to string, (somebody must have had influence in the right places), and eight children in green butter muslin Greek tunics were to carry a vastly long garland of paper flowers and leaves, winding it prettily between ourselves and around the hoops.

It was an ambitious plan. Even with eight experienced, naturally graceful and biddable children, it would take some doing - but the teacher who planned it had seen something like it done at a Dancing Display, and was so impressed by its charm that she managed to persuade Maggy to let her try. Beaky, I am sure, had a much more accurate assessment than either of them of the difficulties, but she was in a minority, and we began rehearsals.

Actually, as long as we were practising with jumping ropes with a weighted bag at each end to keep them taut, the routine went, not well, but passably - not bad enough to be condemned out of hand.

That was a pity.

When the day of the Concert came, Giulia, Barrie and Sally were all perfect in their graceful movements and managed the papery garland as easily as they managed their knitting wool in Handwork lessons. But the rest of us .....

I can only speak for myself. When I was put into my butter muslin shift, I felt a fool. Mother had consented to my doing without my vest just for the dance, and that was a blessing because the tunics only went over one shoulder. But of course, I had to keep my knickers on. Even if they were only my linings, they were still made of thick white stockinet and the butter muslin stuck to them and rode up. I had to keep taking a hand away from its vital routine with the garland to pull my hem down to a decent Plimsoll line. This was distracting and I feel sure some of the others had the same trouble, as nothing else could really account for the series of disasters that befell that garland of paper roses.

Bella, of course, was a problem anyway. She was slow, and stout, and it had never been possible to do more than place her in position with the garland and tell her to hold it woodenly until the next move. Josephine, who was next to Bella, was supposed to pass the garland on to her neighbour on the hoop, but Bella kept an obstinate grip and Josephine's impatient tugs finally broke the string and paper roses and leaves showered in the air around them. Further along the line Sally and Giulia were posing exquisitely, and Rosamund was delicately winding the garland round the hoop. Rosamund took ballet lessons and she rather fancied herself. She moved with grace and austere elegance, but unhappily she also planted her foot, firmly, unbudgingly, on the garland as it passed her on the floor. Cynthia, always grittily practical, growled at her to get her hoof off it, but Rosamund was lost in the misty footlights of Covent Garden, with King George and Queen Mary applauding rapturously. Cynthia dug her heels in and tugged - in vain.

At the other end of the line - anchor man, as you might say, I was taking the feed-back of the garland fairly successfully from Barrie, a veteran of Dancing Displays, when I felt my sticky knickers trapping my green butter muslin yet again. I put a hand down swiftly to yank at my hemline lost my footing, accidentally found a slippery bit of stage, and full in view of all the parents, including my shrinking Mother,

198

skidded, slithered and landed resoundingly on my bottom, bringing the whole beautiful passage of choreographic delight to a ludicrous and inelegant conclusion.

Our uniform dresses for dancing class were black velvet tops and pleated chiffon skirts. When Sally joined the class, her father  objected to a child of her age being dressed in black. So powerful was his personality that he talked Miss Margaret into changing the dress for everyone, and we went into sea-green tussore Greek tunics with 'knickers to match', that article of faith in the middle classes of the time. Swedish cousins of Ursula's used to fall about laughing at our 'knickers to match', and though I was indignant then, I wonder now what their purpose was. After all, knickers are knickers and recognisable as such, whether they are white or pink, or rosebud cotton like our dresses. We did spend a good deal of time upside down, turning cartwheels or standing on our heads - but why was it less immodest to display bloomers made of the same material as our dresses than plain regulation navys? We all had a thick pair of white 'linings' on underneath, anyway.

Each morning's school began with everyone lined up round the edge of the Big Room. We had roll-call, Christian names only, and on my very first day I made a fool of myself and was sniggered at by the whole school. Miss Margaret had stumped in and settled herself at the big teacher's desk. She began calling out names. "Octavia" - "Here". "Pamela" - "Here". "Orinda" - "Here". "Evelyn" - "Here".

Voices answered from the other end of the room where six tall girls, all of twelve years old, were standing - there didn't seem to be any boys among them as there were among us little ones.

"Dorothy" - "Here". "Joan" - "Here". "Pat" -

"HERE" I called out, immensely proud to be noticed, and to know just what I was supposed to do.

Heads turned towards me and a titter broke out. What had I done? They called my name.

"Pat", again said Miss Margaret, and a big girl - come to think of it, I knew her by sight - Pat Tait - answered "Here".

It was a kindly little school and I have no doubt that a teacher explained to me after prayers when I should expect to hear my own name called, but for a good while my shame coloured Prayers and made them an embarrassment.

We sang a hymn - that was easy - then a psalm - that was not! It had no tune, and the words seemed to fit in all anyhow. Then we all had to repeat the Collect for the week. Our family was Nonconformist and those prayers in their stately English were alien to me. Our Scripture homework each weekend was to learn the new Collect, and I came much later to be glad of this; familiarity with the English of their period was not only a help in understanding Shakespeare and Milton, but also the language, so direct and clear, was not a bad yardstick for judging style.

Our reading in the Transition was helped by a phonetic method, and this needed to be offset by spelling lessons. Each week we had to learn a certain number of words from Dr Grenfell's Spelling Book. The big girls had to learn six, and we only one. But every Monday, Miss Margaret would ask someone in each class publicly to spell one of the words. A chart was kept to show how each form was doing and the winning form each term got a coveted gold star. I was not a good speller. I have a standard test we all did about this time and out of 100 words I only got five right.

"Onward Christian Soldiers" was a favourite because in the chorus we all turned smartly to the right and marched noisily round the room while Miss Margaret flung the windows open and breathed deeply. Another excitement might come at the end of prayers. Before we dismissed, some child might put a hand up eagerly in the air, stretching so far in her excitement that she would look as though she had been hung from the ceiling by her wrist. "Please - please -

200

please", she would be panting, longing to be noticed.

"Well, Diana?"

"Please, Miss Margaret - it's Betty's birthday!"

Lucky Betty. She would cast her eyes modestly downward and shuffle her feet.

"Then we must have the Birthday March! Miss Myland, please?". Miss Myland, would begin searching the music on top of the piano, while Betty only said how old she was, and what presents she had been given. Then once again, we all turned to face right and followed each other marching in a ring round the room and singing,

> "To thy loving parents
> On this very day,
> God in heaven did send thee
> Here on earth to stay.

Then there came an Angel
From a distant land
Who through life will lead thee
Gently by the hand.
God in Heaven protect thee
From all sorrows near.
May a happy Birthday
Come in every year".

As we pranced and sang, Maggy would stump from window to window flinging them open to welcome the wild North-eastern, while the Birthday child basked happily in the joy of being the centre of everyone's attention. It was almost as good as opening the first present.

12. A PENNY TO SPEND

 y shopping was limited to those times when I had a penny to spend. This did not happen very often; I had no pocket money until I was nearly thirteen, when Father gave me a princely shilling a week, sixpence for a National Savings stamp and sixpence for myself. I was getting the same at eighteen!

A penny to spend had to be begged from Mother, when the craving for a few sweets grew too great. We did not get tips, or money for birthdays. Our uncles and aunts all lived in Ireland and neither Gerald nor I had godparents. Once, when I was seven, I found a corroded grey disc in a rubbish heap and took it to Father. "It's a shilling", he said, "but you couldn't spend it like this. The shopman wouldn't accept it". And he offered to carry it about in his pocket where it would rub against the other coins and gradually clean itself. Meantime I could be thinking what I really wanted to spend it on.

No shilling in the world ever bought so much joy. It was limitless wealth to me - enough money to buy anything I wanted, and I was never disillusioned as I changed my mind so often. It was months before I asked Father if I could have it. I had accepted his word trustingly, and it was only many years later that I realised what he had done. My corroded disc was almost certainly a washer, or a foreign coin, and he had swiftly thought up this plan so that in due course he could give me an authentic shilling from his pocket and I would feel it was my treasure trove. I have forgotten what I spent it on at last, because I had enjoyed so many hours of vivid day-dreaming of the wonders I could buy, but never did. To travel hopefully is better than to arrive.

Aladdin's cave, of course, was Woolworths. "Nothing over

sixpence" they proclaimed and a child with a hot sticky penny could while away a whole wet afternoon, nosing from counter to counter weighing up the merits of all the cheap and gaudy novelties that came from Japan, the tin toys from Germany, the pencils, rubbers and books, paint-brushes and pencil sharpeners marked proudly "Made in England". Those were the days of the campaign to make us "Buy British" and beat the Slump but with only a penny to spend I could not always afford to be patriotic.

I think I could easily write a whole book about Woolworths and the miracles sixpence could work there. The toys come crowding through my mind, bright banana coloured cricket bats, and composition balls that left a red kiss on everything they touched; birds made of compressed cotton wool, bright yellow like canaries, with two long tail feathers that whirred when you whirled the bird round your head on its stick; divers in glass jars of water. A red rubber skin was stretched over the mouth of the jar. Inside a little china diving doll floated, his helmet bobbing on the surface. When you pressed your thumb into the rubber skin, you increased the pressure inside and the little diver was forced to descend to the bottom of the jar. Release your thumb, and he floated back again to the top. But he did cost sixpence. There were magic painting books, where the outline pictures had to be brushed over only with clean water, and the colours, thin and metallic, bloomed on the paper. There were enchanting little packs of cards, doll-sized but complete, Joker and all. These I was told, were for playing Patience, but I loved them just as miniatures. There were pencil boxes galore, from the swivelling, sliding multi-storey wooden ones, with a hollowed out compartment for each item, to the very up-to-date leather pouches that became popular after zip-fasteners swept the market. A tin globe of the world, an inch across, hid a pencil sharpener in its base, and exercise books with ribby red covers had tables of invaluable information printed inside, about bushels, grammes and drams, rods, poles or perches, gills, pints and quarts, acres, fathoms and Troy weight. There were bundles of wooden spills in puce and shocking pink, yellow, acid green - colours so strident they set even my teeth on edge. There was Japanese china, incredibly cheap, patterned in blue or terracotta; strings of gaudy glass beads, pretence wedding rings, enchanting miniature tobacco pipes with drooping stems like meerschaums, and meant to be used as cigarette holders. Bubbling crowds of glorious balloons on sticks were tethered high above the counters, and box-kites and bundles of cotton flags for festivals. But best of all to me, at two a penny, were the Japanese paper flowers. The two halves of a cockle shell were glued together, and when you dropped them into a tumbler of water, the glue melted, the shells opened slowly, and ribbons and streamers of fantastic blooms crept out and up, to unfold and hang marvellously bright and crisp in the brilliant light of the water. They would last a day, or even two, before the thin folds and fans of tissue paper began to disintegrate and the translucent purple, crimson and emerald collapsed in sludge about the shell.

We all shopped at Woolworths. We went there for our Jacobean tumblers, for the white cups and saucers with a gold clover leaf that were used in the kitchen, for fireworks and decorations, for bathing caps - in a jumbled heap of thin rubber fantasies, as colourful and varied as a tropical flower garden. Anything seasonal came from here - the snowman, or Santa Claus for the Christmas cake. The pink sugar roses that held birthday cake candles, the little cards with charms for the Christmas pudding, packets of gummed paper circles to cover the pots of summer jam. While Mother chose, I could feast on the brightly coloured gimcracks and the tin toys with keys to wind up their clockwork. Mice that scuttled and frogs that leaped. For a short while too, Germany exported delightful little cast metal dwarfs. They pushed a wheelbarrow, and they had large delicately curved feet, so that if you put them at the top of a sloping board, gravity walked them sedately down it to the ground. Under the yellow electric light, treading the creaking diagonal board flooring and sniffing up the mingled smells of turpentine and rubber, biscuits and mice, the old Woolworths offered colour and fulfilment. Nobody felt impoverished in there.

If I went shopping on my own, it would be to one of the little local corner shops. There were two on the cul-de-sac that flanked our back lane, and three more if you crossed the road and explored towards the cemetery. Each shop had its peculiar charm and speciality.

Ursula, Carl and I knew them all. One was really a small grocery, and had a very scanty selection of sweets, but they did sell a kind of malt-flavoured butterscotch which Carl liked. He and Ursula had Cod-liver oil and Malt by the spoonful, out of a big brown glass jar, and it was really quite pleasant to eat, like half set toffee. Carl used to help himself when he got the chance, and he let me lick the spoon sometimes to taste. I was given Scott's Emulsion. That also was quite tolerable, not fishy at all, but no one would have got hooked on it as a sweet. The malt-flavoured butterscotch came in uneconomically large lumps, but could be broken down, leaving needle-like sugary splinters to be picked up and sucked on a wetted finger.

Opposite was a real sweet-shop. When you pressed down the brass thumb-latch and opened the door, it brushed a bell on a spring and the jangle brought the shop-lady out of her back parlour. There was worn basket-patterned lino on the floor and heavy brown lino on the counter. Rows of glass bottles stood glinting in the sideways light from the window, pear drops, acid drops, chocolate drops, enormous,

exotic buttered brazils, Dolly mixture and jelly babies, satin cushions fizzing with sherbet inside, aniseed balls, liquorice allsorts, and treacle toffee. Hardly anything in those days came in wrapped bars except chocolate, and not many kinds of that. The counter was crowded with novelties which cost a farthing or a half-penny, and made up in variety of choice what they cheated you out of in real value. Sugar pigs and sugar mice with white string tails arrived for Christmas trees but were still there, pink or white and slightly dusty, at midsummer. Lollipops like red and green tennis racquets, liquorice ribbons with a blob of hundreds and thousands in the middle; metal trays of toffee that the shop lady cracked with a little hammer, packets of pretence cigarettes made of floury white sugar, and best of all, mystery Monster Lucky Baskets. These cost two pence, and were not really good value, except that the excitement and anticipation they generated were as important as their contents. Ursula and I got one once and rushed away to sit in the lane among the nettles and dogs' droppings, to see what was inside. The "basket" was two strawberry chips fitting one over the other, and inside we found a celluloid Kewpie doll an inch high, a fluted tin patty pan, paper riddles and mottoes, a tiny rubber ball the size of a marble, and a dab and sucker in a triangular bag, to be shared fairly, lick and lick about. There was a liquorice tube up which, in theory, we could have sucked the fizzy Lemon Kali powder, but it got blocked up with spit almost at once. But the toffee lollipop could be licked, dipped in and then sucked until all the powder was gone, and there was still quite a lot of toffee to be shared on the end of the wooden skewer.

I was never allowed gob-stoppers and I envied Gerald, who was, and whom I had watched taking the great ball of hard sugar out of his mouth to see what colour it had turned next. You could do the same with aniseed balls, but I did not like the flavour.

You could buy sheets of scraps at this shop as well, printed in Germany and forty years out of date when I remember them. They came in stamped-out sheets joined by little paper links. They were shiny, slightly embossed and brilliantly coloured. The children, puppies and kittens were all fat and sentimental. The flowers were rosy-cheeked hausfraus of bloom, healthy cabbage roses, robust lilies, sturdy forget-me-nots. The angels and cherubs were small cousins of the oleographs in our Family Bible, languishing in long white nighties, or pink feathers, but still well weighted at the base, and clearly unable to fly. There was plenty of choice at these little shops, and some more respectable sweets too, like the gold wrapped bars of Rowntree's "Pieces of Eight" chocolate that Auntie Charlotte liked when she came to stay. She used to send me out for a bar to share with Mother as the sisters sat chatting. She would give me a penny to spend for myself as well, so I was eager for the errand. Those were rich times and I would have enjoyed them except that I was uneasily aware that there was some mystery, some sadness about Auntie Charlotte's visit, something to do with a little boy dying. Years later I discovered that she had had a breakdown. As an overworked fever nurse, in the middle of a bad 'flu epidemic when most of the staff were ill, she had been so exhausted that she had made a mistake and given a child an overdose that killed him. She had resigned after the enquiry, and gone to pieces through a sense of guilt, grief and loss of confidence in herself. About ten years later, lonely and hopeless in the middle of the War, she jumped over a cliff.

At the end of the cul-de-sac where our little shops were, a five-barred gate closed off the road. Beyond lay allotments, a market garden and the open fields that bordered the LNER line. Old Arthur ran the market garden alone. He can not have been so very old, for I can remember him twenty-five years later, still in his khaki great-coat and straggling ginger soupstrainer, selling papers outside the Red Lion in town. We used to be sent down to Old Arthur, with a broken-down shopping basket, to buy potatoes, carrots and lettuce. He was the nearest thing to a farmer we met often, but he wasn't really a countryman, and his talk was all of motor cycles, cars and the great Schneider Trophy races, as he weighed out potatoes on his black, earthy scales.

Up near the railway, at the little station entrance, was the last of our local shops. It was our final resort on Sundays or when the corner shops were closed - which hardly ever seemed to happen. It was a little wooden kiosk, a lozenge shaped hut built to fit into the obtuse angle made by the road and the railway cutting. It was called the "Handispot", and was open early and late to sell newspapers, tobacco, sweets and chewing gum to the workers who travelled daily to Lutterworth or Leicester. Here when all else failed, Father could get half an ounce of Three Nuns Empire, or Mother a twopenny bar of Fry's Chocolate Cream. The railway was closed down, the station buildings demolished, and the prim little Handispot, so small only one customer at a time could get inside, had no further reason for existing. Its yellow ochre boards and starchy little ruffle of railway fretwork round the eaves, melted away in the wake of Dr Beeching. But our two little corner shops are still there, though the worn brass thumb-latches have gone, and when I cross their hollowed steps and greet their smiling, kindly young owners, I think I can smell again the malt butterscotch and the pink sugar mice that drew me there fifty-five years ago.

13. EDUCATION

t Summerlea, we stayed in the Transition until we had mastered the three Rs in a rudimentary way. Until we had, we did not work as a class, except for singing, games, or painting. The rest of the time, one child might be doing sums from a card while another was learning to read with the teacher. However, we now stayed for the full school day, and at 9.15 every morning we lined up in a great oval with the others, round the Big Room, and our names were called for the Register. There were competitions, too, and we took part in these. Who could grow the best flowers from bulbs - a bowl of daffodils, or a hyacinth in a glass? We kept them at home, and brought them in for judging as they reached their best. The winner would be a form, not a single child and the chances were fairly equal.

Joining in for Prayers and Call-over made the change an easier one when we were moved up to the Lower First. We did not go all together as a form, but were promoted as we were ready. This could mean one solitary child going on alone into a new group, and it was just as well that in prayers we had grown familiar with the names and faces of our new companions. I do not remember feeling any dramatic sense of strangeness, or fear when I was sent on up, but I do happen to remember my first day in the 'proper' school because we had a History lesson.

I imagine most children of seven are like me and have very little sense of the past. I know I was not capable then of realising that there had been a time when I was not. Gerald was six years older than I, and I know stories about him when he was five, being lost for a day, and discovered down at the Cattle Market in Father's cap and walking stick, 'helping' the drovers drive the herds, or asking Sally's mother, calling at school for her elder daughter Mary, whether she wanted "nice Mary", or "the other Mary who fights". I understood that he had been a very small child then, not a big boy of thirteen, but that he had existed and I had not was past my grasp. "Where was I then?" was my constant enquiry when told old tales.

That day in the Lower First, I sat at a folding desk, varnished like butterscotch, on a rush-seated chair that was printing itself off on to the backs of my legs, and faced a blackboard on which Miss L had written

William I   1066

William II   1087

Henry I   1100

Stephen   1135

This was all a novelty. It was something called "Normans", and we read it out several times as quite a satisfying jingle. But after that we were expected to answer questions on "Dates". The board was turned over. "Barbara, what was William II's date?" "Ten eighty seven".

The whole business was loaded with unsolved puzzles. What were Dates? What was Normans? Why did these boys, William and Henry have capital 'I' after their names? Why did Stephen not have one?

How did people know that William Eye Eye should be called William the Second? (No one had explained Roman numerals to me at this stage, and my Prayer Book had the Psalms numbered in Arabic figures). Above all else, what <u>was</u> "Ten sixty-six"?

I had a quick memory and very soon was able to rattle off correctly the "Dates" of Normans and Plantagenets as well, but I think

my understanding of time existing centuries ago developed very slowly indeed. If someone said to me "Once upon a time, long, long ago ....." I was perfectly happy to listen to tales of how a girl and boy lived in a mediaeval village, or in an Elizabethan manor house, and be content to know that these things had once been and now were no more. But a sense of the continuity of Time, which is so necessary if you are going to tackle "History" from the Romans, working forwards, was not mine to command. I might have developed an understanding of it from the other end through parents and grand-parents and their way of life as children, and so being led back gradually until the moment when I could have recognised what a hundred years meant. I could have used as a yard-stick Great Grandma Fleming, sitting nodding and mumbling at the window in the house where Father had lived as a child. She died when I was seven, and she was nearly a hundred years old.

The school was very old fashioned in many ways and some of the textbooks we had dated back to the 1880s. I remember "Ceppi's French Course" with pictures on every page, but they were of a family of children dressed in the Norfolk knickerbocker suits, the frilled pinafores and immense goffered hats of starched broderie anglaise that the children wore in the E. Nesbit books. Pictures are more powerful than words and we accepted these children as like ourselves, in spite of the clothes. A good deal of the learning we did was learning-by-heart, but at seven and eight, few of us had any objection to this. It

Marie et son frère arrosent les fleurs.

was something we could all do well and most of us very well, except Bella who was decidedly a slow pupil, and was a legend among us for putting up her hand in a Composition lesson and asking how to spell "Hat". But no teacher mocked her or harried her, and she plodded on at her own pace. Accuracy in multiplication tables, History dates, spelling and grammar was encouraged by turning the lessons into quizzes, where you moved up or down the line according to your success. The chance to move about, and the smallness of the forms - (ten to twelve children was average) meant that school was usually not so very unlike a game played at home with Mum and some friends. There was a chance for everyone to shine at something. Geoffrey was good at Maths. Betty shot better than anyone else at Netball. I recited with the most "expression" (it must have been excruciating!). Sally wrote the prettiest hand and Ursula, despite her being much younger, was exquisitely neat in all she did. Diana was by far the best at being a bouncing ball in dear Mr Aspey's Gym class, and Barrie, crisp, saucy Barrie, danced. One day, after Prayers, we were all told to sit cross legged on the floor and Barrie came in wearing a neat little dress-suit with a cane and topper, and scarlet tap shoes, and while a teacher played the piano, she sang and tap danced dazzlingly to a tune called "Crazy People". We had a wireless by then, but it was home-made, and our few gramophone records were all Gilbert and

212

Sullivan or Harry Lauder, so 'Jazz' and 'Dance Music' were entirely strange to me. The only cinema in town so far was known as the Flea-pit, and though Gerald was considered flea-proof and allowed to go, the rest of the family did not. The world of Jessie Matthews, Shirley Temple, Mickey Rooney, did not burst on me until the grand new cinema, temple of the thirties, was built and Father would take us all now and again, to wonder at suitable musicals, or history films that were recommended at school, like "The House of Rothschild" and "The Iron Duke". Then I caught on to the catchy tunes of Carroll Gibbons and Henry Hall. But when Barrie danced, I was amazed but bewildered. The only popular tune I was aware of was one that Henry sang in Guernsey -

"Felix keeps on walking
Keeps on walking still.
With his hands behind him
You will always find him -
Blow him up with dynamite, but him they could not kill
He just murmured "Toodle-oo"
Landed down in Timbuctoo
And kept on walking still".

The Big Room was divided for lessons by a screen that pulled down from the ceiling and separated the Lower and Upper Firsts. Our desks had to fold so that the room could be cleared to use for Gym. The side frames swung inwards and the top flap hinged down. This vulnerable design sometimes collapsed spontaneously, and the inkpot would roll across the scrubbed boards, ink soaking into the thirsty wood. Then the culprit would be sent racing downstairs to the dark and beetle-haunted kitchen for milk and a cut lemon from Miss Hetty. The lemon was supposed to bleach the ink, but I think the milk must have been only for sympathetic magic. White milk and black ink cancel each other out. Later, one of the maids would come puffing up with a scrubbing brush and a bucket of hot water and ammonia. A spilled inkwell could be quite a fulfilling diversion, but I do not think we spilled them on purpose at all, because the scolding for clumsiness and the rather terrifying venture into the alien cave of the kitchens, ruled by sharp-tongued Miss Hetty, were too frightening.

My desk was close to a window. A conker tree in the next door garden hung across the passage and tapped at the glass. Miss Margaret, who loved birds, hung half-coconuts in the branches, and from where I sat, I could watch the tits turning somersaults as they picked at the white meat. There were necklaces of monkey-nuts, too, and at the opposite window, the dinner scraps were put out each day on a bird-table nailed to the window sill. Here, the guttersnipe

sparrows yelled coarse abuse at each other while they paddled in the remains of the rice pudding. I had a fluttering circus to watch on either side, and my mind would drift off the mental arithmetic sums as they droned on "and seven ... and four. Take away five ... add three ..." A great tit, dazzling smart in his black hood and green coat, was considering me with a beady eye, only four feet away. I eyed him back, and after a while, he hunched a shoulder, swung by his toe nails and nibbled coconut.

·123456789·

Arithmetic was my nightmare. I managed all right through adding-up, and "taking away", though "borrowing" was always a puzzle. But when we came to long-division, I was hopelessly lost. I wanted a formula to work by, but I did not want to understand it - only to use it. Father tried to help me with my homework, but he had a different method and I frantically pushed it aside, fearful of becoming even more muddled than I was already. He in turn grew impatient because I refused to listen to the logic. It all ended in

214

shouting and tears and Sunday evenings were the blackest time of the whole week. Monday mornings when we corrected the sums were bad too, but not so bad because I was not alone. We were taught by an intense, springy little Welsh woman with crinkly hair, glinting black eyes and a temper on a very short fuse. My idiotic mistakes piled up and I made more and worse ones as her temper and her voice rose. When she finally slammed the book down on my desk and raged, showering me with spit, my mind would crumble to powder, and I would sit, numb in fingers, feet and head while the lightning played around me and the other children watched in open-mouthed awe. Firecracker Miss W gave me a fear of figures that has blighted me ever since. And yet, it was only a matter of personality - and my fear of being shouted at. When Miss L began us on Geometry, and told how the Egyptians needed to be able to mark out their lands each year when the Nile floods had washed away the landmarks, I was caught. This was practical - we made squares and triangles and cut out accurately the shapes of paper windmills. With compasses we drew six-petalled flowers and filled them in with colour. From this start I was able to carry right through my school days a pleasure in geometry, a liking for Euclid, so that at fifteen I could get 98% in a geometry exam, though I only scored 32% in arithmetic and a stupefying 11% in algebra! Miss W's hectoring was still numbing my brain.

Arithmetic apart, everything else was fun. Mlle Guibert taught us French. A devout Catholic, she used to shake her fist in anger at the foursquare portrait of Henry VIII that hung beside Mercator's map of the world with all the British bits coloured pink. Gentle, gray Miss Savery came up in the afternoons from the Montessori, and read to us, or encouraged us to write our own stories and descriptions. New, young, college-trained teachers came and went, rarely staying more than two years. They were liked or hated, judged crudely and immediately on no grounds at all. As we grew more conscious of ourselves as children, we banded together against the "grown-ups". We were not so frightened by the outside world as we had been at six or seven. Grown-ups were no longer our refuge and reassurance, so we automatically despised them, laughed at them and treated them as enemies. It was not until many years later that I was able to be open-minded enough to consider Miss L as a real person and appreciate what she was. She was enormously intelligent enquiring, well-read - an imaginative teacher. She was born a bit too soon to be able as a 'lady' to make the kind of career for herself that would have fulfilled her powers. She would have been a splendid M.P. - or a History don, or a head of a successful business. But to us she was automatically "silly old Beaky". We were blind to her remarkable good looks and too bigoted to have any idea of her breadth of mind or even to profit from it. To us it was hilarious that she worked as a V.A.D. in the war, and we sniggered at the thought of her in uniform. We were, in fact, growing into the nasty little savages children do grow into when they live in groups and are cut off several hours every day, from the civilising and controlling influences of their parents. We were just as intolerant about the other teachers. "Bobby" was popular because she was young, cheerful and unpretentious, but "Dicky" was sneered at because she powdered her nose, had her hair done at the hairdresser's, and took trouble to be well turned out. ("Bobby" cut her own hair with the nail scissors, and wore amorphous tweedy sacks!) Maggy, dear cherry-nosed little Miss Margaret, who loved us and sympathised with us and never made unreasonable demands of the young and silly, was mocked and giggled at; we made up insulting verses to be chanted privately behind the bandstand in Recess. We became a sly-eyed, sideways glancing secretive group, whose dumb insolence and unexplained bursts of laughter must have been galling and very hard to bear, to women who had given us nothing but encouragement and help. It was our nastiness, not their failure, and I doubt if it can really be avoided. Children, from eight to fourteen, are generally savages.

A tiresome little boy called Francis brought a toy car to school - one of the early Matchbox toys. He had it on his desk and kept playing with it and naturally the other boys who sat near were more interested in the car than the lesson. Francis was often a nuisance in this way. At last, Miss L confiscated it and put it in the pigeon holes at the back of the room. We heard about this and held a great moral indignation meeting. Miss L had been entirely right, very mild in her action, and Francis clearly was not bothered anyway, since he did not even ask for his car back at the end of the afternoon. But we saw him as a Martyr and Beaky as a monster of cruelty not far removed from Count Dracula. We laid an elaborate plan to steal the car back and restore it to Francis. Sally and I were delegated since we walked home and had no bus to catch. We made a tremendous adventure of it, though in fact there was no difficulty about it at all, and we went about for days afterwards behaving as though we had relieved Mafeking single-handed. We encouraged the others to glower at Beaky, and make pointed remarks (which might have puzzled her if she bothered to listen to them) about unfairness, and bullying. In short, we made ourselves wholly obnoxious at about ten years old. We behaved badly on buses, and nudged each other and giggled when Miss Margaret scolded us, and said quite seriously how ashamed she had felt of us. We got up a secret society whose aim was to spy on the teachers in the hope of uncovering something discreditable which we assumed must exist. About this time Miss Margaret, who was taking a less active part in the teaching by now, was heard bidding goodbye at the front door to a certain Mr Caldwell, and we immediately decided that he was 'a spy'. For whom or what purpose we neither guessed nor cared. We excitedly built up a web of vague intrigue and treachery that was to end in Maggy and Beaky being tried and shot! We based all this on the fact that there was no child called Caldwell in the school, therefore the man could not have been a parent - therefore he was something sinister - therefore he was a spy. Q.E.D. In fact as I realised several years later, he was an agent acting for the sisters who had decided to sell the school and retire. We, our age group, were the last to be able to finish our time at the school. What a pity we could not have been a more wholesome and rewarding lot.

Learning to read was not a dramatic or sudden process for me as it seems to have been for many people who struggled uncomprehending until one day they were looking at a page and without warning, everything slipped into place and they were reading. I remember being taught the alphabet as a kind of gibberish charm to be rattled off, before I went to school. Then in the Montessori class, my finger was traced over letters cut in fine sandpaper and stuck to attractive shiny pink cards. I think it was a good method. We learned what the letter was, the sound it made and how to write it all at once. But of course, it needed one teacher to one child and a very small class. I dare say, given those conditions, any method could be a good one.

Next we had readers, well printed with many pictures. The words were divided into syllables, and that, too, I believe is important. 'Flash cards' give a child no idea of how a word is built up, or how to break down new ones and find what they are saying.

As well as coloured pictures, these books had coloured print. When two consonants were pronounced together as one sound, we were reminded by their being printed in yellow, and two vowels in red, so yellow "ch" and red "ai" in "chair" would have two reminders about how to say the word. The "e" on the end which made "star" into "stare" or the "c" in "race" soft, was printed blue. I have one short glimpse of myself sitting at a low table by the open window and reading very slowly about Ann and Pe-ter go-ing into the shop.

Once we could read that much we moved up to the Transition class where we learned to write between double lines, well spaced, with good big heads and tails to our letters. We were taught "script" first, as it was almost exactly like print, and later on we were encouraged to join up our letters. I so liked the firm squareness of script that I was unwilling to join, until it was forced on me by sheer pressure of note-taking when I went to secondary school. Sally wrote differently from the rest of us, as she had a governess until she was seven, and learned with an old fashioned copy-book. Her letters had interesting twirls and loops which I thought very pretty but puzzling. How, for instance was her "F" related to mine? Hers went $\mathcal{f}$ and mine went f.

I was not spectacular in my progress at these skills. There were no delightful surprises in the reports that I took home each term, nothing to follow up the amazing day of the "Three Babies", which for a few short hours made my mother think she had produced a genius. On my fourth birthday, someone gave me a book in a shiny cardboard cover, with thick paper, big print and a picture on every page. It was about three children visiting a farm. (Looking back to those days, I sometimes think that ALL children's books then were about children visiting a farm). I knew some farms - Dowther's, McGowan's, MacIlgorm's - and Mother took a few moments off from the kitchen to read me the whole book. I suppose it took three or four minutes, with pauses to look at the pictures. When she went back to the cooking I brooded over my present, and when, later in the day, she sat down, in her afternoon dress, to do the mending by the fire, I announced importantly that now I was going to read the book to her. She smiled tolerantly and I began. Presently, she put her needle down and looked over my shoulder. I came to the last page; she was silent - and then said doubtfully "Do it again".

Delighted to capture the limelight I turned back to the beginning. Page after page I went through the story, exactly the words printed, stopping to point out the appropriate pictures and turning the page over at the correct time. Father came in from school and Mother looked at him bemused. "Tom, I've no idea how it's happened, but she can read!"

I was made to perform again for Father. Twice I went through the book. But on the second reading, he stopped me. His finger pointed to a word in the middle of a page - then another, and another. "What is that word? What does that say?"

Of course, I had no idea. I simply had a very good memory and repeated Mother's reading and the moment of turning over the pages after one hearing. Anyone who has told a story to a toddler knows the indignation with which your audience reacts if you alter so much as one word of your original version. I had only added a book as a stage property.

Anyway, learning to read very early is not always an advantage. Father could read fluently by the time he was four and by then he was being rigorously dragged off to Church twice every Sunday by the Presbyterian aunts who brought him up. Each time he was taken into the Church he went through a paroxysm of terror, but no one troubled to find out why. Sixty years after, he told me. There was a text painted as a frieze round the walls above the pews. It read, "The Zeal of Thy House hath consumed me". He knew what "consume" meant all right, but not what a Zeal might be. So he pictured it as a huge wild beast that lurked wheezing and growling in a dark den behind the harmonium, and he entered the Church in dread, always expecting the moment when its hunger would be uncontrollable, and the minister would toss it little Thomas, spectacles, sailor hat and all, as the handiest morsel to appease its monstrous appetite.

No one tried to teach me anything more than the alphabet and I did not go to school until I was five and a half. Missing this one term did not matter as we were such a small class we could be taught individually anyway. I was not specially quick but I was able to read simple books by my sixth birthday when I was given "Tiny Tots' Annual", and absorbed into my experience such matchless verse as

"I like Augustus. Wouldn't you?
He thinks of lovely things to do.
He gives me sweets with pink inside
And often takes me for a ride.
I like Augustus. Wouldn't you?"

It is a sad reflection that, looking at that verse now, I am extremely suspicious of Augustus for offering children sweets - pink or any other colour - and taking them for rides. That sequence spells danger in our decades, instead of the bland innocence of 1929.

If "Augustus" was a fair sample of the literary standard of children's annuals, I am not surprised that was the only one I ever received. Our home was stuffed with books, but very few for children. I can remember only two - "Tales of Uncle Remus" which I could not understand because the dialect and spelling defeated me, and "The Seashore Shown to the Children" which I read ritually every summer from the time I was seven. As soon as "Where we were going for the summer holidays" was settled, I would abstract it from the bookcase in Gerald's room, where it lived with "John Graham, Sub-Lieutenant" and "The Mystery of Desborough House", and take it to pore over. Every other page had a coloured plate - three sorts of Sea-lettuce, a Razor-shell, open and shut, the Common jelly-fish (a sort of rainbow parachute) and the Stinging jelly-fish (segmented, clear tan and as big as a saucer). All sorts of shells were there in full colour, and all my childhood I yearned to find one called the "Painted Top". Cowrie shells were shown there too, and I failed to understand that some of the shells and fishes would not be found in our cool Northern waters. The Sea-horse, the Dragonet, the Cowrie and Painted Top never came my way. Neither, thank heaven, did the Portugese Man of War, or the Squid, but I did meet an Octopus once in a scene of horror which has stayed with me always. It was at Petit Port when I was nine. Late in the afternoon when the tide was lowest, and even the deeper rock pools were warm all through from the sun, a little girl of about three

was paddling up to her rubber knickers in a pool with a carpet of sand on the bottom and waving rags of bladder-wrack on the walls. She began to scream and struggle and her father came running. He lifted her out of the pool, and, twined round her legs and body, waving blindly, was a full grown octopus. The father tried furiously to prise it loose, but as fast as he grasped one tentacle another would clamp round the child. It was worse now she could see the terrifying creature that entwined her, its parrot beak and black eyes seeming full of malice. The suckers are very strong and it was not safe to try to pull them off the baby's delicate flesh. I stood watching, feeling ill with horror and I think the whole thing might have ended tragically with a strangled child if a fisherman who for some reason was in the bay had not come running - an angel in a Guernsey and sea boots. He turned the creature's inksac inside out and this either killed it or shocked it so dreadfully that it loosed the child. It sounds, it was, fearfully cruel, but there was nothing else to be done. You could not even have used a knife safely with that writhing, hysterical baby thrashing in terror in her father's arms. Poor child. I wonder what legacy of nightmare that hideous ten minutes left in her mind.

Three years in a row, I caught one of the infectious childish ailments in the Spring Term, and had to stay home from school for several weeks - three full weeks for Chicken-pox, four for Measles and six for Whooping-cough. For these periods, I was made to spend my whole days in Father's study, a south facing room, sunny and evenly warm from the continental stove which he had wisely installed. Those were the days when servants to carry coal buckets could still be got, and the English said loftily that you couldn't feel really warm except in front of a good open fire. Germans and Austrians with their funny habits were properly despised, and it took an independent person like Father, who worried about nine tenths of his coal bill going straight up the chimney, or Ursula's Swedish family who knew from experience, to see that stoves meant a warm house, not a scorching hearthrug and a draughty cold Hell everywhere else.

Father's study was warm and it was lined with bookshelves. Two walls were full right to the ceiling. I could read anything I wanted. I think Father argued that if I could not understand a book, it was not going to do me any harm, and if I could understand it, the damage was done anyway. So in the long mornings and afternoons when I was alone, I could take out whatever I could reach on the shelves. There was a Buffon's Natural History with plenty of woodcuts of animals. There was "Swiss Family Robinson" in French, with steel engravings of Ernest riding the ostrich, the Tent House, the great iguana, the dogs in their spiked collars, the raft and the pinnace, the house in the salt-mine. I pored over these pictures so often, so long, and asked so many questions about them that during my second term of imprisonment (for measles) Father bought me "Swiss Family Robinson" in English and it filled my mind to overflowing. I read and re-read it, almost non-stop, for five years. It had everything I wanted in a story - an island world, little homes made in odd places, security in the wilderness, a spice of danger, but never enough to frighten seriously, and above all, everything always turned out well. No matter what wild scheme the boys thought up, it worked; no matter what unobtainable item was needed to carry it out, Mother was able to produce it from her enchanted bag. It would be interesting to know how many miles of 'Pack-thread' Mrs Robinson must have collected from the wreck that day they made their first precarious boat from casks nailed together and bound by planks. I revelled in such enterprises as the making of the drinking fountain in Francis' pretty turtle shell, and the manufacture of manioc bread, and sago from the palm tree. I never closed the book without feeling the glow of virtue rewarded, as if I too had been observant, had been enterprising, and had turned my education to good account.

For other reading, I had a system. It began when Father picked a dull looking brown book out of a low shelf and said "You could try reading this". I was only seven and my reading still went pretty slowly, but there is nothing like loneliness and boredom to develop this skill. The book began agreeably, with a sickly crippled boy in a wheelchair, and a strong young lad in a ragged shirt, who talked to him. Good. It was about children and I was prepared to read on. It turned into "John Halifax, Gentleman", a success story by Mrs Craik. I loved it and read it many times with gradually growing understanding and sympathy as years went on. At first, though, one reading was enough (and I doubt if I read the whole book anyway). I looked further for variety. "John Halifax" was in the "Nelson's Classics" Series, and there were a good many of these in Father's shelves. I took the next one purely because it had an identical cover.

This was stronger meat, and more enticing because it also began with children, but this time the main character was a girl, and nearer my age than John and Phineas. The book was "Jane Eyre" and its terrors and extremes fed my imagination and held me so that sometimes I could not bear to turn the page, but neither could I bear to put it down. The wicked stepmother theme, the cruelties of John Reed, the awful unexplained suggestiveness of the Red Room, the sufferings at Lowood, Helen's death - that fearful night in the Thornfield attic with the unseen mad woman growling and pacing next door - the mysterious voice at the end that called half the length of a kingdom "Jane, Jane, Jane" - all were thrilling beyond belief and at the end of my illness, I managed to carry off the book for my own, to be read fearfully before going to sleep, and to be re-told in whispers to terrify poor Ursula, who suffered from nightmares.

This system of reading books because they had identical covers led me over the years to relish some most unlikely and a few highly unsuitable books, but as I say, nobody censored and I could read what I wished. "Hiawatha" in dark red and black curlicues, led me on to "The Faerie Queen" in the same overcoat. The language of "The Antiquary" did not daunt me because I had heard the dialect spoken in Northern Ireland. I could hear the sound in my head of such words as 'aiblins', and 'callant'. "Get out o' the gate, ye little sorrow" - that was how I had heard impatient mothers address their offspring in the streets of Larne, and something even of the poetry of Auld Edie's words came through to me when he spoke lovingly of the 'burnsides' where he would 'gang daundering'.

"The Antiquary" did me nothing but good, but I am not so sure now about a rather puzzling book called "The Blue Lagoon", which started off in all the right ways with a young brother and sister shipwrecked on a desert island, but ended up with the mysterious arrival of a baby. Where did it come from?

The best book, and by far the most influential on my whole life, was Father's present to me on my eighth birthday. It was produced by the Warnes who had published Beatrix Potter, and it was (is in fact, I still cherish it) the most beautiful children's book I have ever seen, "Once Upon a Time, Tales from the Classics told for Children".

224

Thick, soft paper, clear print, immaculate prose, often ¥
the Latin or Greek original, but with most of the r
suppressed and fifty breathtaking water-colour illustrations. He
the sugar-loaf mountains round Delphi, and the dark spire
cypresses; blue, purple and lavender of the landscape, the peaco
jade and wine of the sea. One of the pictures, one which was also
stuck in a panel on the cover (whence I lifted it off and put it in a
photo frame) quite literally made me gasp with its beauty. It showed
Proserpine delicately pretty, dancing amid meadow flowers, in a froth
of pink almond blossom while hidden in the branches gazing out
hungrily at her, is the stern, rough-haired and black-avised Pluto,
waiting his moment to spring. The enchanting girl, her delicate robe
afloat, the candyfloss bushes and the fierce dark king made my heart
hammer with almost unbearable emotion. It was beauty, sheer visual
beauty, that I had discovered here, and unlike the passing beauty of a
flower or a soap-bubble, this was there whenever I wanted it - open
the book and I could drown in its sensuous delight.

I cannot praise this book enough. Harry G. Theaker - that was the
painter. Thank you, sir for your beautiful Greeks, who have never
dated because you did not make them 1929 fashion plates. Thank you
for those mountains and valleys, glowing in colour, for golden
Atalanta, and "poor lost weeping Ariadne", Icarus with rainbow
feathers springing towards the sun, and Phaeton plunging oceanwards
in a haze of flame.

Father taught me to pronounce the names properly, (so that now
I can hardly bear it when Keats himself rhymes "Prosperpine" with
"wine") and I lived for the next five years with the glory that was
Greece. The horrors in Homer were glossed over (unlike my Grimm's
Tales which often sickened me) and I had in my mind for ever the
colour, shape and beauty that really is there. The oracle at Delphi is
among mountains that plunge almost vertically. The flowers do grow
in spring as in the fields of Enna where Proserpine danced in my
lovely picture. The whole book is pure gold.

It was pictures I craved at this time. I read books and I told stories
to playmates, but if there was something inside me that was fighting to
come out, it was as a picture that I tried to release it. Self-expression, -

225

for it - was in colour and shape. Father could
...en his pictures of places were finished I could
...and be there - see it, feel it, smell it. I longed to
...ld not draw things right - and would chuck my
...ly after ten minutes because they failed entirely
...at I saw in my mind's eye. Father encouraged
...little at a time how to "make things real". He
showed me that a tree was not a mophead on a stick but a series of
Vees branching out smaller and smaller. When you tired of dividing
up Vees, you could add some spongy lumps at the ends of the
branches, and oddly enough, it did look quite like a tree. My friends in
the Lower First were full of admiration, but did not seem able to get
the knack themselves and continued to paint green mops on sticks,
sometimes with a legless bird as big as a cow sitting on top.

I learned about simple perspective and the Vanishing Point, and
I could make brick shaped houses and long straight roads that looked
convincing; I was taught also how to put in a background if I coloured
the Easter egg and chick, or the bunch of primroses that were printed
on the Children's Page of the newspaper, for a competition. I enjoyed
colouring printed pictures because the drawing was done already and it
was right. But in painting lessons at school, only disappointment came
of my efforts. I could not be happy just slapping the paint on the
paper. I saw a scene in my mind before I began, and what I produced
was a horrible travesty of that ideal. Sometimes I could forget for a
few minutes the disgust as I mixed a purple or a green that sang to me
and laid it on the page. We had not got round to mixing colours yet at
school, and my companions depended on the coarse purple, the orange
and the impossible Green Bice in the paintboxes. This last was a green
so crude that it made my tongue curl up as though I was eating alum.
I might enjoy my purple sweep of heathery foreground, but as soon as
I sat back and looked at the whole painting, I knew it for what it was -
a mess - a childish, formless, disgusting mess.

Except once. It was after I had learned to do trees, and it was a
windy day in April. "Painting" was for all afternoon. We had given
out the boxes, and after carefully removing the white china ink-wells
from our desks, and setting them on the deep wooden tray Miss L

carried round, we had each collected a ribbed glass fishpaste jar, filled it from the enamelled water jug, stood it in the ink-well hollow, and waited. What were we to paint today? Miss L sat at the big teacher's desk with a book. "Listen", she said, "then paint what it makes you think of". And she read "I wandered lonely as a cloud". I saw in my head the bare trees, like the ones outside in the Rec, their branches raked by the bouncing wind. Then below them, the waters of the lake, quaking with laughter, but above all, the crowd, the host of golden daffodils. They made a sheet of colour, heaving in ripples like corn in the wind, but they were also a million individual flowers hurling themselves from side to side, lying almost flat, falling about with joyful laughter. I was in a daze as I began to draw. Trees first - a few - then a line for the shore, and I reached hungrily for my brush and the paints. Cobalt sky - brown trees - they ran a bit because the sky wasn't dry. Blue again for the lake. Then like someone keeping the cherry on the cake till last, I rinsed my brush and turned to the glorious rich Chrome yellow. Those daffodils - I brushed on stroke after stroke of solid gold - the very essence of the flowers, until the paper was filled, and I sat back seeing it all in the splendour of the imagination.

My picture was praised. It was given Purple Plus - the highest mark we could get - and I was not allowed to take it home. Instead, as a great honour, it was to be kept and pinned up on display at the end of term when parents were invited in to see some of the best work we had done. I floated home like a gas-balloon, dreamy with achievement and pride. I thought about my wonderful picture and longed for the day when I would see it again, when Father would see it too and praise it because it was "Real".

It was only a few days till the end of term, and even my patience was not unduly strained, The afternoon of Breaking-up day came. Father was busy himself at school and could not come, but I would be taking the picture home. Mother came, to see my Composition book (Imagination good; Spelling v. poor) and my wonderful painting that I had been crowing about for a week.

I could not be bothered with books. I scoured round the walls where our paintings were pinned on great sheets of sugar paper.

"Teddy Bear" by Hubert, aged 6, Transition, "Spring scene" by Pat, aged 9, Upper First. I could see the bold yellow and blue of my masterpiece, and dragged Mother over to it. We stood in front, and even as she was saying, "Yes. It's very good. Daddy will like that" my heart fell through my boots. It wasn't good at all! It was rubbish, like all my others. Just a crude mess of colour. I didn't think Mother even knew what it was meant to be. Yet I had been so sure this time I had succeeded. In my mind I had carried my vision all week and now I looked at the real article, it was a delusion, a fraud. When I was given the picture to take home at half-past three, I took it uncaring - almost hating it. Mother, who had endured my boasting for the last seven days, talked on the way home of how pleased Daddy would be, but I just clutched my shoe bag, my case of exercise books and my sheet of spellings for the Grenfell test (5 correct out of a hundred) and plodded on in misery. <u>Why</u> had I thought it so good?

Looking back now, I believe I know the reason. A very short time after this, in the following autumn, I became actively conscious for the first time of the power of words. I always enjoyed "Recitation" and did it well, "with expression", and I welcomed any chance to show off. I think I was ready to feel the impact of language which has been the real force in my life, and what happened that day was that Wordsworth's poem, or at any rate the simple vision which is part of it, swept like fire through my mind, and as I painted, I was only seeing the vision, not my picture. The vision was still what I was seeing as my picture was marked and put away. The vision - Wordsworth's - was what I carried home and described, what haunted my eye in the dark, and what I waited in longing to see again on display. Then, when I did see it, the reality and the vision parted! I had been, I believe, affected by poetry for the first time, but I did not recognise what it was that was happening.

14. SPORTS AND GAMES

ports Day at Summerlea was the high point of the year. Even when we had a school field of our own, the Sports went on being held on Caldecott's Piece, one of the Rugby School Games fields, and practically in the centre of the town. It is the innermost of a line of playing fields that spears into the town's flank, at the apex of a triangle of green grass and trees that probes unbroken, except by one thin line of houses, right up to the shops, the banks and the bus terminus, even today. So it was here, in a quiet extension of the countryside that we were allowed each summer, to set up a hundred yards running course, to carry out every chair, bench and stool the school contained, and then to pray for fine weather. I don't think it ever rained us out in the years that I was there.

Invitations went out early in the summer term to all the parents, who were invited to attend, to take part perhaps in the Family Race, or enter their very small ones in the Babies' Race, but much more important, to contribute a Prize. This was the secret of the popularity and excitement of the Sports. It was the open policy of the School that every child should win a prize. It might only be a packet of sweets which showed that your team had won the Relay, but no child was to go home feeling he had been left out and was a failure. I think it was a good idea, and saved the day from being besprinkled with tears, and loving mothers feeling faintly indignant on behalf of their disappointed young. But it was only possible because the parents were so generous.

Every parent gave a prize, some more than one. The races were arranged to cover the age groups fairly and every race had a first, second and third prize. These were carefully allocated by the teachers, and then one day, all the prizes were set out on long tables down the middle of the Big Room. They had tickets on them, saying "8 Years Race: First Prize. Junior Three Legged Race: Third Prize (this had to be two equally matched items). Senior High Jump: Second Prize."

We walked all round gazing. We had long ago entered our names for all the events we wanted to try to win. I was swift-footed and could confidently expect to come first in my Age Race, so the first (and, just in case, the second) prizes for that were scrutinized very closely. I do remember one year being caught in a trap caused by my own greed.

I was ten, and the second prize for my Age Race was a red oiled silk model aeroplane with an elastic band to power the propeller. Gerald had had several of these and they had never flown well, being prone to nose-dive splinteringly, five seconds after take-off. All the same, I WANTED that aeroplane. I resolved not to win but to come second. Our Age Race was quite simply a contest between Sally and me, and when I really felt determined I knew I had the edge on Sally and could always beat her by just that few inches and last spurt that took me to the broad white tape ahead of her.

As we stood lined up at the starting point, waiting for Beaky's "Ready - steady - GO!" I whispered to Sally, who was next to me, "I'll let you be first this time!" Rigging a race did not seem shocking to her, or to me, though I knew uncomfortably also that I was pretending to be generous, but my motives were bad. Sally gave me a glance of admiration and pleasure. Kind child, she had no idea about that red aeroplane that was dancing along my mind as I spoke.

"Go" came Beaky's voice. We spurted off, Sally and I well ahead of the others. That is not saying much - we were a dozy and uncompetitive lot on the whole, complacent through never having had to fight for position or survival. As we neared the end of the course, I dropped back a little, artistically, and Sally breasted the tape just ahead of me. I think Mother was quite pleased. It grew embarrassing when year after year your leggy tomboy left nice little girls like Sally and Diana to take second place. I was safely second. Hubert came third. I waited in a glow of pleasure for the prizegiving at the end, under the lime trees that fringed the field. My name was called. I walked up through the scatter of clapping to receive my aeroplane - and was handed - what on earth was this? A stupid, silly shaped case with a loop on it, to carry your slippers in to parties or dancing-class! I went back to my empty spot on the grass unbelieving, while Hubert went up and received the third prize - MY red aeroplane!

It was obvious, of course, to the grown-up mind that a case for dancing slippers was not going to be much use to a boy, and a quick re-shuffle was needed. But my dismay at the failure of my mean little plot was enormous. If I had known, blow Sally, I'd have gone for the gold, and won the bead mosaic that was earmarked "First". I detested that silly slippercase. It was just the kind of girlish and prissy object that made me feel embarrassed. To make things worse, Mother was delighted. It was what she called a 'useful' prize. Something useful was what she always urged us to ask for if we were to be given a present. But this cut clean across my acquisitive nature. 'Useful' if it was 'necessary', would be produced somehow, whatever happened. It was the things that were not necessary that I craved - the joyful, impractical, daft, unexpected nonsense.

We had no serious athletics and no records were kept. The nearest we got was a very mild High Jump and Throwing the Cricket Ball. That was done in another part of the field as our erratic aim might well have blacked the eye of a visiting Mother. High jump was over a rope with a weight at each end - a comforting rope, since it was quite hard to dislodge from its pegs. We jumped straight on, bunching our legs beneath us, and clearing a good 18 inches. A young teacher recently out of college taught us to jump obliquely, scissoring our legs. We did not actually jump any higher this way, but the rope could be up to the level of our behinds, not our dangling feet and it all seemed much more impressive. I was doing rather well at this until, for some reason, I lost the knack of getting my feet back on the ground, and time after time I landed with a jar on my bottom with my legs still straight out. Father, who had dropped in after school to see the last few events, stepped in and put a stop to it before I damaged my spine.

Almost all the races were novelties, and simply good fun.

Three-legged race, Sack race, Egg-and-spoon - all these are run at the Church Fête every year still. But I have not seen the Crab race since my childhood. You stood closely back to back with your partner, linked arms and skipped sideways - easy if you practised first and learned to keep in step. We had a wheelbarrow race when one child ran along on her hands while her partner held her legs up like the handles of a barrow. "Late for the Train Race" meant starting off in pyjamas over our clothes, running to a jumbled heap of shoes where you had to discard the pyjamas, and find and put on your own shoes from the heap.

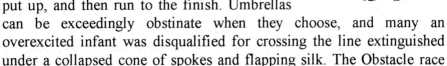

It was an advantage here to be a girl and have buttoned shoes, not lace-ups. Then you ran on and sorted out your own coat, then your hat and finally your umbrella, which you had to put up, and then run to the finish. Umbrellas can be exceedingly obstinate when they choose, and many an overexcited infant was disqualified for crossing the line extinguished under a collapsed cone of spokes and flapping silk. The Obstacle race

meant everything from crawling under a great strawberry net held tight to the ground by four teachers, to blowing away a saucerful of flour until you uncovered the jelly sweet buried in it. You had to eat the sweet before you could run on and catch and kill a sticky bun on the end of a yard of string. Hands were not allowed. Speed depended on how much dry flour you could bear to swallow along with the sweet.

The Family Race and the Babies' Race ended the programme. Mother threaded a needle with which she ran to Father, halfway down the course. He had to sew a button onto a scrap of cloth and the child raced with this to the finish. This was about the only time that we envied our sweet-tempered, gentle family of millionaire's children. They had what amounted to two lots of parents, and for such riotous occasions as the Family Race, their well stuffed Nanny in her grey coat and sensible felt hat was "Mother", and the chauffeur, full of fun and nonsense, did Father's job. Most of the real Fathers were very sedate, but Bean was like a clown, or a child himself in his enthusiasm and excitement, and we all cheered madly if Diana won, pounding down to the tape with Bean bouncing behind her, urging and laughing and pace-making for her.

Last of all, the egg-shaped toddlers, straddlelegged, heavily weighted at the base in great balloons of nappy staggered the whole fifteen yards to where Mummy crouched, calling and waving a favourite toy. Some made good speed, their little legs going round like wheels. Others gave up running, elevated their behinds and made their way grinning gummily on all fours. And inevitably a few sat down with an unexpected thump and remained rooted, while eyes screwed up and mouths squared like letter-boxes. The tears of frustration and bewilderment had to be mopped away when baby was scooped up and patted and crooned over. Somebody always seemed to have a Dolly Mixture or a Jelly Baby to pop into the bawling mouth and silence it with sweet surprise.

All this time, under the trees where the Montessori class sat on a rug every fine morning for a story, a tall tinkly piano was being played. A modest caterer would have set out card tables and bent-wood chairs, and Mothers had drifted down from the races to drink tea and eat tiny buttered scones and little sugared cakes in paper cases, with hundreds-and-thousands sprinkled on the icing. A thin flouncy lady in a flowered voile dress and a droopy Leghorn hat had fingered out an endless stream of tunes - Charmaine - Lily of Laguna - Roses of Picardy - The Merry Widow,- Alice, Where Art Thou - tea

room music sounding strange and thin in the afternoon air, with the cuckoos across at Springfield blowing flat notes to mock her sprinkled runs and trills. All through the long hours her wrists bounced over the yellow keyboard and her bony ankle pumped her foot on the loud pedal, until the last race was done and the visitors drifted across to where the fathers and children had grouped the chairs around the table loaded with Prizes.

Anyone who won more than three prizes was asked to bring back the surplus the next day, and some "Consolation Races" were run for the few, very few, who had not won any. Dear Geoffrey, in our form, was always one of these. He was by habit late for everything, his mind being happily far away exploring new ideas and fantasies. He would pound in last, even in the Consolation Race, but as he was perfectly happy that way, it did not seem to matter. We were all used to mothering "The Professor", tying his shoes, winding up his muffler, putting his cap on, and then pointing him in the right direction for home and giving him a little push to start him off. He generally got there, though once or twice he was diverted on the way and had to be searched for by his mother and the maid. After we moved to '106' it was better because Diana and I passed nearly by his gate and could launch him safely on the home stretch.

The Sports Day at my father's school (proper athletics with cheering, records to be broken and a gun to start the races) was always on a Saturday so that fathers could come and watch their sons. This was a grand occasion. Mother gave good deal of thought to "what she should wear" and I had to have my Sunday dress and a hat. We were under double scrutiny since Father was both Staff and a Parent. Gerald must have trembled in case we put a foot wrong, and Mother especially had to be very careful as she had blotted her copy book badly in Gerald's first week at the school.

He was only ten. Form One in a Secondary School was for ten year olds then. Mother had to pass the school field on her way to town, and as she walked by the palings, the boys were out for Break. A knot of younger boys caught her eye. They were holding a little lad upside down by his legs and bouncing his head on the turf. Horrified, she realised it was Gerald. A tigress aroused she threw all caution to the winds, dashed through the Field Gate and stormed into the group of boys who were initiating Gerald into the realities of life. "How dare you! Wicked behaviour - little boy - no business to hurt him ..." Gerald was reversed again, the ring of torturers goggled at Mother. Gerald wiped his nose on his sleeve and glared at her with positive hatred as she moved off with threats of exposure and punishment, if they dared to hurt her son again.

Of course, she could not have made a worse mistake if she had sat down and worked at it. Not only was Gerald a new boy, who must be taught his place; he was also a new boy who was the son of a master, and a master who was not very well liked at the junior end of the school, being merciless with idlers and oafs - that is with almost every ten or twelve year old. Now, to this handicap, Mother had added the shameful one of having a Mum who <u>interfered</u>, who ran to the rescue of her baby boy. It was not that Gerald enjoyed being bounced on his head, but he had the wits to realise that it would have to be borne for a while, and was infinitely less painful than the long torment of mockery and contempt he now had to face. Any mother would have felt as she did when she saw what was happening, but what she should have done was to walk straight on and leave them to thump his head flat! It would have been better in the long-run than what he now had to live down!

Fifty yards along the footpath from our school was the town recreation ground, the 'Rec'. It was a big square field with a fringe of lime trees and horse chestnuts all along its perimeter paths, and flower beds where it fronted the road. Here we went every day at playtime, which was called "Recess", and here also we could use a grass netball court in winter. Recess must have been long - half an hour at least - to make it worth while to lead the whole school there and back in a crocodile along the pavement. First, the children who had milk sat in a row in the cloakroom, which was a long greenhouse at the side of the school. Miss Hetty came down the line with a tray of glasses of milk and each child had to ask in French. "J'ai soif, Mademoiselle. Voulez-vous me donner un verre de lait, s'il vous plaît?" And when you had received it, "Merci beaucoup." When this daily ritual was over we lined up in twos and Beaky led us out to the Rec. Here we could play as we wished until her whistle went, when we lined up again at the great Memorial gates and were led back. Shoes must be changed each time, coats and hats hung up, then we were shepherded off to our proper rooms for the next lesson.

The Rec was a good place for play. Nearest the road, where we might see our mothers going home from town, was a broad asphalt walk with a ramp half way along, surrounded by an iron railing. Here, on the ramp, perpetually rearing up like a mastodon, stood a German tank on its caterpillar tracks - a war memorial, grey, ugly and menacing. The island it made was big enough to race round and dodge, as you could be out of sight of your enemies behind its rivetted sides. But better far than the tank was the line of pink chestnuts that edged the grass in either direction. Groups of children had their favourite trees and clustered daily about their warm, familiar trunks. Sally and I always made at once for the third from last in line - a tree which was somehow more gnarled and ancient looking than any other. The other trees sank decorously into the soil with only a token thickening at the base, but our tree put out great splayed roots above ground, that dug in like a monster hand, grasping the earth with mighty strength. Between the roots were sheltered coves, smooth and mossy, like three cornered rooms, and here we could play at keeping house. Early in June, the ground was enchanted - frothing with the rich pink fallen blossoms. You could sweep up great lapfuls of the flowers, bathe your arms in them, shower them down in lavish rain. The strange dog-faced florets fascinated us, and for a couple of weeks while they poured down from the rich branches overhead, our games were all of bridals and royal receptions - nothing more commonplace would do while the magic earth was pink as an icecream under the chestnut trees.

In October came another benison. Midland clay and Midland damp do not encourage brilliant autumn colouring, and almost the only trees that change colour reliably are horse chestnuts. A dry, sunny autumn will turn the limes lemon yellow and the hawthorns a sullen red, but mostly the leaves just darken and fall, still green, in early December. The conker trees were different. Every windy October day, we raced down the line while other children were in their tarmac playgrounds, to sift eagerly through the whispering drifts of leaves, orange, yellow, biscuit, for the spiked fruit, split like a sleepy cat's eye, with the polished conker gleaming in rich mahogany. The lining of the rough cases clasped the precious jewel within so closely, so perfectly, nesting it in sweet white leather like the finest kid. The gloss wore off soon and the lining tarnished brown like a cut apple, but the moment of finding and opening the shell and holding the perfect glowing conker with its gleaming white scar was magic then and is just as magic now - though now I always put the conker back for a child to find. However much children of the eighties spend their time in darkened rooms, nearly flat on their backs and watching "Star Trek" between their elevated and filthy trainers, they still feel the primitive conker greed when those green bullets come bounding down in the late September winds.

We played Netball in the Rec in winter and cricket on our own field two miles out in summer. Cricket was largely for the benefit of the little boys who started at our school and moved on at eight or nine to Prep school, or Grammar School. Tennis courts were too expensive any way, but one cricket pitch could be kept mown, and half the field roughly cut. The other half was left for hay. We had to go out there by a village bus, and wait, hopping up and down in the shallow ditch by the road verge for it to pick us up on the return journey. Dead oak leaves smell of raspberry jam. A new pot of raspberry takes me straight back to the roadside at four o'clock, and the smell of the crushed leaves as we scrambled in and out of the shallow dry ditch, under the oak that grew beside the field gate. Sometimes the bus was very late - sometimes it did not come at all - and then Miss Margaret, who was small and cheerful and cherry nosed, like a garden gnome but dressed in green, would squash seven or eight of us tightly into her little open topped Austin Seven, and drive us in leaps and curves back to Town. She learned very late and was never a safe driver, but she made up in verve what she lacked in skill and Ginger Bill, the Police Sergeant, used to tuck his thumbs in his belt and gaze skywards, tactfully, if she skittered round Dead Man's Corner on the wrong side when he happened to be within sight. She never lost a pupil anyway.

We played a pat-ball sort of cricket. To make two teams we had to cover an age range from twelve down to eight and though we did use a hard ball, bowling was strictly underarm. I longed to bowl overarm and go flailing down to the crease with my arm going like a windmill. I practised quite a bit for one summer in the back garden, but when the neighbours from five gardens away began to complain, I recognised that though I might have power I lacked precision.

We played a match once, against one of the boys' Prep schools that some of our brothers went on to. Our team began with Betty, a tall eleven year old, and finished with Patience who was very small for nine. She faced the bowling of twelve-year-old Clifford who was

already five foot six, a sturdy country boy. His first ball bounced and hit Patience in the eye. She was carried off the field. The following week educated us all in the astonishing and murky colours a really good black eye assumes on its progress. Long before Patience had paled to the hue of stale mustard, it had been decreed that we would play no more cricket matches, since no one else could produce a team as feeble as ours. Patience was a heroine. Her father was the Rector and was shortly to become a Bishop. Patience was the only one of his four children that I shared classes with, but older friends of my brother's told me that the other three were traditionally irreverent about their father, and that his eldest son used to say that "Father preached the same sermon Sunday evening as he did Sunday morning, only Sunday evening he took his dentures out and nobody could recognise it".

The School Field was rough pasture that needed taming as a games field. So every afternoon we spent up there, we had a stint of "work" to do. We were doled out daisy spuds and set to go about the mown part, jacking up dandelions and plantains, or else we were all given a pair of scissors with dull blades and blunt noses, and we had to crawl down yard wide rows, cutting off bents. The slowly revolving mowers of those days would not sever those wiry springy flowering stems of the tough grasses.

The term after the famous cricket match, we challenged one of the elementary schools to a netball match, to be played on the grass court in the Rec. They undertook to send a team of similar age to ours, and we eyed them when they arrived with a certain snobbish contempt. They were one of the poorer schools, from the far end of town down by the railway. They were small - mostly a lot smaller than we were and had peaked faces, or else enormously fat cheeks like half balloons. Their school hats were like the caps our housemaids wore, only of navy blue wool. Most of their gym tunics were grey with age and had been handed down from older and larger girls. Our sea-green serge and cream tussore, that had to be ordered specially from Liberty's, looked exclusive and superior as we waited in a huddle, not quite sure how to behave as we had never been hosts at a match before. "Slum children" I am sure was in all our minds. I know it was in mine. I was not concerned about winning, since the game bored me, but I took it comfortably for granted that we were socially superior and would naturally win.

We went to our places and the whistle blew. It was like playing against a team of well-trained cats. We flumped and blundered about in our usual self-satisfied way, with soggy knees and ankles, and arms flapping uselessly like wet fish - and among us darted and snatched the thin, eager little girls, literally running rings round us as we lurched, bewildered by their speed and grimness. They were there to win. They cared. They knew about competition and the effort needed for survival. We had spent our lives in cotton wool, the good things coming to us by right, we felt, and without our effort. Before the shriek of the whistle was out of our ears, the other side had a goal. If we ever did get near the goal-post, our shooter might have five or six shots and the ball would bounce off the post uselessly. Their shooter would poise for a second, one foot backward, balance the ball on her spread fingers and shoot. First time, every time, it slipped sweetly through the net, and twenty-three times it did that in the course of the match, while we scuffled and fell over each other fruitlessly. I trundled about helplessly trying to mark my opponent, but she moved with the speed of light and I could just as well have stood still, for all the good it did. They were used to playing on tarmac - they were neat-footed, alert and aggressive.

At the end of the match, 23 - nil, when Beaky led us along the pavement back to school, she scolded us all. She was red faced with the humiliation, but we were merely stunned. Those "slum children" I had despised, had shown us up as incompetent, and a gleam of understanding came upon me that the social order might not be irreversible; in fact, it might not even be right!

The winter of 1932 was very cold. There was no snow, but the frost deepened day by day, stifling sound and slowing life down to a crawl. We stayed in school for Recess and danced "Sir Roger de Coverley" and "The Post Horn Gallop" in the Big Room, rather than face the whistling cold in the Rec. At lunch time Ursula, Sally and I, John, Giulia and Christopher, gathered in the cloakroom, huddling over the hot water pipes in our coats and gloves, until we were shooed out and told to go home. Then we scampered in a bunch - past the Rec - Ursula spun in at her gateway. Giulia next, then me. John and Sally, scarlet cheeked and blown, had to stand in the cold on the edge of the road until the maid slipped on her coat over her apron and dashed out to see them across.

One morning, Miss Margaret announced at Prayers that the ice was bearing on the old arm of the canal, and those of us who had skates might bring them back to school after lunch, and would be taken skating for the afternoon. How many thought they would be able to go? Perhaps ten eager hands shot up, straining their owners sideways with enthusiasm. Mine was among them. But I had no skates.

Since 1927 we had had mild winters and there had been no skating. That winter, though, when Father made us the toboggan, there had been a flash frost after the snow had melted, and the flooded fields of St Thomas's Cross had frozen over. The water was shallow and here and there grass blades and twigs poked up through the glassy floor, but day after day, the schoolboys and masters had cycled out there instead of Games, to skate. Then one day at tea time Father had been brought home in Colly's car, semi-conscious and bleeding from a great gash on his temple. He had tripped on the rough ice and knocked himself out. He was lucky not to have killed himself.

I had often pondered over his skates since that alarm. They were screwed to the soles of his fine leather boots and the more I looked the less I understood how people could stand up and move about on knife blades! As Miss Margaret spoke, my plan came full blown to my head. I would go skating too. I would wear my own shoes and put my feet inside Father's boots and skates and so make my feet large enough to fill them adequately. It never struck me that I would look like Mickey Mouse, and in my desire for this new experience, I certainly never allowed myself to think that the whole scheme was utterly impossible. I skimmed home for lunch and announced my plan over the stew and boiled potatoes. Father looked at me with amusement. "Well, of course you can't go", he said. "You haven't any skates or boots". I explained my idea in a tumble of words, and I had built up such a total belief in it all being feasible that when he continued to deny me, I did not believe him. As repetition and "No, no, no" began at last to penetrate, the disappointment was more than I could bear. Of course, the child who began to cry into her pudding was being silly and spoiled, but I had so utterly believed I could go skating. It seemed to me I was being wilfully frustrated. I was not given to crying desperately by this time unless I was frightened, but that February dinner time, the sun darkened, the world was hostile and my own family became a ring of cruel, jeering strangers. I was coated and hatted and sent off to afternoon school too wracked to know or care what was going on and the sullen heaviness wrapped me all day.

Father seemed to have understood the depth of my disappointment. He came home after school with a pair of skates for me. They were clever. They had expanding clamps and a key to wind them open and shut, so they could be screwed onto the thick soles of a boot of any size. They were a beautiful blue steel, hollow ground and sharp, and I had them nearly all my life. But boots - they were expensive. I only had shoes and my feet grew fast. Buying a pair of boots for perhaps a few days' skating, to be out-grown by the next time we had ice, was beyond the budget. Father called on a friend who had three boys and a girl and was able to borrow a pair of sturdy boys' boots, a bit too big, but nothing that a couple of pairs of Gerald's socks would not take care of, and the next day, a Saturday, Father took me off down the road, over the railway line and to a shallow field pond where cattle drank. Here on a piece of ice about the size of the Big Room, I learned to keep upright, most of the time anyway. Skating was a surprise - rather like the surprise I felt when first put on a horse - nothing stayed still! You had to cope with a fluid situation and be in control though your feet were slithering off and there was nothing to steady yourself by.

The ice held for a long time that year, and at weekends we were able to go to the lake in the grounds of Newbold Revel, once the home of Malory of the "Morte d'Arthur". Here there was space for ice-hockey games organised by our friend Mr K and in the bays near the bank, where bleached rushes stood locked in whispering ranks, I and the other novices could shuffle and stagger and occasionally feather stitch a few glorious yards on the ice. It was mysterious and awe inspiring to gaze down through the clear surface, seeing the stalks of the rushes recede into bottle green dark below, to see the trapped bubbles frozen to their stems, and realise that we were walking on the water. The forget-me-not blue of the sky, and the lavender and damson etching of the bare woods sharpened as the sun went down, and groups collected round the few cars, to drive home. I had to sit on the spiky frozen grass for Father to loosen the clamps of my skates with the little cranked key like the starting handles of the cars waiting for us. Then with our skates tied with string and hung round our shoulders, we tramped across the slippery grass banks and the sugar candy gravel to pack into the draughty cars. The starting handles were swung, the engines spluttered at last, and with blue exhaust blown into the cold air like the wind from Cherubs' cheeks in the old maps, we shuddered off into the dusk, towards the beaded loops of soft yellow lights where the town straggled up its long hill to the church towers at the top.

Skating was wonderful, the nearest we can come to flying. You move with swiftness, little effort and no friction. I loved it and could feel the motion still as I closed my eyes at night, rather as you feel the ground unsteady even after you have stepped off a rocking boat. But I never had the smallest wish to go to skating rinks. Skating, and swimming, for me, must be under the sky. Indoors they are like trapped butterflies, caged and unnatural. So skating has remained a rare pleasure, only to be indulged when the frost was long, open and hard. Four inches thick the ice had to be on the old canal, and six at Newbold Revel where the lake covered some acres and had running water through it. Flooded fields froze quickest and were safe if the ice did break, but they were dangerous too because of the broken branches and tufts of grass and weeds that jutted through the surface.

The children played games they made up - stories they invented, or embroidered onto real incidents. I was chief story teller and the games would grow from my tales. But some games seemed spontaneous, like "Gianty". This was played on the huge, solid, highly polished dining table in Ursula's house. I think now that it was very forbearing of Ursula's mother to let us do it, because buttons and belt buckles would have scratched the polish badly. But she always was most forbearing over our games, and I suppose we can not have done any damage or Gianty would surely have been stopped. It was played by one of us lying face downwards on what felt like half an acre of

table top, and sliding and spinning round on our tummies, trying to catch the other two with a hand over the edge, as they crawled round the carpet and in and out beneath the table. It could be hot, riotous and dizzy as Carl and I grew reckless in the risks we took and Ursula spun red-faced to either side, stretching until her legs waggled in the air, and trying to touch us as we scrambled to safety in the dead centre underneath. If we both made for this haven at the same time, she could reach underneath and touch us with a fingertip, so one or the other had to break for safety. It was a good game. It was just as exciting to be the hunted rabbits on the floor as to be Gianty, and so there were no quarrels or peevish complaints of "It's my turn now". The game would go on until the rabbits' knees were so sore from scraping over the carpet that we all thankfully gave up.

Telling a story and acting it out is the most universal children's game. It may be Mothers and Fathers, or Doctors and Nurses, or, more likely, some adventure that starts from a book and develops as it goes along. With Ursula and Carl, the game always involved Secret Passages. There was a secret passage in their garden and it came into every game. A tall doglegged fence shut off the back yard and outhouses from the lawn outside the drawing room. A yew hedge had been planted against it long ago, and allowed to grow up into trees. Beneath this, between the trunks and the fence, it was dark. Branches had died, leaving a tunnel through which children could crouch and run. You slipped into it through a thin place low down by the house wall, and could creep along within arm's length of the grown-ups in their deck chairs, and not be seen. The tunnel emerged into sunlight by a rockery, overgrown with alkanet and ferns. It was a wonderful 'prop' for a game, and our stories would always involve an underground passage from a castle, or more likely, one behind the panelling of an "Elizabethan Manor", since they were my passion at the time. It would involve danger, escape from enemies and the bonus of a hidden treasure at the end. I am quite sure that as Ursula's mother and the two beautiful grown-up sisters sat in deck chairs in the sun, they registered every brushed twig and stifled giggle in the yews behind them, and probably realised that they, a graceful and elegant group of lovely young ladies, were, in truth, coarse and cruel foreign soldiery, or the grasping relatives of three intrepid children, striving to save their rightful inheritance from the plausible and cruel uncles and aunts who had superseded their own dead parents. What is it about being an orphan that is so appealing in the games of childhood? Is it a half-realised desire to be free of the control of adults, or is it a playing with pathos, injecting emotion into lives that, with luck, have never yet known real sorrow? Whatever it is, we were always orphans, and in all our best stories as well there were twins - brother and sister. That, I could believe, might be the expression of the child's desire to be of both sexes. But if that is so, it ought to be less evident now, when conditioning to sex early on is at least recognised and frowned on. Even now, the stories written for homework by my twelve-year old pupils have just as many twins in them as they used to have forty years ago.

My memories of games with Ursula and Carl are always of summer, Saturdays, or long, flatly lit evenings when both sets of parents felt it was fighting the grain of the wood to require us to go to bed at a sensible time. From the age of seven, I was allowed in summer to stay up and play until, say, nine o'clock. The battle over bedtime used to begin about six years old. We said among ourselves that "when you are six, you go to bed at six; when you are seven you go to bed at seven; when you are eight ... " and so on. This broke down for me in the long light evenings, when Mother realised that forcing a rebellious brat, brimful of energy and annoyance, to go to bed while the thrushes were still triumphing outside was only asking for trouble. Once I realised that no pressure was being put on me to go to bed, I would peaceably drift upstairs with Pussy, when I was tired, or there was nothing else outside worth waiting for. Modern parents have a more difficult job. Whatever time they try to drive their children off to bed, there is always some highly unsuitable T.V. programme just half-an-hour, later, which their offspring are furiously determined to watch, especially when it is the Late Night Nasty!

Play with Sally was emotionally and socially very important in my development, but it was more restricted than with Carl and Ursula. There were places and times when Sally and I could be together, outside school. In the simple black and white of my very early days, I had decided to hate Sally. But our mothers were friendly and exchanged tea visits, so I found myself expected to play nicely with Sally in her home, when on school days I was one of the hallooing mob that chased her through the Rec on the way home.

About this time I had taken to reading snippets from the newspaper as I followed the daily adventures of Japhet and Happy and the Noah family. One day I read in a sob-sister column about two girls who had been inseparable friends for the astounding, enormous time-span of nine years! I felt I would like to have been the heroine of such a news item, so that afternoon, when I was taken to tea at Sally's I said abruptly to her "Sally, let's be best friends, and then when we've been best friends for nine years, we can write to the newspapers about it".

Sally agreed. She was always an agreeable person. From that time on we did all the things that best friends do. I called for her in the mornings and we walked together to school. We sat next to each other in class, and chose each other first when picking up sides for games. This tremendous change had taken place on the last day of the Easter holidays, and must have bewildered some of our mates, who were used to seeing me organising ambushes for Sally and watching my bottle green coat chasing like a demon after her purple tweed as she fled down the pavement to the sheltering presence of Rhoda, the maid, waiting to take her across the road. But childhood memories are short, and it was soon accepted that you need never send two people to look for Pat-and-Sally.

Sally's mother was a widow with one young daughter when she married Sally's father. He was naturally more possessive about his only child than most of the other fathers in our circle who would have been delighted if their children had melted into thin air except at such times as it was congenial and convenient to have them around. Our fathers loved us, but they did not want us children cluttering the place up all the time. Sally's father did. So play with Sally was limited, and was probably more precious to me for that reason.

My games with Sally were largely based on a history book we had at school. It was full of pictures and was called "The Manor House". It showed the way of life, the clothes, food and customs, the sports, work and games of a Lord of the Manor's family and servants in the late sixteenth century. This was backed up by the stories Beaky told us, all the proper tales of the period of the Armada, the game of bowls on Plymouth Hoe, of the Golden Hind, of Queen Elizabeth and her three hundred dresses, and above all Raleigh putting down his cloak for Gloriana to walk on.

Then there was a book of sample Christmas cards that had been thrown out at Sally's father's office. One card drew us back again and again. A rose brick front of a great house with stone mullioned windows and a porch. A man in doublet and hose and a short cloak was dismounting from a black horse, and being greeted by a girl in a farthingale. The house walls were draped in the scarlet of Virginia Creeper. I am sure that was an anachronism, but to us in our dull Midland town, it spelled Romance. We called the house Guilford Hall and invented a great serial story about it and its inmates that went on after school day by day for years. Everything Elizabethan seemed wonderful to us then, even those clumsy, over decorated clothes. No, especially the clothes. My dreams were haunted by the desire to be allowed to cut long slits in a pair of my green serge bloomers so that I could put another coloured pair inside, stuff them enormously with newspaper and have a pair of puffy knickers worthy of Sir Walter Raleigh. Sally and I would scheme and contrive for a whole winter afternoon, with borrowed nightgowns, a velvet party cloak, cushions and string, to dress ourselves as Queen Elizabeth and Sir Walter, all to enact a little scene lasting about one minute -

Q.E.   Alas, if I walk across this road I shall get my shoes
         muddy!

Sir W.   (whipping off the party cloak and laying it the length
         of the hearth rug) Gloriana, pray walk upon my
         cloak.

Q.E.   (primly) Thank you Sir Walter, you are gallant. (She
         walks down the rug, and Sir W. kneels on one knee
         gazing after her).

                    Curtain.

Then, with perhaps a few minor adjustments with pins or string (Gloriana's farthingale had an unnerving tendency to slip) we would go through it all again, and part at six o'clock to dream up further perfections, rarely attainable, in our costumes.

Sally's mother did add one item of dress which made us feel we were the genuine article, and allowed us to boast that when we dressed up we had "real ruffs". She gave us a box of twelve elaborately pleated paper pie frills, which could be stretched round our necks, and carefully coaxed together again afterwards for use another time. They were exceedingly uncomfortable, scraping our skin but the authenticity they gave was worth it. And I dare say Sir W. and Q.E. suffered even more from their starched ones. I had at one time a dress with an organdie collar that nearly sawed my head off. I hated it but I was happy to tolerate our paper pie frills.

Ursula, Carl and I acted plays as well. The drawing-room in their house was a double room divided by a curtained arch, and such an arrangement demanded use as a theatre. We were not usually allowed in there - after all, their long-suffering Mother needed some refuge in a house where three children were given the freedom from attic to cellar. But we did once make up a play and got a concession to present it in the drawing room, with the brown chenille curtains that opened and closed with a string. The play was about a King, a Queen and a Prince - because Ursula's great longing at the time was to be a boy. I do not remember the play, but I do remember the audience - Ursula's mother, and Betty and Doris, the two maids, invited in to swell the ranks. And when we took the hat round afterwards, we netted three halfpence, riches that justified a thoughtful visit to the corner shop, and the immediate planning of

250

another and more ambitious play. I don't remember that second one ever being performed. I expect the audience had taken all they could bear.

Play changes, of course. Two toddlers squatting in the gutter, crooning over a leaf-boat or a little pile of mud and sticks, are often glad of each other's company, but their "play" is quite independent. A companion toddler gives the impression that the world is on their scale, and that is comforting, but there is no exchange of ideas or constructive game. Our game of 'Gianty' was the invention of seven-year olds. The play we acted, which required the three of us to work together, came when we were eight, as did the drama of Sir Walter and Good Queen Bess. By the time Sally and I were nine, one of our form who was ten, had read a detective story - the Butler had "dunnit" and at Betty's summer birthday party, in her large and mystifying garden, where I could never make out how one part linked with another, this story was transformed into a game - a game of chases and deceptions that somehow caught all our imaginations, so that we went on with "Beach the Butler" every Recess through that whole long autumn term. There was no particular story, although Elizabeth would gather us all round now and again and refuel us with another situation. All I remember of the game was the breathless excitement of it all - events did not seem to be necessary - or even two sides in the struggle. I think we were all on the same side, and it only needed one of us to point to empty air and say "Look - I'm sure I saw him slip in among the trees" for us all to race off, hearts pounding and thrilling, in pursuit of the entirely imaginary butler. Wordsworth speaks of the "organic pleasure" and the glad animal passions of childhood and I think he was right. Excitement and joy are there, fizzing in the blood, and need little, or no stimulus, to bring them gushing out..

It was playing this game, on the afternoon it began, that I jumped a flowerbed in my excitement, from lawn to crazy-paving path, and tripping over a lavender stump, fell and gouged a good teaspoonful of flesh out of my knee. Up till that moment, a fall if it brought blood, meant crying. Perhaps that day I was too excited - or perhaps Betty's mother was on hand too quickly, tactfully praising me for being so brave - but I was mopped up and bandaged - even had some iodine put on, without fuss. I discovered, to my surprise, that it didn't seem worth crying about, and I remember resolving as I walked home after the party, that I would not cry any more. It was a stage in growing up, but a very early one because I was not able to imagine, at that moment, any reasons for tears other than injury and pain. I had experienced grief, when my little cat was killed, but I somehow thought that crying belonged to infancy, and grief would not affect me in that way any more.. I still lived, at nine, inside the glass bubble of childhood, and imagined that grown-ups were a different kind of being, and were invulnerable and immune to suffering.

15. THE KEYS OF THE KINGDOM

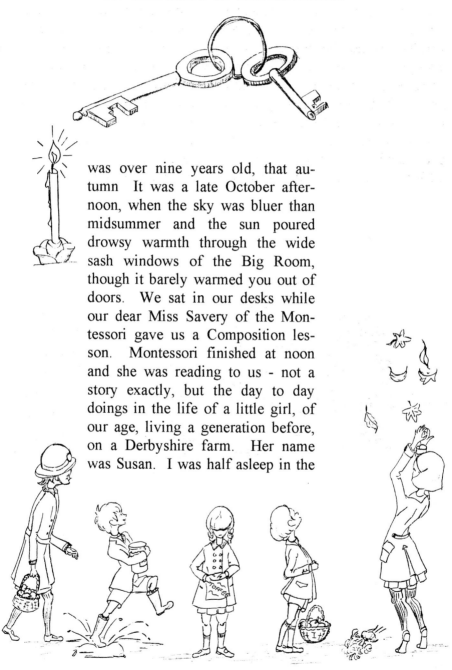

was over nine years old, that autumn It was a late October afternoon, when the sky was bluer than midsummer and the sun poured drowsy warmth through the wide sash windows of the Big Room, though it barely warmed you out of doors. We sat in our desks while our dear Miss Savery of the Montessori gave us a Composition lesson. Montessori finished at noon and she was reading to us - not a story exactly, but the day to day doings in the life of a little girl, of our age, living a generation before, on a Derbyshire farm. Her name was Susan. I was half asleep in the warmth, and my drowsy eyes wandered from the great billowing elm tree in the garden, still harsh and blackish green as in summer, to the acid yellow of the limes in the Rec, and beyond them the cloud shapes of our beloved conker trees, pale orange, gold and copper, glowing in the sun, and clear and crisp against the deep blue sky. Some windows were open and I could smell dead leaves, and bonfire smoke. We were quiet and sparrows had come to the bird table outside the window to peck and scuffle for the dinner scraps.

I liked autumn better than spring. There was nothing special to do in spring, unless you counted bringing sticky-buds indoors and watching them unfurl in a vase of water. But in autumn there was colour and warmth. We had Harvest Festival, when we picked long trails of Virginia creeper off the garden wall, and wound it, unbelievably scarlet, round the balancing beam and the screens and on the dark wood of the window frames. We threaded hundreds of conkers on strings and hung them like swags of beads among the creeper. We picked the yellowest, the reddest, the most brilliant leaves and gummed them in patterns for the walls. We took our offerings of apples and jam and honey to an orphanage on the other side of town.

Miss Savery's voice murmured on as I dreamed. Scraps and details of what she read swam in and out of my mind. Milky mist, curling in the hollows of the ground; a triangle of cobweb, strung thickly with diamond drops; someone's cap filled with mushrooms, white suede like wedding gloves. The little pictures followed one another, until I found myself sitting up and paying attention to what was read. I had a tingling at the back of my neck and a stretched feeling over my scalp - the physical signs which in after years signalled to me that I had met poetry, the real thing, head on. I was seeing the pictures, seeing them because of words! Words could paint pictures - paint them on your mind and it did not matter if you could not draw. The words would do it all. It was a time of revelation - when I strode from one kingdom to another, when I grew ten feet in half an hour, when horizons melted and fell limitlessly away - when everything was possible.

Still dizzy from this amazing discovery, I took my chewed bone pen when Miss Savery finished. "Write your own description of Autumn", she said, and the words tumbled crudely on to the page, but I looked, and saw, and what I saw I had words for. One chestnut tree in the next door garden nearly touched the window where I sat. Its leaves were large like fingers, I said, and some were brown, some yellow, some orange. But when I looked at the trees further off in the Rec, they seemed orange all over. I knew, I said, that if I went to them, I would find their fallen leaves thick on the ground, smelling a bit like mushrooms, curled with crisp edges, and shiny conkers hiding under them. The bonfire smoke was blue, I said, but not the same blue as the sky. But Autumn was nice, I said, because of the colours; I liked to see the leaves yellow or gold, or scarlet or the colour of plums.

Drunk with new power I wrote on and on until I was stopped with amusement when the tubular bells were rung by the monitor whose pleasant task that was for the week. "What", I asked Miss Savery, "was that book you read from?"

"The Country Child by Alison Uttley".

That was the first time I had asked about a book because I wanted to read more of it. Mrs Uttley gave me the keys of the kingdom.

That was an experience of complete happiness. Words could paint pictures, flawless ones, with no bad drawing or muddily mixed colours. A few months later I was taken farther, to the knowledge that words can be the complete experience, sight, sound, emotion and understanding, and it came without any warning and left me thunderstruck, actually rather frightened at the force I had discovered.

Dent's "King's Treasuries" Series had two little volumes of Modern Poetry, and mooning about the bookshelves (they were like a drug to me now) I leafed through one of them. I had known them in a vague sort of way ever since my measles and whooping-cough spells in Father's study, when I had read and enjoyed the following:-

"Three Jolly Farmers
Once bet a pound
Each dance the other would
Off the ground."

and "It was early last September,
Nigh to Framlingham-on-Sea"

Now an angel led me to John Freeman's

"Music comes
Sweetly from the trembling string,
When wizard fingers sweep
Dreamily, half asleep,
When through remembering reeds
Ancient airs and murmurs creep,
Oboe oboe following..."

and the sounds of the instruments were heard in
my head.

"Flute calling clear high flute,
Voices faint, falling mute
And low jarring drums."

I felt it again - the tightening of the skin over the temples and crown, the tingle in my spinal cord - as I read on

"Was it the wind in the reeds?
Did the wind range
Over flute and oboe pouring
Solemn music sinking, soaring
Low to high,
Up and down the sky?
Was it the wind jarring
Drowsy, far-off drums?
Strangely to the brain asleep
Music comes."

The return in the last line to the words of the opening, the echoes of sounds, the unanswered questions - the dream state - it was all an experience so full and overpowering that I could hardly bear it. I could not have talked about it. It was not like my daffodil picture when I wanted to boast and show off. It was too big for that. It was something almost dangerous, and I returned the book to the shelf guiltily, as though I had pried into secret matters not meant for me. I was afraid, even ashamed. But I knew I would never again be able to keep my hands off for long. This was force, strength, angels of thunder and lightning. It might dissect me, destroy me, but I was the elected victim. I would have to know more.

Learning is what we do mostly in school and is a slow, step-by-step business - but it advances steadily. Education, which is knowing how to cope best with life, goes forward in leaps, and is unpredictable. I asked for music lessons (Sally had music lessons). They turned out to mean practising five-finger exercises and scales instead of going out to play.

"I want to play tunes".

"You have to do exercises if you want to be able to play tunes properly. Sally practises half-an-hour every day".

Sally's front room had a fire in it every day. She did not have to sit in a draught from the cold north window and pound blue fingers up and down the icy keys. But that was learning. Eventually I was allowed to master a piece lasting forty-five seconds called "Lullaby", and I was very pleased to play it, with a great deal of fussing with the piano stool, and insistence on total silence, when Mother had ladies in to tea. But when after Prayers one morning at school, Roger was asked to play his "examination piece", and he sat down quietly, forgot all about us, and played a Chopin Study, that was education - mine, not his. Not only because the music was immeasurably more advanced, but because it really mattered to Roger, and what was more, he was two years younger than me I was silently humbled. I saw myself in proportion for a moment, just as I had done years before when I smashed my little tumbler in an imperious bid to get my own way, and was coldly told that unimportant small persons must await the convenience of their elders, even when the elder in question was the maid.

Groups of children are like dogs - they work out who is the pack-leader, and as with other wild creatures, the leader is under constant challenge. Pack leaders among children are often saved from defeat and humiliation by passing on and up to a new level of their society - a new school, a new form, a new activity which takes them beyond the reach of their ambitious peers. I would boss anyone I could induce to accept my bossiness, but in turn I was quelled by other children. Carl and I were amicable equals for a couple of years. Then Carl began to develop beyond me. He was going on to his "boys only" prep school and part of the new ethos was to despise girls. I began to fear his roughness and contempt, and to turn more to Ursula. The two of us together could just about match Carl, though I remember a day when we failed. We had settled down to have a private girls' tea-party, using the child's tea-set Ursula had been given for Christmas. Kind Betty and Doris in the kitchen had given us sugar and milk, small bread and butter, and made tea for us in the little flowery pot. They had even found coffee-spoons, small enough for the saucers, and put dainty tea-knives out and jam on a minute glass dish. We sat in a glow of pride at the corner of the great dining table where we played Gianty, and sipped with little fingers crooked. Ursula was mother and poured pale fawn tea into egg sized cups. Then Carl arrived and demanded to be included. He had a wicked light in his eye, that warned us that he meant to break up our girls' play.

He started by raiding the bread bin and coming back with a couple of doorsteps and a seven pound stone dripping jar which he dumped on the lace-edged cloth laid for us. The scale of our dainty party was ruined. That great stone pot loomed over the flowery cups like a coal-scuttle, and his doorsteps were bigger than the plates. Next came the Lyle's Golden Syrup tin. Carl plastered dripping on his bread and syrup over the dripping. He demanded tea. Ursula drained the pot but there was only half a cup, so first he drank the remains from the milk jug, then he up-ended the pot and turned the tea leaves out on to a plate. Finally he emptied the sugar basin into his half cup of tea, stirred it to a gluey sludge and slurped it noisily. All this time, though Ursula had at least protested, I had sat numbed and cowed. I did not even go to fetch Betty, who would have put a stop to it at once, as he

was covering the cloth with tea-stains and smears of dripping.

This is the power of the aggressor; shock can hold the victim silent. I recognised the behaviour when I read Sally's "The Tale of Two Bad Mice" - sheer pleasure in offending. All children do it when they get the chance. I would lord it over Ursula in my turn, as long as I could, and as she was more than a year my junior, I could pull rank fairly easily. But one day, we were sitting at my dining-room table, colouring pictures in books. I had my "Tiny Tots" Annual and she had brought a similar book of hers. Heady with colour, I was painting in a group of children. Their clothes could be any colour I wanted and I joyfully followed my fancy, ignoring probability. A dress was orange with big purple spots. A boy's shorts yellow with green zig-zags. I raced from picture to picture, while Ursula concentrated on one. I jeered at her slowness. "I've done four and you haven't finished one yet".

"I must not" said Ursula calmly, "go over the line".

I was arrested. I watched her. She was younger than me, but her concentration was complete. She kept her hand, still a dimpled baby hand, rock steady as the loaded brush moved carefully. Not a smudge, not a blur, marred her picture. She took the details one by one. Her boys' shorts were grey. Her girl's dress was pink. Nowhere did the brush stray outside the printed lines. Silently I admired, and uncomfortably had to admit that though she was younger, she was better at it than I was. That took some swallowing.

"I'm tired of this. Let's go and play in the lane".

When you are not winning, always change the rules!

With two men and a tomboy in the family, Mother always had a workbasket full of darning. Socks were made of wool, and we walked everywhere, so large holes known as "potatoes" wore in the heels. Mother tried desperately to keep abreast of them, but to do so she had to cobble the holes. The first thing was to go over all the socks as they came out of the wash, and darn over any thin parts. This would save them for a week or two, but meant that when they did wear into holes, the remaining fabric was taggy with darning wool. Swiftly Mother would weave from side to side, darning needle threaded with double or quadruple wool to fill the hole more quickly. If the criss-cross proved too loose and was letting her fist show through she would go over again roughly from corner to corner. The mended sock would in the end have the hole filled all right, but filled with a thick, lumpy and bristling patch rather like a bit of badly worn doormat. That was darning. I never felt any surprise at it. That was how you had to deal with potatoes.

At school, we had a family of sweet-tempered children who had a lovely old-fashioned milk-bottle shaped Nanny in a grey gabardine coat and felt hat. She looked after their clothes, and one day when I was about ten, I was putting on my shoes in the cloakroom next to Diana when I caught sight of a big darn in the heel of Diana's neat grey sock. I stopped to stare. Nearly the whole heel had obviously been a potato, but now it was a neat fine square of meticulous weaving, perfectly matched and as smooth and regular as a piece of cloth. This was the first time it had ever struck me that such a mundane and boring task as darning could be done well. I had a hole in the thumb of my woollen glove and I walked home considering. I had seen Ursula's mother darning socks. She had a wooden mushroom, and I could see the advantage of having a surface over which to pull the work taut. My glove? I laid my plans quietly, and after tea I searched the knife drawer for an old dinner knife with a thick handle which would fill the thumb of my glove. Then I carefully wove up and down, so that I had a thread for every row of knitting, and caught the worn stitches at the outsides safely. There was real pleasure in the accurate weaving back and forth and by going very slowly and carefully I produced a neat, close even patch on my glove that won praise and approval from Mother, harassed as she was with her mending basket boiling over. This was a step forward for me; for the first time I had enjoyed the results of patience, and I was able to believe that patience could bring rewards to other, and more forbidding tasks. This learning how to learn, and how to outface difficulties is a lesson we all need and it had better not be left much later than ten years old!

Not long after this, in my flush of pride, I consulted the section on Mending in a six volume "Book of the Home" my parents had been given as a wedding present. There I found how to do "Swiss Darning", which is a way of mending a hole in knitting so that the mend looks like knitting itself. I was allowed to try it out on a hole in the front of one of Father's old pull-overs, and the result was so good that I was appointed invisible mender in chief when some garment had a hole in a very conspicuous place. I was not overworked - our socks continued to have Mother's doormat heels - and I smirked with pleasure whenever my work was pointed out to visiting ladies for tea.

Most of the steps forward I took in adjusting myself to the world were painful or embarrassing ones - exercises in humility, since I thought a lot better of myself than anyone else did. The darning was a pleasant exception. Social matters were constantly tripping me up. The number of things you were not supposed to mention was bewildering. Why was it so wrong of me to tell Mrs C that we did not buy those linen tea-towels with a red stripe down the middle and 'Glass' woven into it, but used instead worn-out sheets torn up and hemmed by Mother? Why did Sally's father frown and tell me sternly I must never mention "that word" when I said I had read in the paper that Mr and Mrs George Arliss were among the few couples in Hollywood who had never been divorced. The world was very puzzling and after many, many occasions when I was scolded as soon as the visitors had gone for my stupidity in letting the side down, I grew afraid to open my mouth in company. Then I was scolded as well for sitting glumly, and contrasted very unfavourably with Mary, and Ruth, and Janet, who could chatter brightly and make charming conversation while handing round the cups of tea. That summer, we went, after a gap of many years, to Ireland to see the relatives on both sides again. That was the summer I got my head full of nits, and had no idea what they were. I met a family of children to play with and one day their mother asked if I would like to stay and have tea with them. They lived in a low stone cottage near the shore, but I knew many families living in similar humble houses. We sat at table and there was a big steaming aluminium pot of tea, a pile of soda bread made on a griddle, half a pound of butter on a plate, and as a treat, a delectable sort of thin biscuit called "Slims". The girls reached for soda bread and handed me some. I split my triangle across and took a lump of butter from the dish. I had been taught that when I was out to tea, I was to put butter and jam on the side of my plate, never directly on to the bread as we did all the time at home. This saved me from total disgrace that day. With a hunk of butter as big as a golf ball on my plate rim, I was just about to spread it all, lavishly, on my soda bread when I caught sight of Amy, the eldest girl, staring at me in astonishment. What had I done wrong? Surreptitiously I scanned the table, and saw the two younger girls buttering their bread. They had each taken a slender scraping of butter, no more than a curled shaving on the knife, and were spreading it thinner than tissue on the cut surface of their scones. We did not reckon ourselves well-off at home and had many economies that I knew my friends' families did not have to practise, but it now came to me that to these new friends, butter was an extravagant luxury, and what I had on my plate and had only just stopped short of spreading thickly on one side of my triangle, would have done all three girls for the whole meal.

I did what I could. I took a shaving off the lump and meagrely skimmed the scone. Amy's eyes dropped, and hot with discomfort, I munched dry soda bread, leaving the shaming yellow nugget on my plate when I had finished, without comment, and I have no doubt it was restored to the butter dish in the kitchen when the table was cleared.

Being cut down to size is a painful but necessary part of education. Gradually, I learned what I could do and what I could not; my attempts to boss everyone round me were foiled - my playmates were as self-willed as I was. Sometimes, my exalted ideas led me into really public humiliation, as when I decided, without consulting anyone else very much, that we would act a Form Play and perform it to the whole school. Sally thought it would be fun and so did Ursula, so I gathered all the others one wet Recess and told them. "We're going to do a play. You'll all be in it and I'll be the Producer". Betty, Jean, Diana, Geoffrey, Norma agreed doubtfully. "What play will it be?"

"Oh, I'll choose the play".

"What shall we wear?"

"We'll find something".

The next day, largely I believe to show off my superior knowledge of the Classical stories, I brought along a one-act play from a book at home, about Ulysses and his men on Circe's island. The others didn't like it. Not that I gave them a chance to read it; I was taking it for granted that they would do what I told them. Ursula always did when it came to acting (provided she played the part of "The Prince", never "The Princess"). The mutinous cast took a look at the book and decided that any play including characters with impossible names like "Eurylochus" was not their cup of tea. I had no idea of compromise. I simply doled out the parts, keeping Ulysses, Eurylochus and Circe for myself, Ursula and Sally. The slaves were ordered to learn their words and be available for rehearsal after school the next Monday. Meantime I burned my boats by going to Miss Margaret and telling her we were doing a play and would like to perform it to the School. She was all smiles and encouragement, and wholly unsuspicious, bless her, so she booked us a date in about three weeks when lessons would be suspended for the afternoon and we could put on our show. She arranged for us to have the Big Room to rehearse any day we wanted and promised the Acting Box would furnish us with Greek tunics. There were plenty of these, luckily - two squares stitched at the shoulder. What school acting box does not overflow with these, and with large baggy sateen bloomers which are vaguely 'Elizabethan' as the tunics are vaguely Greek?

I remember that rehearsals were few, ill-attended and stormy, and only two days before our performance, I was still raging fruitlessly at my crew who did not know their speeches, their cues or their moves, and who were only concerned at the time with scrapping over which costumes they should have. If I had possessed a cigar I would have bitten it in two. I was worried, but still had no idea of what lay ahead. "You must learn your parts" was my last word to the cast, and two days later, afternoon lessons were cancelled, chairs and the gym benches were set out in the Big Room, all the rest of the school including the Transition sat waiting for us to emerge from the top of the Cloakroom Staircase.

At last, down in the Cloakroom, Jean and Betty had fought it out over the purple satin tunic and Geoffrey had been persuaded to take off his thick grey socks, and was being chivvied barefoot and protesting up the stairs. Sally and I made our entrance backed up by the Crew. For a few moments all went well. We two knew our parts, but when the dialogue spread out to the rest, the prompter had most of the work. I was furiously hissing directions. "You're supposed to go off over there, you silly".

> "Well, don't shove- 'I think, I will go and explore the island' ".

Prompter - "Come with me, my friends".

> "Oh - 'Come with me, my friends'. What do I do now?"

The audience was bewildered; Miss Margaret tried to look patient, but Beaky was furious. After five minutes more, she spoke aside to Maggy, who nodded. Beaky got up and clapped her hands.

"It is quite plain that your play is not nearly ready to show to anyone. We will stop now. Get changed into your proper clothes and we will have lessons as usual".

My shame was unbounded, and I brooded over it for several days. I was ten at this time. I tried to take out my disappointment by blaming the cast bitterly. "You never tried properly", I complained.

"You fooled about and didn't learn your parts or anything". I got the answers I deserved, bluntly and openly. "We didn't want to do the play. You chose it. We didn't like it. It was dull, and anyway, why should <u>you</u> give all the orders?"

It was a hard lesson to learn, but I was lucky to learn it relatively young. Of course, I tried again, many times, to carry others along with me in schemes about which I alone was enthusiastic, and failed. I started magazines and had to write the whole of issue two after a fairly co-operative issue one. I tried other plays, and organised picnics and team games and secret societies. They failed - but I was at least prepared for difficulty; it never shocked me so much again, and I did learn gradually to give way, to persuade, and to listen to others' wishes instead of expecting to bulldoze them all my way, believing that I was admittedly better than they were and had therefore a right to be obeyed.

Not long after we had moved to '106', I was in the kitchen with Nellie, the last of "The Darlings". Even in the seven or so years that I remembered, feeling had been growing against 'domestic service', and there were other ways for girls to earn their living. Work in a shop or in the light bulb factory was probably harder, but it was more sociable. Poor little Nellie worked for us only till 3 in the afternoon, but she was solitary. There were no other young people for her to chat with. Three of us were out at school and Mother had to go out for shopping and visits. I think Nellie had been reluctant to come to us, and after she left Mother decided to do without a maid as we were no longer babies and could very well help with washing up and errands. But the idea of future change had not occurred to me. I was leaning on the table while Nellie polished the brass and copper kettles. It is typical of the way I took privilege for granted that I was standing there idle and never offered to polish too.

Nellie was youngest but one in her family; after her came the Twins. I said "First we had Elsie, then Marjorie, then you came, Nellie. I suppose when you leave us, Vera will come".

"No", said Nellie firmly. "Vera's not going out to service. She's going to the High School".

I absorbed this. The High School was a County Grammar School.

Girls from Summerlea did not go there; we went to another private school for the "Daughters of Gentlemen and Professional Men", and the school buildings were only a few doors away from '106'. It was approaching the time when I would have to be transferred to this more advanced establishment, and within months my comfortable complacency was shattered. The school moved to a country estate twenty miles away and pupils had to be weekly boarders. Father did not beat about the bush. Gerald was within a year of University and Father announced that he would not be able to afford to send me to a private school. He did not pretend to be sorry since he knew that I would get a better education by going to the High School.

My first, shameful reaction was horror. I saw myself as losing face among my friends who were all going away to boarding schools. My second was the appalling realisation that I would be separated from Sally, whose father would have no financial problems. But deepest and darkest was my feeling of shock that I was to be sent to the same school as the maid's sister. Sheer, inexcusable snobbery of the nastiest kind, for I loved and admired the Darlings, and I am thankful to recall that I kept this particular objection to myself, because I was just old enough to realise that it was disgraceful. But it was deep all the same, and when a year later I went alone, in the summer term, to the High School, I went resentful and prepared to find fault. I was amazed to find when I got there that I was in the same form as one of my old playmates from the lane behind '62', and several other girls I had known all my life were there as well. The following term, I was joined joyfully by Sally, whose father could not face the prospect of sending her away and seeing her only for a day and a half at weekends. From the moment Sally arrived, we took possession of our inheritance and grew, learned and laughed our way through a wise and generous education for which I could never show enough gratitude.

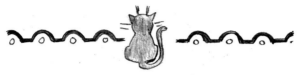

rowing gradually as the years went on, was my understanding that other people were real, like me. At seven, Brian was my best friend for a while. On Friday we were happily planning what we would do in Recess next week. On Monday he was in school. He never appeared again. I asked no questions, scarcely even wondered where he was. By Tuesday, Norma had replaced him and he was - not so much forgotten as swallowed by oblivion. If I had seen him fall overboard from a liner and sink into the ocean I would probably have turned away and looked for a new playmate just as indifferently. It was not that I cared for nobody, but Brian was not real. He only existed at school. I knew nothing more of him, not even, perhaps, his family name. I had never seen his home or met his parents. He was printed flat on my mind with no depth. If Sally, or Ursula, had vanished I would have been in distress, angry, lonely and rebellious, demanding to know where they were and to have them brought back. But they were people, like me. I ran in and out of their homes and recognised and greeted their parents if I met them in the street. But the other children with whom I never played except at school were no more than faces in the class, and evaporated like puffs of smoke when the school bell rang at half-past-three.

Cautiously I began in time, to probe for the depths in other children's lives. I started to piece together the facts that Christopher wore a kilt and sporran at parties, that his father spoke in the same way as my uncle and aunts spoke in Northern Ireland, and that Christopher brought heather and Edinburgh Rock back to school from his summer holidays. Giulia's mother redecorated her nursery for a girl of eight instead of for a toddler. We were taken to see it when we went to Giulia's birthday party. The carpet was pink and covered the whole floor. Curtains, dressing table and bed were draped and frilled in crisp spotted muslin, tied with rose coloured ribbons. Privately, I was awed and carried the picture home in my head, to imagine Giulia reading a book in that pretty pink velvet chair, sleeping in the canopied bed, burying her toes in the rosy pile of the carpet, and doing all these things when I was not there to see! I began to realise that she had a life independent of me.

At School, a few children had to stay to dinner, and a handful actually boarded there from Monday to Friday. Their double isolation began to draw my curiosity. I had seen the maids setting up the trestle table for dinner in the Big Room as I withdrew down the boxed-in stairs to the cloakroom, outdoor shoes and home. I questioned a dinner girl.

"What's it like staying to dinner?"

Pause for thought, then, "Miss Margaret says Grace".

Yes. I could picture that. We never said Grace at home, but at Peggy's summer parties out at her aunties' farm, we all had to stand round the jellies and the birthday cake while a strange formula was mumbled.

"What do you eat?"

"Mutton stew".

Ugh! grey meat with weirdly shaped neck bones, transparent blubbery gristle and lengths of white nerve like worms.

"And semolina".

"Do you have to eat it all up?"

"N-no. We can put it on the bird table sometimes".

Most of mine, I felt, would have ended on the bird-table.

But if the lives of the dinner-children were strange, what about the boarders? When I was safely home having tea, with a fire crackling behind my shoulder, Pussy purring and Gerald enthusing about Neville Loveitt's motor-bike, they would be eating their tea in the yellow electric light of the room where we learned French verbs. What did they do all the long evening? Did they take any of their toys

270

to school? What would they do if they had a tummy-ache in the night? I tried urgently to imagine the daily routine of my life transferred to school, with TEACHERS to replace Mummy and Daddy. The more I thought, the odder it became. Think of meeting Maggy on her way to the bathroom, in a dressing-gown and slippers. Think - how extraordinary - of having breakfast at school. My imagination could just encompass dinner or tea, but breakfast somehow seemed impossible. And imagine having Maggy enquiring if you had "been" satisfactorily afterwards. My thoughts shied away with a snigger of sheer embarrassment. But throughout my speculations, the idea was developing that the other people in the world did have backgrounds, routines and feelings just as I did, even if I knew nothing about them.

Transition, Lower First, Upper First, Second Form, Third Form - gradually we climbed the ladder, going up in groups as time went on, since we were now taught more as a class and less as individuals. The boys mostly left from the Upper First, to go on to Prep Schools or to Form One of the Grammar School. Girls generally went on to boarding school after the Second Form, so the Third Form was an elite of only half a dozen children. Sally and I were among them. Sally's father did not want to send her away from home but otherwise did not really know what to do with her. My father could not afford boarding school and in any case preferred that I should get the more demanding education of the Girls' High School. I did not know this and still snobbishly imagined that I would join Ursula, or Betty or Giulia, who had already left. Diana's father did not want her to go away either, so he compromised; he persuaded the Headmaster of the boys' Prep School her brothers went to, to take Diana, the only girl in a school of boys. So I lost my companion in the campaign to evade Terrible Theresa who ambushed us on our way to school. So many of us were leaving that dear little Maggy gave us all a picnic on the last afternoon at the field. Instead of cricket and catching practice and a ten-minute stint with a daisy-spud, digging out plantains, we had lemonade and sugar buns, and plates full of raspberries brought from Beaky's garden in huge glass sweet jars. There had been eighteen of us in the Second Form, a stable group of old friends, with a well-established pecking order. We had almost all been Brownies; we had had our Secret Society; we had acted plays - successful ones, not like my disastrous "Ulysses and Circe". We acted "Toad of Toad Hall" with lively Dorothy in a marvellous Toad costume of green eiderdown, her legs and elbows bent outwards and her eyes gleaming through the open mouth of the wide flat head. We did two plays in French. Mother was annoyed when I was cast as the Ogre in one. I wore a crêpe hair moustache stuck on with unreliable sticking plaster. "What shall I do if it falls off?" I asked Mlle Guibert.

"Just say 'Oh, la, la, cette moustache', and stick it on again", she replied.

What a pity it stayed on after all.

By ten we had all found self-confidence. We no longer clung to grown-ups for safety, venturing out a little way only when we could speed back again if things got awkward. We now saw ourselves as a strong, clever, self-sufficient group, and grown-ups as silly, fussy, grotesque, in fact "the enemy", and we despised them. Of course, we still required their services, to prepare treats for us and look after all the tedious details like seeing we had food to eat, and our socks mended, that pennies were supplied for bus journeys and the Swimming Baths, that we were up to date with the latest crazes, and had Yo-yos when everyone else had Yo-yos, and leather pencil cases with zip-fasteners when these put out of fashion the old wooden ones with three layers of slides. But nevertheless, grown-ups were foolish, outdated and inferior to US.

This smug self-confidence, irritating and unjustified though it was, had its uses. Because we supported each other, we no longer looked out on the world as a place of danger, where we were at a disadvantage. Instead, we began to watch its antics as we would have done a circus, seeing the behaviour of its inhabitants as a comedy which only we could appreciate. The grown-ups might have been fish in a tank for all the sympathy we had for them, but we did observe them, and if we laughed, we also became aware of some of the problems of life. Maggy's old father lived at the school. He would shuffle about quietly, and if he met one of us in the passages, would point his walking-stick at us, twinkle his rheumy blue eyes and say

"Bang, You're dead!" One of Maggy's sisters had a minor accident in the Austin Seven, and their Father was bruised and shaken. That, of course, was hilarious. "Trying to kill off the old man", we crowed in the Rec at Recess. But a few weeks later, 'flu and pneumonia took the old man in earnest, and we were silently shocked and I hope a bit ashamed. His little pointed silver beard and shuffling slippers vanished from the quiet corners of the school.

The Town became a Borough and Mr McKinnell, our grocer, was the first Mayor. We were all taken to a great ceremony in the Rec, and I discovered to my secret surprise, that the bandy-legged delivery man in polished leather gaiters, who drove a pony trap and brought our weekly order on Thursdays, was not, as I had imagined, Mr McKinnell. Mr McKinnell was not even the tall thin man in a calico apron down to his ankles, who leaned over the counter and discussed pickled walnuts and candied peel with Mother. He was a smoothly convex gentleman in a long red robe and a three-cornered black hat!

Little Patience, whose eye was blackened in a cricket match by Clifford's bowling, was going to leave us to live in Cornwall. Her Rector father was going to be a Bishop. We knew quite a number of Rectors and Vicars, Curates and Ministers, but Bishops were getting a bit too close to God for comfort! I was glad I was not Patience.

We had an election, another eye-opener. It seemed that "the grown-ups", so united in keeping us under their thumbs, did not agree among themselves.

There were different Parties to which you could belong and Sally started coming to school wearing a big blue ribbon rosette, like a prize cow at a show. I demanded a similar rosette and was good-humouredly supplied with a purple one. "Why purple? Sally wears a blue one."

"Sally's father is a Conservative. Daddy is a Liberal".

It seemed - or at any rate it was rumoured - that there was yet another party, vaguely shocking, which wore RED rosettes. "Labour" they were called, and my ten year old friends said, quoting their parents no doubt, that they were dangerous and would destroy the country "if they got in". I was not at all clear what that meant. Surely they were "in" already, that was the trouble. They lived down near the Railways and their children went to elementary schools, and were uncomfortably swifter and sharper than we were, as we found when we played them at Netball. It came as a very considerable shock when I heard Father at the dinner table speaking with sympathy and some respect of the aims of this dreadful Labour Party, though he was still voting Liberal at that time.

If our little Form group had been the only one to which we belonged, it would have been very bad for us. We were exclusive, self-satisfied, cold and sneering about the rest of the world. There was no one in a party of ten year olds to make us think, or feel, or care. If we mothered Geoffrey, the last boy among us, who was too delicate for another school yet, it was because he was one of us, not because he needed extra care. But we were lucky; other influences were there to give us standards worth following, so that for part of the time at least, even if not always for the right reasons, we learned to think a bit about other people's needs and to try to be less savage.

It is easy to laugh at the Brownies and all too many youngsters do so cynically now. It is not their fault that advertising and the entertainment industry have encouraged them to model themselves on monsters and perverts, but it makes us all the more thankful for those who do care about justice, sympathy and restraint. Brownies caught us just as we were ready to enjoy being part of a gang and gave us group activity and a naive pride in making the world a pleasanter place. This was nicely fitted to our age and ability. One good deed every day; be helpful; speak the truth; learn useful things like reef knots. A Brownie meeting was largely team games and stories as we sat round in the Fairy Ring, but it taught us a bit, too. We had Sixes, and the older ones in the Six had to help and teach the Recruits.

When it was time for the Fairy Ring we came prancing out of our corners in a line, chanting

"This is what we do as Elves,
Think of others, not ourselves".

or others singing,

"Here we come, the friendly Pixies,
Helping Mothers when in fixes".

Childish, ridiculous - maybe. But if a child is to be "conditioned" to a way of thinking, and they all are, I would rather it was by this kind of propaganda than by sleazy sex and the drugging effect of heavy rhythm.

Brownies did us a great deal of good and Brown Owl, a gentle girl who lived a lonely life like a Princess in a Tower, in a dark house shut off by high walls in the town, was one of the very few grown-ups who never raised her voice to us and never needed to. If we were too unruly, she just waited, and we quietened down. She brought us so many pleasures and treats that we knew we were robbing ourselves if we went on rioting, and excluded her suggestions

Dr Barnardo's was another good influence on us. A speaker came to talk to us and get support among schools for the Homes. We were ready and eager for anything that seemed like belonging to a Society. The speaker caught our interest because his speech was almost all stories about orphans who had come to the Homes. If we were to form a group, we would pay a shilling a year subscription, (that meant asking at home), would get a magazine quarterly and, most enticing of all, a collecting box which we could keep at home and bring in to be opened when it was full, or once a year. It was the collecting box that did the trick for most of us, because it was well and sturdily made in the shape of a little house about eight inches long. It had a porch, chimneys and gables in the roof, and was papered with windows and doors, bricks and tiles, roses up the walls and children peeping from the casements. It was so enchanting that I could not wait to belong and have one of these little houses to stand on the hall table at home. I am sorry to say that my box never got more than a few pennies in it in a year and I expect that was the case with most of them, but it gave me a glow of virtue to think I was collecting for children who were not lucky, like me, and glowing with virtue was a fairly rare experience for me about that age!

The magazine was far more effective. Sally and I, poring over it, found much of it devoted to the names of children who had made special efforts to raise funds for the Homes, and the amounts they had made. Joyce and Betty Hudson of Leicester had raised £5.00 by a Sale of Work. Alan Wright had made £1.00 by exercising the neighbour's dogs. Linda Rowe and her mother had held a Bazaar and made £17.

We were fired to try as well. We would hold a Bazaar.

When we talked it over with Sally's Mother, we began to realise what a lot of preparation and organisation would be needed, but that in itself was a gain; we had gone to a grown-up sensibly to discuss difficulties. She helped us with scraps of material to make needlecases and penwipers. Father got us offcuts of leather from the Art School and showed us how to make bookmarks. Later he borrowed us a punch and we made simple purses. Scraps of the left-over parchment from his belly-dancer lamp-shade became bookmarks too, and he showed us how to paint hollyhocks on them with simple blobs of colour. Sally knitted square kettleholders; I made woolly balls for babies.

When we felt we had enough, we got on to the interesting part, the selling. We decided to put all our goods in an attache case and go from door to door. Father told us we would need a Hawker's Licence to do that and we were stopped dead in our tracks. Then he relented. He did not think anyone would complain about two little girls selling for Dr Barnardo's, as long as we only went to people we knew already. So we had to promise not to go to any strangers. We counted up all the houses in the area where we could claim at least nodding acquaintance and felt there was a profitable number. So one sunny Saturday morning we set out, feeling enormously important with our case, and well-drilled by our Mothers in doorstep politeness.

We were going to work down the road from Sally's and then back up on our side. We came to a corner house. "It's Miss Grey's". said Sally.

Miss Grey (that was not her real name) was the sister of a Very Exalted Person Indeed!

"Do you know her?" I asked.

"Well, we say Good morning on the way to Church". Sally replied. "I think that's all right".

We knocked at the door. The Charlady opened it, not the maid. She had concertinaed stockings, three aprons and a holey cardigan. Sally eyed her, disapproving. "May we speak to Miss Grey," she said at her haughtiest.

The charlady looked us up and down. I began to feel uncomfortable and to make a move to retreat. At last, in ringing and cultivated tones, the charlady spoke. "I AM Miss Grey", she stated.

I escaped, blushing to the ears, but Sally stood her ground and sold her a twopenny book mark!

Our reward came, not from feeling we had done something to relieve the needs of the orphans, but when we read our names in the magazine - "Sally C and Pat R held a Bazaar and raised eight shillings and sixpence".

It was not exactly a fortune, but ten shillings, they told us, kept an orphan for a week in those days.

The Town was spurting into growth. Our solid Victorian houses, three storeys high with cellars, and coloured glass panels in the front doors were rented, but now land was cheap, and people were beginning to build their own houses further from the centre. Father bought a plot on the way to Summerlea field, and set about saving what money he could by designing his own house and doing most of the architect's drawing. It was all too remote to have any impact on my mind. '62' was home and always would be, and I peered contentendly through the yellow, the blue and the red glass in the front door, and wondered why the neighbour's porch looked so attractive through the yellow and so dismal through the blue; I bounced on the boughs of the laurel below the yard, and wore a groove up and down the lane to Carl and Ursula's, never imagining that anything would ever be different. But change was coming. Ursula was going to boarding school. Her father was about to retire and Sally's father would succeed him as Chief Engineer of Steam Turbines. Sally's father was buying a big house on a hill slope, with a huge garden where only part of the grass was mown short, and the rest was a-flutter with tiny wild daffodils and grape hyacinths in the spring. Even in the holidays, we would all be separated, a mile at least between each of our houses. But then, a mile was not as long as it used to be, and we were beginning to be trusted out on bicycles. The changes, when they came, brought more freedom, new people, an inrush of fresh ideas and stories. There was a ghost that began to haunt Bilton churchyard, and we went on our bicycles to shudder deliciously round the place. An old lady, Mrs McQueen, who lived opposite Sally's new house, was a miser. She dressed in rags, and always pushed an old barrow full of mysterious bags when she went out. Her house was locked like a gaol and the postman, looking through the letter-box, saw rats running up and down the stairs. The mound where our new road crossed the Sow Brook at the bottom of the hill was where they buried suicides, because there used to be no cross-roads in the town. There was a marvellous place down a little side street off Dead Man's Corner, called the Public Library, and you could have a ticket for nothing and borrow a new book every day if you wanted.

Books, by this time, had become something I could share and talk about. When at ten, I found Freeman's poem, "Music Comes", it was a secret experience, one I would have shuddered at having to explain or even reveal. Now the Library gave me limitless reading to fill long hours when I could no longer go out into the lane and play with Ursula. I could show them to Gerald and he put me onto some writers I was proud to enjoy because I felt superior when I said I was reading Hugh Walpole's "Jeremy", not "Peg of the Brownies". I had looked at the newspaper daily anyway, for years. It was the old News Chronicle, and had Horrabin's comic strip, of the Noah family. They lived in Ararat Avenue, and the chief characters were Japhet, the youngest son, and Happy, the dumpling-shaped little bear. Oswald the tortoise, Belinda the ostrich, and Polixenes the parrot, shared their adventures, and they sailed on a voyage in the Ark, and were wrecked on a desert island where they lived on the fruit of the Golobosh Tree, a sort of giant raspberry with a pineapple tuft. As I followed Japhet and Happy daily, an occasional headline or advertisement or scrap of verse would catch my eye. Re-armament was an issue and a weekly column of satiric comment provided me with jingles that stuck in my head even when I had no idea what they were about.

"First it was hats, then it was peas,
Then it was Oswald Mo -
Now by Golly, it's aeroplanes,
Aeroplanes all in a row.
Forty thousand aeroplanes
His Lordship wants to buy.
Others may rule by land and sea,
But Britain shall rule the sky".

I knew something about Oswald Mosley, but who was the
Lordship who grew impassioned about peas and hats?

The Cricketers' names attracted me in this next rhyme, but what
fixed it in my head was the enchanting picture it conjured up of a
bow-fronted Bishop in a poached-egg hat, his gaiters twinkling like
Pickwick:

"When Bishop Jardine dances,
The Loves and Graces sing;
Pomona featly prances,
When Bishop Jardine dances,
And Flora leads the Spring.
Each bud doth now unfold it,
The which the sweet bee robs,
When Bishop Jardine - hold it,
I mean Archdeacon Hobbs."

It was certainly not about body-line bowling, but what cricketing cause célèbre was it?

Headlines caught my eye and I read about the kidnapping and death of the Lindbergh baby, and later had my sympathies roused by the plight of Bruno Hauptmann as the courts played cat-and-mouse with him. Experiences beyond my own or my friends' were just beginning to claim my interest and feeling.

Father decided it was time I saw a little more of the world and took Gerald and me to London, sightseeing. Gerald had been taken to the Wembley Exhibition before it closed in 1929, but apart from that,  all we knew of London was from hasty taxi rides from Euston to Waterloo station to catch the boat-train. We did a lot and saw a lot that day with Father, but the memories I carried away are not the ones Father took me for. I do recall the unbearable glitter of the Crown Jewels in their barred glass cases. We went to the Zoo but I remember no animals except the grey squirrel on the entrance drive in Regent's Park. I offered it a piece of biscuit as it swirled like a leaf around me, and bit my finger. We went on a ride upstairs in an open topped bus and saw no end of famous sights, but I noted only Fleet Street, because it was where Japhet and Happy came from. At Madame Tussaud's I insisted that I wanted to go with Gerald and see the Chamber of Horrors. We went down some dungeon stairs with painted canvas walls, and the second step from the bottom let out a dreadful groan and scared me rigid. I refused to go any further. I hope Gerald did not miss his treat but Father had to take me back upstairs. I think my instinct was right. Years later I did visit the horrors and have been haunted ever since by the bloody spectacle of a medieval Italian method of putting prisoners to death by slinging them up from the roof, impaled on enormous meat-hooks driven through the living flesh.

Of Westminster Abbey I recall nothing and at St Paul's I shamed Father dreadfully. We got off a bus and I saw those huge broad flights of stone steps soaring up to the portico. Spiritually cramped by a day on my best behaviour, I weighed them up with my eye, and then set off to shake the fidgets out of my legs by racing to the top. A man in black with a funny hat was walking sedately down and I was not looking where I was going. I thumped into the buttoned cushiony waistcoat and heard the air forced out. Muttering "Sorry" I sped on and turned at the top to see Father, very embarrassed, with his hat off, obviously apologizing for me. He came on up, looking flushed and most annoyed at my rudeness. "It would have been bad enough", he said, "whoever it was, but - that was DEAN INGE!" When I was asked at school what I had done on my day in London I was able to reply with pride that I had knocked the wind out of the great Dean of St Paul's!

That summer, after several years in Guernsey, it was time to go and see the Irish relatives again. Granny Gillespie was dead and Aunt Charlotte lived alone in Mother's family home. We were able to stay with her and visit Father's aunt and uncle across the ferry at Larne. I had not seen them since I was four and now I was old enough to judge them as people, not as overshadowing shapes of authority. Aunt Rose, the merry one, had died, and Aunt Mary Ann was short, dark and sharp tongued. She seemed to quarrel and scold perpetually, and drooping, ineffectual Uncle Tom took his depressed-looking six-foot four out of her way when he could. Father tried to keep the peace between them but I never wanted to visit at the Nursery.

There was another uncle of Father's, Malcolm, whom I had never heard of before. He also had a Nursery, at a place called Glynn, on the other side of Larne Loch. Father borrowed a boat, a heavy rowing-boat with a single mast and a lug sail, and took Gerald and me out on the loch to teach us a little about sailing. Larne Loch is shallow and we stuck spectacularly eleven times on sandbanks in the falling tide. Father made us each take the tiller, but I was confused at having to push in the opposite direction to the one we wanted the boat to go. Eventually, he told me the story of the skipper who said to the novice: "Look, I don't mind you steering Ss, and I don't mind you steering Zs, but when you begin steering Os, I give up!"

We landed at Glynn and took this new Uncle Malcolm by surprise. He was just like Uncle Tom, six foot four, grey and stooping, but he lived alone with no one to sour his temper, and he gave out a warmth and joy that I had come to think the Nursery folks could never possess. He drew Father beaming into the kitchen exclaiming "Dear Tom, DEAR Tom!" He held us both at arm's length searching our faces lovingly, so that you had to smile only looking at him. He gave us stale mouse-smelling biscuits and tea that would have tanned your boots, and they tasted delicious. He carried us off to see his gardens,

283

where he picked me a green rose - a wizened looking little curiosity, but I kept it and pressed it. He talked with Father about plants as one expert to another and described how he got most of his scanty income from selling pittosporum to the Belfast florists' shops. He told us how to make a green carnation, by putting a red one into a bottle with a little ammonia. It worked too, but smelled awful. As we walked reluctantly back down the village to the shore and our boat, he was followed by a tail of shy little children, and when we reached the jetty he dug his great knotted hands in the sagging pockets of his coat and brought out a bundle of penny sticks of chocolate which the little ones had clearly been expecting. Father protested gently, but laughing. "Uncle Malcolm, I'll swear you have nothing to eat for yourself in the house but you buy chocolate for the weans". (Wee ones).

We waved him goodbye and rowed offshore. I saw him that one day and never again, but I loved him and never forgot him. He was poor, shabby, a failure and a darling!

My education continued. We had Runabout tickets on the railways and saw the Mountains of Mourne and the Giants' Causeway. The train ran through flat boggy land where the air swam with the vile reek of steeping flax. We went on the Belfast and County Down line which was reputed to be so unreliable that when the train was heavily loaded, as on an outing to a football match, the passengers had to get out and push. That may or may not have been true, but Father was certainly not lying when he said that on some gradients it travelled so slowly that he used to get out, pick flowers on the embankment and get back in again before the tail of the train had caught him up.

He took us to Belfast, where many of the streets were still paved with wooden blocks that could be rooted up and made good ammunition in "The Troubles", not so long past. We had lunch in a restaurant, a new experience for me, and I had to be taught not to whisper but to speak out if I wanted something, and how to work from the outside inwards through the regiment of cutlery that flanked my plate. At home I was used only to a knife and fork, and a pudding spoon across the top.

After lunch, Father took us on a sentimental journey to "Inst", the great Belfast Public school where he had taught before he came to England. The building was empty. It was the middle of the summer holiday and only the dusty sunlight shifted on the stone floors. "We'll just take a wee look at the Staff Room", said he, pausing outside a door. "There'll be nobody here".

He pushed open the door and we walked in. A shaggy grey man with an untidy moustache was sitting sideways to us, writing at a table. Father's face lit up as he looked at him. He touched his lip to signal us to silence, and stepped across to stand before him. He stood for a while not speaking. At last, the grey man looked up, a little annoyed at a stranger invading the place. "This is the Staff Room, you know. Can I do something for you?"

"Hello, Carl", said Father.

The man looked puzzled, scanning Father's face. Father deliberately took his pipe out of his pocket, held it between his teeth and began to ruffle up tobacco from his pouch. Something in the action struck a chord in the grey man's memory. He leaped out of his chair and strode round to Father, arms flailing in exuberant welcome. "It's old Tommy Rodgers, by God! It's old Tommy Rodgers".

For me in the doorway, the world stood on its head. My serious, sedate, highly respectable, awe-inspiring Father being called "Old Tommy Rodgers" and liking it! I think that was the first time I saw Father as a man in his own right, independent of me, a man who had a life before me and apart from me, a man who could appear young, not much more than a lad, to this dusty grey old mop who was thumping him on the back and beaming, and saying "I knew you as soon as you stuck that damned pipe between your teeth, you old villain!"

For the rest of the afternoon he entertained Gerald and me with tales of Father's misdeeds as a young master at Inst, and his skill at eating and talking at once at the dinner table, while his colleagues hung on his outrageous words, all so that he could finish before they did, and have time for a pipe before the table was cleared. I did not mind if Father and Carl Brierley forgot Gerald and me altogether. I was entranced. Listening to their talk and shouts of laughter, horizons melted and vanished, never to return again, as my world expanded, and I could see that the years before I was born, or Gerald, even before Mother was "Mrs Rodgers", had been real. Father had been young - must once even have been a child, playing with his brother John who had died so suddenly four years earlier, leaving my unknown cousins Pearl and Balba fatherless.

I will not try to convince myself that that afternoon at Inst in Belfast changed everything for me. I know it was not so. But it was one step on the journey over the watershed. Somewhere between ten and twelve, I crossed a dividing line between the world of childhood, where the streams flow backward, into the world of adults where the current moves forward, and which is still my world though then I was only twelve and now am past sixty.

Wordsworth, who has given a lot to my understanding of things, describes in "The Prelude" how he and a friend on a walking tour, were crossing the Simplon Pass to Italy. They missed the proper road and it was some time before they met a peasant and could ask him which was the way over the Pass.

Wordsworth describes his bewilderment when he was told that all unawares, this momentous boundary line had already been passed and that "we had crossed the Alps!" Even remembering the moment, as he writes, sends his mind into a swirl of confusion, a spiritual tempest like an Alpine storm, out of the mirk and whirlwind of which, great events seem striving to be born. In some similar way, over those two years, I passed unaware over my watershed into the world where adults were real people and I felt my kinship with them. True I was smaller, much younger, and inexperienced, but though they might be twenty or forty or eighty, we were of the same kind. I was no longer a child and THEY outside my world. I do not know when it happened or how, but I know that at ten it was not so, and at twelve, I looked around and amazingly it was. I had crossed the Alps.

The End

March 1986.

Patricia Ecker

9 St Mark's Avenue

Bilton

RUGBY

CV22 7NP.